Imperialism and Colonialism

Recent Titles in
Contributions in Comparative Colonial Studies

Moral Imperium: Afro-Caribbeans and the Transformation of British Rule, 1776–1838
Ronald Kent Richardson

Black and White in Southern Zambia: The Tonga Plateau Economy and British Imperialism, 1890–1939
Kenneth P. Vickery

The Carrier Corps: Military Labor in the East African Campaign, 1914–1918
Geoffrey Hodges

Germans in the Tropics: Essays in German Colonial History
Arthur J. Knoll and Lewis H. Gann

War, Cooperation, and Conflict: The European Possessions in the Caribbean, 1939–1945
Fitzroy Andre Baptiste

No Country for a Gentleman: British Rule in Egypt, 1883–1907
William M. Welch, Jr.

Railway Imperialism
Clarence B. Davis and Kenneth E. Wilburn, editors, with Ronald E. Robinson

Countdown to Rebellion: British Policy in Cyprus, 1939–1955
George Horton Kelling

Science and Social Science Research in British India, 1780–1880: The Role of Anglo-Indian Associations and Government
Edward W. Ellsworth

Journalists for Empire: The Imperial Debate in the Edwardian Stately Press, 1903–1913
James D. Startt

Imperial Diplomacy in the Era of Decolonization: The Sudan and Anglo-Egyptian Relations, 1945–1956
W. Travis Hanes III

The Man on the Spot: Essays on British Empire History
Roger D. Long, editor

Imperialism and Colonialism

Essays on the History of European Expansion

H. L. WESSELING

Contributions in Comparative Colonial Studies, Number 32

GREENWOOD PRESS
Westport, Connecticut • London

Library of Congress Cataloging-in-Publication Data

Wesseling, H. L.
Imperialism and colonialism : essays on the history of European expansion / H.L. Wesseling.
p. cm.—(Contributions in comparative colonial studies. ISSN 0163–3813 ; no. 32)
Includes bibliographical references and index.
ISBN 0–313–30431–9 (alk. paper)
1. Europe—Territorial expansion. 2. Europe—Colonies. 3. Netherlands—Colonies. 4. Imperialism—History—19th century. 5. Imperialism—History—20th century. 6. Europe—History, Military—19th century. 7. Netherlands—Foreign policy. I. Title. II. Series.
D539.W47 1997
325'.32'091821—DC21 96–53847

British Library Cataloguing in Publication Data is available.

Library of Congress Catalog Card Number: 96–53847
ISBN: 0–313–30431–9
ISSN: 0163–3813

First published in 1997

Greenwood Press, 88 Post Road West, Westport, CT 06881
An imprint of Greenwood Publishing Group, Inc.

Printed in the United States of America

The paper used in this book complies with the Permanent Paper Standard issued by the National Information Standards Organization (Z39.48–1984).

10 9 8 7 6 5 4 3 2 1

Copyright Acknowledgments

Chapter 1, "Colonial Wars: An Introduction," was published in J.A. de Moor and H.L. Wesseling (eds.), *Imperialism and War. Essays on Colonial Wars in Asia and Africa* (Leiden, 1989), 1–11.

Chapter 2, "Colonial Wars and Armed Peace, 1871–1914: A Reconnaissance," was published in *Itinerario* 5, No. 2 (1981), 53–73.

Chapter 3, "Knowledge Is Power: Some Remarks on Colonialism and Science," was published in the festschrift for Sartono Kartodirdjo, *Dari babad dan hikayat sampai sejarah kritis* (Yogyakarta, 1987), 351–368.

Chapter 4, "The Netherlands as a Colonial Model," is an extended version of a paper presented at the First Indonesian-Dutch Historical Conference, held at Noordwijkerhout in the Netherlands, 19–22 May 1976.

Chapter 5, "The Debate on French Imperialism, 1960–1975," is an updated version of an article published in *French Colonial Studies*, 1 (1977), 1–16.

Chapter 6, "The Giant That Was a Dwarf or: The Strange Case of Dutch Imperialism," is a revised version of an article published in the *Journal of Imperial and Commonwealth History* 16, No. 3 (1988), 58–70.

Chapter 7, "The Berlin Conference of 1884–1885: Myths and Realities," is an elaborated version of a contribution to S. Förster, W.J. Mommsen, and R. Robinson (eds.), *Bismarck, Europe and Africa. The Berlin Africa Conference 1884–1885 and the Onset of Partition* (Oxford, 1988), 522–541.

Chapter 8, "The Netherlands and the Partition of Africa," was published in the *Journal of African History* 22 (1981), 495–509.

Chapter 9, "Toward a History of Decolonization," was published in *Itinerario* 11, No. 2 (1987), 94–106.

Chapter 10, "Post-Imperial Holland," was published in *The Journal of Contemporary History* 15 (1980), 125–142.

Chapter 11, "Overseas History, 1945–1995," was published in Peter Burke (ed.), *New Perspectives on Historical Writing* (Cambridge, 1991), 67–92.

Chapter 12, "Overseas History in the Netherlands after the Second World War," was published in *Itinerario* 18, No. 2 (1994), 97–115.

Contents

Preface

The words that appear in the title of this book, *imperialism* and *colonialism*, are well-known expressions often used in political debate and mostly with strong, negative connotations. The word *expansion*, on the contrary, is a much less commonly used term and has no special connotations. It is more a term for the professionals. All three words, however, refer to the same phenomenon, albeit in some slightly different forms. All three words also have their histories.

The word *imperialism* has such a long and complicated history that an entire book has been devoted to it.[1] Let us simply observe that the word originated in France in the nineteenth century, where it referred to the political friends of Napoleon III and the Second Empire before crossing the Channel, where it was used in the debate concerning the future of the British Empire. Only in 1902, when J.A. Hobson published his book *Imperialism: A Study*, did the word *imperialism* develop into a concept with a specific meaning.[2] From that time onward it has referred to a specific form of colonial exploitation, connected to a particular stage in the development of capitalism. From then on the term has also become *en vogue* both in political debates and in scholarly discussions, and it remains so today. According to the *International Encyclopedia of the Social Sciences*, "the concept refers primarily to attempts to establish or retain formal sovereignty over subordinate political societies, but it is also often equated with the exercise of *any* form of political control or influence by one political community over another."[3]

Colonialism is a somewhat younger term, although its sister, *colonization*, is of much older date. But *colonization* is a technical term, originally only used to describe the phenomenon of people migrating to other parts of the world and starting there a new life as settlers (*coloni*). Colonialism, like imperialism, came over from France, where it was used for the first time in the title of *Le Colon-*

ialisme, a book by French socialist and anticolonialist Paul Louis in 1905.[4] To quote once more the *International Encyclopedia of the Social Sciences*, "Colonialism has now come to be identified with rule over peoples of different race inhabiting lands separated by salt water from the imperial center; more particularly, it signifies direct political control by European states or states settled by Europeans, as the United States or Australia, over peoples of other races, notably over Asians and Africans."[5]

Thus, colonialism is at the same time a wider and more limited concept than imperialism. It has a wider meaning because it is not limited to a particular historical period or a specific stage in the development of capitalism. On the other hand, it is also more limited because it refers only to one form of foreign rule (the colonial one), although often other forms with a somewhat different juridical character, like protectorates or overseas territories, are also included.

The concept of European *expansion*, finally, is derived from the British. In 1884, John Seeley gave his famous lectures in Cambridge on the *Expansion of England*. They were later published as a book under the same title.[6] The word *expansion*, of course, is a metaphor derived from the field of physics to describe the extension of bodies. According to Seeley, England was also an expanding body or, rather, an expanding society.

The concept of European expansion is the most encompassing of all three because, like economics and politics, it also takes cultural and social interaction into account. When, in the introduction to a book of essays on *Expansion and Reaction*, I had to give a definition of it, I proposed that "the history of European expansion could be described as the history of encounters between diverse systems of civilization, their influence on one another and the gradual growth toward a global, universal system of civilization."[7]

It is this subject that, in one way or another, is dealt with by all the essays collected in this volume. Some of them discuss questions related to the theory and practice of imperialism, such as French and Dutch imperialism and the partition of Africa. Others are about various aspects of European colonialism, be it war and conquest or more peaceful issues like administration and science. The third part is about decolonization and its consequences, the two last contributions being historiographical essays giving an overview of the writing of overseas history in Europe and, more specifically, in the Netherlands after decolonization.

All these stories and essays have been previously published in journals and collective volumes. They have been checked and brought up-to-date for this publication. As every contribution has been written in such a way that it can be read independently, inevitably there is sometimes some repetition, although this has been reduced to a minimum.

I would like to thank Lise Grünfeld, Janelle Moerman, and Anne Simpson for their help in correcting these essays and making editorial suggestions.

Part I

Colonialism

Chapter 1

Colonial Wars: An Introduction

THE SUBJECT

It is a disputable philosophical thesis that war is the father of all things, as Heraclitus believed. It is certain, however, that war is the father of historiography. Much attention has been given to war not just in the Bible, the Iliad, and other early products of the historical imagination, but also by the first historians in the Western tradition. Many of us learned our first Latin from Julius Caesar's report of the colonial war of conquest *par excellence*, the *Bellum Gallicum*, and our first Greek from Herodotus's description of one of the first wars of national liberation, that of the Greeks against the Persians. In fact, it can be said that Antiquity saw the classic description of the three main types of war, namely, wars of conquest, by Caesar; wars of liberation, by Herodotus; and "interstate"[1] wars in that most famous of all ancient works of history, *The Peloponnesian War*, by Thucydides. The same preoccupation can be observed in modern academic history as it has developed since the nineteenth century in Europe. In addition to the development of the state, relations between states—war and diplomacy, in other words—have received the most attention. In a continent like Europe, where the nation-state became the most important form of social organization and where these states were born in conflict and remained in conflict, this should not be surprising. In addition to this, academic history long retained its strongly literary quality and therefore wars were ready subjects, as they offered many opportunities for lively descriptions and dramatic scenes. "War makes rattling good history," as Thomas Hardy wrote.[2] Nevertheless, criticism developed both of the exaggerated emphasis on the state and its vicissitudes, and of the *l'art pour l'art* character of military historiography. Just as war, as Clemenceau famously said, is too important to be left to generals, so historians discovered that war is too important a subject to be left entirely to the military chroniclers. Thus the old, abandoned *histoire bataille* returned in a modern form as the history of "War and Society." The history of war once again became the concern of "ordinary" historians.

European history itself has enough wars to keep historians and others occupied, but colonial wars also have always excited great interest. The conquests of Cortez and Pizarro, the operations of Coen and Clive and later the great imperialist *fastes*, the Mutiny, the River War, the Mahdi War, the Tonkin Affair, Aceh, the Boer War, and so many others have received much attention in literature and historical writing. This is, of course, in itself no reason to devote a special study to them. The questions have to be asked whether they are worthy of all this attention, and whether they are suited to a general analysis. The answer to the first one can be brief: these wars were undoubtedly of such importance and had such consequences that they still deserve our attention today. The second question is more complicated. A general analysis of colonial wars requires two premises. The first is that colonial wars form a separate category. That is to say, that they have something in common which distinguishes them from other wars—in short, that they are *sui generis*. The second is that war forms a specific phase in the history of colonialism, clearly distinct from another state—that of peace. In other words, it requires that the dichotomy between war and peace, so well-known from European history, can be recognized in overseas history too. Both premises are open to discussion and lead to a number of questions, which we will examine further.

COLONIAL WARS: A CHARACTERIZATION

The War Aims

The first question that arises is, which wars can be described as colonial? In the widest sense of the word there are very many. The three main types of war (conquest, liberation, and interstate war) can all be distinguished among colonial wars. The American War of Independence was the first in a long series of wars of decolonization, of which the struggle for the Portuguese African territories was the last one (unless the Falklands War can be so considered). Wars such as the Anglo-Chinese, the Russo-Japanese, the Spanish-American, and the Boer War were, in contrast, not wars of liberation but rather interstate wars (although they can all be considered to be colonial wars, or at least overseas wars). They were not colonial wars in the classic sense of the word, that is to say, wars of conquest. The main characteristic of these wars was that their aim—usually achieved—was not merely to defeat the opponents but also to annex their territory and to subject their population.

The first element that these colonial wars have in common is thus their war aim. This is, of course, very important. As Clausewitz's famous formula has it, "war is the continuation of politics by other means." In other words, political aims determine the war. In "normal" wars in European history, the war aims were generally limited. The peace conditions often included territorial provisions, but normally they only concerned a portion of the territory. In colonial wars, in contrast, war aims were absolute. Colonial conquerors came to stay. Their aim was the permanent and total subjection of the population, or, in other words, the establishment of a lasting peace.

The special nature of the war aims had consequences for the result, that is to say, the end of the war. Normal wars ended in victory or in defeat. Europeans did experience defeats in colonial wars, but they were rare. The majority of wars ended in victory. But what does that word mean, exactly? How can victory be defined? When was it achieved? A normal war is won when an opponent is beaten, that is to say, when he accepts the victor's terms. But when is a colonial war won? When is an opponent defeated? There were usually no peace conditions, and often it was not even known who the opponent was. Callwell, the author of a classic book on colonial wars, pointed to this problem. In contrast to "civilised" wars, in "Small Wars," as he called them, it was impossible to aim against a clear, central target, such as the ruler, the government, the capital, the centers of population, because these do not exist.[3] Callwell exaggerates somewhat, but the opponent was indeed often difficult to find or even to define.

In this respect a distinction can be made between two sorts of wars, namely, those against better-organized states and those in areas with a very low level of state organization, or, in Sir Garnet Wolseley's words, against "uncivilised nations."[4] Paradoxically enough, it was not the weak, but rather the strong and well-organized opponents who were the easier adversaries for the Europeans, both militarily and politically, both during the conflict and thereafter. In military terms, the advantage was that the latter sometimes could be tempted to do precisely what they should not do, namely, give battle. Set battles were generally won by the Europeans. Once the enemy was defeated, the existing political organization could be taken over and continued under colonial supervision. An enemy with a lower degree of organization, and which limited itself to guerrilla activities, was much more difficult to deal with.[5] In these cases the colonial state had to be built up.[6]

Admittedly, this distinction is somewhat theoretical, because in practice both types of war often occurred together or in succession. In Madagascar, in 1895, several campaigns were conducted, resulting in a French victory, or at least in a treaty in which the French terms were accepted. But there then began a guerrilla war which would last many years and which cost the French more effort than the official war. In Morocco they fought first against the sultan, but thereafter, for several difficult years, together with and in the name of the Makhzen against tribes who had never accepted his authority. In North Sumatra in 1903, the Dutch declared that the war was won, but it is doubtful whether Aceh was ever genuinely under Dutch control.

Because the opponent was not a government or an enemy army but the population itself, colonial wars can be characterized as people's wars. This does not mean that there was no distinction between citizens and combatants, but that this distinction, which in Europe was becoming steadily firmer in this period, was more fluid. Since colonial wars were conducted to establish a permanent presence, a purely military approach was insufficient, and account always had to be taken of the civilians. In short, it was a matter of conquering not just the country but also the "hearts and minds" of the people. Two schools of thought developed in military theory on this point. One stressed military intimidation above all and the other gave the "conquête des âmes" a central role. With some simplification, these could be called the English and the French schools, since it is in the writings of Callwell, on the one hand, and Gallieni and Lyautey, on the other, that the most detailed formulations of these two approaches are to be found.

Callwell described colonial wars as "small wars," yet did not see their scale or extent as their main characteristic, but, rather, the nature of the opponent. The core problem was the absence of a clear political structure. For Callwell there was only one solution, an assault on the population itself. They must be intimidated.[7] In the Netherlands Indies army this was known as the "Indische taktiek."

In contrast, the French school of Gallieni and Lyautey stressed the socioeconomic aspects of war. In the wake of victory, the colonial army received other tasks to perform, such as the founding or restoration of markets, schools, and so on.[8] The Americans in the Philippines used the same strategy. When their army retired after the war against Spain of 1898, it left behind more than a thousand Western, English-language schools.

Because colonial wars were so different from more orthodox wars, and because colonial armies, unlike those in the mother country, were active and fought battles, the armies in the colonies developed their own cultures. This was a world of action, initiative, and energy. Here men worked and did not just wait, as at home. Those men who wanted to perform useful work, who craved action and wished to make a career for themselves, entered the colonial army. Here it was possible to prove one's courage and to release one's energy. The colonial army was a preeminently practical army. The lessons of the military academy were of no importance and book-learning was not needed. "You have a lot to forget," said Bugeaud to his officers.[9]

The Means

The specific character of colonial warfare was determined in the first place by the aims, but also, to a degree, by the means. This provides a certain paradox. If the aim of colonial wars was absolute (namely, total subjection), the means employed to achieve this were always limited, at least on the European side. In European wars the matter was reversed. The aims were limited, at least until the unconditional surrender strategy of 1940–1945, but the investment of means has become steadily more massive. Since the French Revolution, war has been a matter of the "nation in arms," even if it is only the male portion of the nation. In colonial wars, this was reversed. On the one side, the European, there was a professional army. On the other, their opponents, the distinction between army and people was by no means always clear. That the Europeans limited their military deployment derived, of course, from the fact that, ultimately, colonial wars did not threaten vital interests, as was the case in wars against—or on—the home territory. In this respect colonial wars resembled those eighteenth-century wars—"guerres en dentelles"—in which limited means were also employed.

The Europeans neither wished to deploy unlimited manpower, nor could they, but it was not necessary to do so, because of their military supremacy. Colonial armies were superior to virtually all their adversaries. This supremacy was first and foremost based on technical prowess.[10] However, this factor should not be overemphasized, or at any rate, not made absolute. The image of impotent Africans armed with arrows and spears being mown down by Europeans with machine guns is not incorrect, but it is one-sided.[11] Technical superiority was not always usable. Gunboats could, naturally, only be used in very limited areas. Heavy artillery was virtually untransportable and light artillery was not always effective, since fortifications in Asia and Africa were sometimes very solid.[12] Cavalry was often not present or presented great logistic problems. The Europeans may have had better weapons, but their opponents also possessed firearms. There were guns in plenty in Africa, although they were not always of good quality. In this respect it is important to note that the military breakthrough in Aceh eventually came when the *Corps Marechaussée* employed not the Maxim gun, but that quintessentially primitive weapon, the naked sabre.[13]

The technical superiority of the Europeans was indisputable and was one of the elements of their strength. But, they also had other strengths. The power of European armies was also of a sociocultural nature. Michael Howard has pointed out that an army forms a world of its own, a social order.[14] European armies were disciplined and well trained, they knew how to maintain weapons, they had good morale and a strong esprit de corps. They were highly developed, ready implements which could be moved as needed and deployed according to military science which, during many centuries of conflict, had elaborated well-thought-out rules of strategy and tactics. While there were gifted commanders in Asia and Africa, they did not necessarily dispose of such armies. The Africans were also weakened by their political division, which gave Europeans the opportunity to employ a policy of divide and rule, to exploit internal divisions, and to make use of African collaborators. On the other hand, European intervention could also lead to the development of African coalitions.[15]

However, there were various spheres in which the Europeans were at a disadvantage. In the first place, there was the lack of knowledge of the terrain and the need to adapt to tropical conditions. Colonial armies often operated in totally unknown regions in which they depended on local cooperation and information. Additionally, they were highly vulnerable to tropical diseases and complaints.

As Joseph Chamberlain once said: "The mosquitoes saved the West Africans, not the intellectuals."[16] Many studies have shown that most soldiers did not die in military action, but of disease. Many never arrived on the battlefield, for they had already succumbed. It was not incorrect of Callwell to describe colonial wars as "campaigns against nature."[17] In extreme cases this could mean that only a low percentage of the troops actually saw action. The French campaigns in Morocco were, in this respect, the first modern wars, as they were the first in which this proportion was reversed: a majority of the casualties died on the battlefield, not in the infirmary.[18]

Finally, there was the size of the armies. The colonial power could only mobilize a limited number of troops. There were enormous differences between them as regards recruiting and financing. The English were in a unique position as their Indian army had an enormous reserve of troops which could be employed anywhere in the world as necessary—and this at the expense of the Indian budget.[19] For other countries matters were different. The Germans mainly used troops from the fatherland overseas. The French, in contrast, did not wish to do this, but, rather, saw in the colonies the possibility to recruit troops for the motherland. The *tirailleurs sénégalais* were the best known example of this. The Dutch East Indian army consisted of one-third European and two-thirds Indonesian troops. The Moluccans were considered to be the Indonesian example of the "martial castes," more valuable in war than the "meek Javanese." Nevertheless, considerable use was also made of Javanese.[20] Colonial wars were also in this respect old-fashioned, as they were reminiscent of the press-gangs and mercenaries of the European armies in the seventeenth and eighteenth centuries. However men were recruited, their numbers were always limited by financial considerations. The attempt was always made to charge these troops to the colonial budget. This was not always possible, however, and thus the mother country also had to contribute to the costs of defense.[21]

WAR OR PEACE?

Colonial wars seem to have a number of properties in common by which they can be considered a separate class. They form a separate category, distinct from the wars in European history. This raises a new question: if these conflicts are so different from "normal" wars, can they be described as wars at all? What is war, anyway? According to the *Concise Oxford Dictionary*, it is: "Strife, usually between nations, conducted by force." This is clear enough, and anyway, dictionaries are not needed to tell us what war is. We know what war is. War is the opposite of peace. Of course, we know that this distinction is not quite absolute. We speak of the Eighty or Hundred Years' War, but this does not mean that the countries involved were engaged in military activities for all of those eighty or hundred years. Nevertheless, in all those years there was a state of war, that is to say, a situation that differed from that known as peace. In the course of history, moreover, that dichotomy would become steadily stronger. The First World War lasted from 1914 to 1918, and those four years were genuinely years of actual warfare. The conceptual distinction became steadily more real. War and peace both became more "absolute," to use another phrase of Clausewitz's.

To what extent was this also the case in colonial history? Was the exercise of violence limited to those periods known to history as the years of war? Was it either war or was peace there too? The situation is much more complicated. We have already seen how in Madagascar an official war was fought in 1895, and then ended by a treaty. But only after that did the real military conquest, the pacification, begin. The French expansion in West Africa saw a number of wars, against Samori, the Tuculors, and so on. But, as Kanya Forstner has argued, it was in fact a continuous process of military expansion.[22] Officially, there were four Aceh wars, but in fact there were thirty years of war! The shift from less to more violence—and vice versa—was fluid, it was never a dramatic break. It has been the European habit to describe the military conquest of Africa and Asia as a series of wars. This answered the needs of European journalists and politicians, newspaper readers and taxpayers, but not to the reality of the other two continents. In the overseas empires there was a permanent state of war, as the great architect of the British Empire, Joseph Chamberlain, knew when he wrote: "In the wide dominions of the Queen the doors of the temple of Janus are never closed."[23]

A second, even more fundamental question follows from this: can the distinction between war and peace be used at all? If there was no war on, was there peace? Was there peace before the colonial conquest or after it? There is no simple answer to these questions. The nineteenth-century Europeans believed that the overseas world was one of anarchy and barbarism, so that war and violence were endemic. Wellesley (the future marquis) said that: "Asiatic government was so infernal in its character and the feuds of various tribes, nations and states were so irreconcilable that the great peninsula . . . must have been a mere hell on earth."[24] The colonizers saw themselves as the great bringers of peace and therefore were keen on the word "pacification." This term can be questioned, but it is not entirely incomprehensible. The precolonial social and constitutional relationships in Africa were very different from those in Europe. Africa had some ten thousand political units. These were regularly in conflict with each other. There had never been true peace.[25]

Europeans were, to Africans, to a certain extent the same sort of foreign invaders as many of their black predecessors had been. It can thus not be said that the colonial wars constituted an abrupt break with a preexisting state of peace. Circumstances were different in Asia, and the constitutional situation there more closely resembled that in Europe. In India, however, the state had no monopoly on violence.[26] This monopoly as it existed in Europe has caused many wars, but it is also a necessary condition for peace and peacefulness. The colonial order was indeed an order, a system which in any event guaranteed a certain degree of rest.[27] The Swiss historian Lüthy has summarized it as follows:

"for the extra-European world the colonial age was, on the whole, an age of peace and security as the bloody history of Asia and Africa had not seen before."[28]

Whether the colonial order can really be described as peaceful is, of course, another matter. Pacification brought order, but did it bring peace? Was there peace in Leopold's Congo when there were no more wars, but hands and feet were chopped off by the hundreds?[29] It can be viewed otherwise, and the whole colonial system can be seen as a form of violence—the term "structural violence" has been used in this regard. In this vision, it does not matter much whether there was open and virulent violence, as at the establishment (and at the end) of colonial rule, or a permanent and immanent form of oppression, as was evident during the colonial period. This raises the question as to the place of colonial wars in the history of colonial expansion.

COLONIAL WARS OR VIOLENT COLONIALISM?

Colonial wars fill a special, and spectacular, place in the history of European expansion. They have therefore always attracted attention, both in colonial historiography and in its nationalist successor which has *fêted* its own heroes, those of resistance. In traditional colonial historiography we find such great conquerors as Bugeaud, Gallieni, Faidherbe, Lyautey, Kitchener, Gordon, Wolseley, Van Heutsz, *e tutti quanti*. On the side of the resistance, originally only the Boer generals, such as Botha and De Wet, were mentioned, but later this group increased to include a large and colorful collection with such stars as Samori, Al Hadj Omar, Dipanegara, Teuku Umar, Abd el Krim, and many others. In fact, the nationalist historiography does not differ much from the colonial, except, of course, in its appreciations.[30] It is the same play, with only the roles of hero and villain reversed. The vision of the colonial period remained essentially the same. It began with a phase of conquest and primary resistance. This was followed by a colonial period of subjection, which was itself succeeded by a new phase of resistance. This resistance derived from the nationalist movement and resulted, with the wars of decolonization, in modern independence.

It is questionable whether this is the right vision. The arrival of the Europeans did not meet with resistance everywhere. There were also those who welcomed their arrival and benefited from it.[31] Colonial rule was, moreover, to a certain extent a continuation of existing forms of indirect or informal control. Independence had not previously been total. Against this, even after the colonial system was well established, the rulers' ability to rule was limited. They were highly dependent on the cooperation of the local population. Equally, decolonization did not entail a total break with domination. In all sorts of ways, dependence and foreign interference have survived. In this respect, the English historian Ronald Robinson has described imperialism in its totality as a system of collaboration.[32] In his vision, all relations between Europeans and the overseas peoples were forms of cooperation. Even during the heyday of colonial rule the ability to rule and control was limited. The changes in the form of imperialism, from informal to formal and vice versa, were only changes in the terms of collaboration. The phenomenon itself remained the same.

In such a vision, colonial wars lose at least some of their importance, if not their spectacular character. This does not detract from the interest of their study. For historians, colonial wars are of great significance for two reasons. On the one hand, their peculiarities are of importance for military history, because they demonstrate the limitations of certain general theories on the development of modern warfare. On the other, they raise essential questions on the nature of the colonial period and on the course of European expansion.

Chapter 2

Colonial Wars and Armed Peace, 1871–1914: A Reconnaissance

WAR AND PEACE

The concepts of war and peace are not as simple as they appear at first glance. Closer scrutiny reveals that reality cannot be reduced to the simple dichotomy expressed by this pair of words. There have, after all, been wars which were never declared and periods of peace which did not follow peace treaties. Yet this made them no less real. Moreover, some acts of war were described euphemistically as ''punitive expeditions,'' ''punishment raids,'' or ''police operations,'' while others were described pejoratively as ''terrorism,'' ''banditry,'' and ''piracy.'' There have been wars which officially lasted seven, nine, thirty, eighty, and even one hundred years, although the actual fighting took place within a much shorter period. Conversely, there have also been eras of peace which were in fact, no more than a truce extending over a number of years. In fact, the concepts are so elastic that not only in George Orwell's frightening *Newspeak* but also in ordinary English, one can say that ''war is peace'' if only one adds two adjectives: cold war is armed peace.

Both concepts are sufficiently well-known to be used without much commentary. Since 1947 the phrase ''cold war'' has become the accepted term for the tense relationships and the concomitant military rivalry which existed between two superpowers and their allies without escalating into direct military confrontation. Between 1871 and 1914 a similar combination of great diplomatic tension, the formation of alliances and an arms race, also occurred, but this is traditionally called ''armed peace.'' The merits and inadequacies of these two terms will not be considered in further detail here. However, one peculiar and dangerous aspect of both of these terms should be noted: they place so much emphasis on the relationship between the major powers that one tends to forget how many acts of war occur in "peacetime." Since the Second World War ended in August 1945, hardly a day has passed without there being some form of active warfare somewhere in the world. It might be an exaggeration to claim the same for the period of armed peace. In fact, our knowledge is too limited to allow any accurate estimation of this. Numerous tribal wars and other conflicts which did not intrude upon the international system evaded the scrutiny of the historians of those days and thus cannot be evaluated today. But we do have material pertaining not only to the "normal" wars but also to the colonial wars which were so abundant in that era. This chapter is an attempt to gain an impression of the scope, nature, and problems of these colonial wars and thus to get a better insight into the character of an era that is known as "the period of the armed peace" but also as "the age of imperialism."

COLONIAL WARS: A SURVEY

For an initial impression of the total amount of warfare which took place during these years, we should look at the statistical material collected by Singer and Small. In their book *The Wages of War, 1816–1965*, the authors surveyed all wars conducted within this period. Before an armed conflict could be included as such in this list, a number of criteria had to be satisfied, the most important being a minimum number of casualties.[1] Subsequently, they classified these conflicts as "interstate wars," that is, wars between states which were part of the international system; or "extrasystemic wars," that is, roughly speaking, colonial or imperial wars. On the basis of these criteria, the following list can be drawn up for the period 1871–1914 (see Table 2.1).[2]

In total there were 28 wars within a period of 44 years. These numbers do not reveal very much. The data are scarce and difficult to compare; the classification appears to be rather arbitrary; the simple sum tells us little about the nature and intensity of the conflicts. However, even without a more detailed and inevitably casuistic subdivision, two salient points can be noted. In the first place, although the wars listed are not comparable to the world wars as regards their severity and magnitude, they most definitely were conflicts of considerable dimensions and significance. Second, there was only one fairly prolonged period without any large-scale war, namely, the decade 1885–1894.

This survey is only slightly altered when we also include the wars which Singer and Small mention but which do not meet their criteria for inclusion. These are listed in Table 2.2.[3] Although the total has now increased to 37 wars, the picture has not changed drastically since once again that same period (1885–1894) is conspicuous in that it was relatively tranquil. This is surprising because it was precisely this decade which marked the climax of European imperialism in Africa. It seems necessary, therefore, to consider the campaigns and expeditions of the major colonial powers in more detail.

In his book on England's *Colonial Small Wars (1837–1901)*, Featherstone lists for the period 1871–1900 a total of 22 important expeditions as well as an

Table 2.1
Survey of Great Wars, 1871–1914

Interstate wars		*Extra-systemic wars*	
Russo-Turkish war	(1877-78)	Aceh war	(1873-78)
Pacific war	(1879-83)	Balkan war	(1875-77)
Sino-French war	(1884-85)	Bosnian war	(1878)
Central American war	(1885)	Second British-Afghan war	(1878-80)
Sino-Japanese war	(1894-95)	British-Zulu war	(1879)
Greco-Turkish war	(1897)	Franco-Indochinese war	(1882-84)
Spanish-American war	(1898)	Madhist war	(1882-85)
Russo-Japanese war	(1904-05)	Serbo-Bulgarian war	(1885)
Central American war	(1906)	Franco-Madagascar war	(1894-95)
Central American war	(1907)	Cuban war	(1895-98)
Spanish-Moroccan war	(1909-10)	Italo-Ethiopian war	(1895-96)
Italo-Turkish war	(1911-12)	First Philippine war	(1896-98)
First Balkan war	(1912-13)	Second Philippine war	(1899-1902)
Second Balkan war	(1913)	Boer war	(1899-1902)
Total - 14		*Total* - 14	

apparently infinite number of incidents and skirmishes along the Northwest Frontier of India.[4] The period after 1900, with the ''pacification'' of Kenya, Nigeria, and the Gold Coast as well as operations in the Southern Sudan and the Red Sea area, was not much more peaceful. A book on the Netherlands Indies Army provides an equally colorful list of ''troubles,'' ''irregularities,'' ''expeditions,'' ''disturbances,'' ''actions,'' and ''uprisings'' in which this army was involved. In all, 32 operations can be listed for the period 1871–1914, even though the Aceh War of 1873–1913 is considered as one single military operation.[5] A similar review of French warfare is lacking. Even so, in the *Histoire des colonies* by Hanotaux and Martineau we find a total for this period of about 40 colonial operations and campaigns.[6] Thus during this period the three most important colonial powers were involved in a total of at least one hundred military operations.

It is obvious, though, that this arithmetic has little real significance. To begin with, the data for Germany, Spain, Portugal, Belgium, and Italy are missing.

Table 2.2
Smaller Wars, 1871–1914

British-Ashanti war	(1873)
Russian-Turkmen war	(1879-81)
British-Boer war	(1881)
Anglo-Egyptian war	(1882)
Anglo-Burmese war	(1885)
Belgian-Arab war	(1892-94)
Germany-Southwest Africa war	(1904-07)
Boxer Rebellion	(1900)
Germany-Tanganyika war	(1905)

Total - 9

Moreover, the criteria and the source material differ considerably. But more important is a fundamental objection to this approach. The facts and figures cited above are the European version, based on information provided by European war records. They do not reflect the actual course of pacification in Asia and Africa.

To obtain an insight into what truly happened, it is essential to study in detail how the occupation and pacification actually took place. Since a comprehensive survey of this process does not exist, the results of regional and local studies will have to be used. Several such studies on black Africa are available. For instance, Helge Kjekshus, who investigated economic developments in Tanganyika since 1858, considered the wars conducted there by the Germans in great detail. The most important ones are known as the Maji-Maji wars, which extended from 1905 to 1907 and brought an end to armed resistance to German colonization. Because traditional military methods could not cope with guerrilla warfare, the scorched earth tactic was applied on a large scale: by concentrating on the civilian population in the agricultural regions, particularly during the sowing season, the Germans broke resistance by means of starvation. But in a fourteen-year period extending from 1888 to 1902—before these major wars and during the ''tranquil'' years of our statistics—there had also been 84 military operations which were serious enough to be defined as ''battles'' in terms of the law of 27 June 1871. (This law stipulated that German soldiers involved in conflicts so classified were granted the right to receive a government pension.) Therefore, in Tanganyika these ''quiet years'' included six battles per year, or one every two months, not counting other no less violent activities such as burning huts and stealing livestock.[7]

Another case study, this time concerning Kenya, provides a similar picture. In "The Politics of Conquest" Lonsdale offers the following summary of British activities in western Kenya between 1894 and 1914. In this twenty-year period there were 50 incidents in Kenya which, according to the English, were so serious that it was necessary to resort to (or at least consider the use of) force. In eleven cases the English refrained from action because they lacked the necessary military equipment; on two occasions the expedition ended in an English defeat or retreat; in thirteen cases the demonstration of British military power alone was sufficient; on twenty occasions a punitive military expedition was carried out.[8] This amounts to one official encounter per year.

These data clearly indicate that the conquest and pacification of Africa by Germany and England was a continuing process. Not one year passed without there being a war, nor one month without violent incidents or repression. Kanya Forstner's description of the French conquest of the Western Sudan, although it does not provide quantitative data, gives a similar impression. In a period of five years and with fewer than 4,000 soldiers, ambitious officers hungry for action and decorations created on their own authority a colonial territory which was larger than France itself.[9]

COSTS AND CASUALTIES

As a result of the marked autonomy and the frequent inaccuracy of the reports, it is difficult to form a correct impression of the actual process of pacification. It is even more difficult to discover what all of these wars meant in terms of human lives and money. In general it can be stated that the colonial powers were determined that the defense of the colonies should be paid for by the colonies themselves. This can also be expressed more cynically: the colonized had to pay for their own conquest. Because only a few serious studies of the colonial budgets are available, it is impossible to specify the percentage of the colonial budget which each country allocated for the armed forces. A study carried out by Davis and Huttenback, however, shows that for the English territories this percentage was about 35–40 percent.[10] For the Netherlands Indies one can use the budgets of this colony to determine how much was spent on military expenditures. This percentage remained fairly constant, the Aceh War notwithstanding. The total budget too remained fairly constant—and low—and did not show a sharp increase until after 1907. The costs of the Aceh War were thus insignificant when compared to those incurred during the so-called "ethical policy" (see Table 2.3).

If, then, it can be stated that the colonial population paid for their own conquest, it can also be said that—to a certain extent—they conquered themselves. Of course, European military power was based in the first instance on superior arms. The unique significance of this fact is clearly expressed by Hilaire Belloc's famous lines:

Table 2.3
Defense Expenditures and Total Government Budget for the Netherlands Indies, 1871–1914 (expressed in millions of guilders)

	I	II	III
1871	116	27	23%
1875	154	52	34%
1880	147	49	33%
1885	131	42	32%
1890	128	45	35%
1895	139	47	34%
1900	146	48	33%
1905	166	54	32%
1910	231	59	26%
1914	347	76	22%

I Total government budget

II Budget for defense

III Budget for defense as a percentage of the total budget

> Whatever happens, we have got
> the Maxim gun and they have not!

But even armed with the Mauser and the Maxim, the European soldiers would not have been able to conduct so many wars without support. The role of the native troops in these colonial wars should not be underestimated.

Because their organizations were so entirely different, the diverse colonial armies are very difficult to compare. It took France some twenty years to organize a colonial army, a process accompanied by complicated jurisdictional disputes and fierce administrative controversy in general.[11] Even when the colonial army became official, this did not mean that it was henceforth always available for action in the colonies. For the French, defense of the motherland took priority. Therefore, most of the French soldiers assigned to the colonial army remained in France itself as reserves for the defense of France. In Britain the situation was reversed. Since the country itself was rarely threatened, England could draw on its metropolitan army for reserve troops for colonial conflicts.

Table 2.4
Colonial Armies of England, France, and the Netherlands

England		*France*		*The Netherlands*	
"*Indian Army*"		"*Armée Coloniale*"		*Netherlands Indies Army*	
		Overseas			
1. English	77,500	1. European	20,000	1. Dutch	9,100
2. Natives	202,500	2. Natives	30,000	2. Other Europeans	6,200
Subtotal	280,000	*Subtotal*	50,000	3. Natives	15,700
Other colonial troops	30,000	In France	28,000		
Total	310,000	*Total*	78,000	*Total*	31,000

Another complication is the fact that India, the Netherlands Indies, and Algeria were so important compared to the other colonial territories of England, the Netherlands, and France, respectively, that separate arrangements were made for their defense. Algeria was looked upon as part of France itself; its defense therefore was an integral part of the military organization of the motherland. England and the Netherlands set up separate military organizations for India and Indonesia, the Indian Army and the Netherlands Indies Army, respectively. Moreover, in many cases the troops were supplemented with local volunteers or ad hoc recruits who served in native companies. Despite these differences the following table presents a reasonably accurate indication of the magnitude of the colonial armies (see Table 2.4[12]). As appears from this, the native troops were very important. In the Dutch and French armies they accounted for 40–50 percent of the troops; in the British army for more than two-thirds of the total. These figures also show that the three major colonial powers together had more than 400,000 men at their disposal for their colonial armies. It is much more difficult to obtain an impression of the opposition. If ever the words of Bertold Brecht are applicable they are here: ''die im Dunklen sieht man nicht.'' Because of the nature of the colonial war, which often took the form of guerrilla warfare, even the commanders generally knew very little about the strength of the enemy. The same applies for the casualties. The casualties of the opposition were seldom counted when lists were being compiled. Van Heutsz, the conqueror of Aceh, was one of the first to introduce this requirement.[13] In general, the figures are only estimates or guesses which are exceedingly speculative and were usually exaggerated—positively or negatively—and for myriad reasons.

Even so, for some of the wars and expeditions, assessments have been made which, in spite of the many uncertainties, provide an impression of the scope of the devastation. The previously mentioned study of Tanganyika by Kjekshus, for instance, clearly illustrates the problems encountered when trying to determine the casualties suffered by the Africans. Even the Germans, such thorough administrators, only recorded these casualties for a few years, and even then only gave rough estimates. In addition, they tended to regard the war as a purely military affair and thus the number of women and children killed was not taken into consideration. Finally, it must be assumed that the chances of survival for the wounded were exceedingly small as a consequence of the poor medical conditions. Some figures are available for the Maji-Maji Wars. The official report, which was presented to the Reichstag in 1907, lists a total of 75,000 Africans dead. Other estimates, however, suggest a total of 120,000 to 145,000 or even 250,000 to 300,000: and this for a relatively small region within Tanganyika! For some tribes more than 90 percent of the population perished.[14] A variation of Tacitus' famous comment is applicable here: they left a void and called it peace.

No less impressive are the figures for the Zulu War of 1879. In total, 50,000 Zulu warriors fought in this war, whereby 8,000 died and more than 16,000 were wounded. Total casualties therefore amounted to about 50 percent. On the British side 1,430 white men died and 1,000 "Natal Kaffirs" were killed in a war that had only lasted six months.[15]

But it was not only the major European powers that conducted wars on such a scale, and not only in Africa. The Aceh War was no less spectacular so far as intensity and casualties are concerned. Here again the figures for the European casualties are more exact and reliable than those for the Acehnese. During the entire conflict, 2,000 soldiers of the Netherlands Indies Army were killed in action and 10,000 died from disease. On the Indonesian side, the casualties are estimated at 60,000 to 70,000 Acehnese killed and 25,000 in forced labor who died from disease and exhaustion. In total, therefore, approximately 100,000 men perished; additionally, 500,000 people were wounded.[16] As mentioned previously, the Netherlands Indies Army was at that time also involved in 29 other military operations, although these were on a much smaller scale.

These examples clearly illustrate that the colonial wars must not be considered modest military operations along the lines of police activity or frontier guard duty, but as a series of real wars comparable in intensity and magnitude with many of the major wars in European history. This is the only point of comparison, however. The major difference between these so-called (and inaccurately, as we have seen) "small wars" and the classical wars was the method of warfare. The European commanders discovered—whether they were French, English, or Dutch; whether they were called Lyautey, Van Heutsz, or Sir Garnet Wolseley; and whether they fought in Indochina, Indonesia, or Africa—that the training they had received at their military academies was of little use in these wars. Hence their aversion to doctrines and theories. This antipathy is expressed in the famous words of the French general Bugeaud who said to his officers:

''You have much to forget,''[17] and those of Van Heutsz: ''Have you come from the Academy? Then of course you know nothing.''[18] How to conduct a colonial war had to be learned in the field. It was not until about 1900 that the experiences of the preceding twenty years were recorded in the form of more or less theoretical papers on the methods of colonial warfare. Thus, the practice of colonial war led to a theory on the small war.

THE COLONIAL WAR AS A PROBLEM

The father of the doctrine of the colonial war was without doubt the French general Bugeaud. Not only did all subsequent French proconsuls, such as Gallieni and Lyautey, follow his principles, the English ''small war'' expert Callwell also lauded his ''great natural gifts'' and his ''ripe experience.''[19] The Dutchman Van Heutsz, too, in his well-known memorandum on Aceh dated 18 April 1894, praised Bugeaud's method of ''restless pursuit, attack, pursuit again,'' although he questioned whether the Netherlands could afford to indulge in such measures.[20]

Although Van Heutsz's summary of the Bugeaud method is not incorrect, it is a highly simplified version of a more complicated approach. Bugeaud was a French general who gained his experience in guerrilla warfare during the Napoleonic occupation of Spain. This experience was to prove useful when, in 1841, he was sent to Algeria where serious problems had developed. The French landing in Algeria in 1830 led to the surrender of the dey but the native populations in the interior continued to resist these new conquerors. The French were not quite sure how to handle this unorganized form of warfare, especially after the rebel leader Abd el-Kader appeared on the scene. This man led a series of quick attacks directed in particular against the communication lines and convoys. It was General Bugeaud, military governor from 1841 to 1847, who broke the resistance. The differences between his approach and that of his predecessors can be found in the areas of politics, strategy, and tactics. Politically, he followed the principle of ''divide and rule'' whereby he attempted to aggravate internal differences and conflicting interests.[21] The dissension among the Africans, who generally recognized only tribal rather than national unity and organizations, was, incidentally, one of the most important sources of their relative weakness. Bugeaud's success can therefore also be attributed to this combination of political and military activity which was to become a characteristic of the French colonial-military school.

Bugeaud's most important strategic principle was that he was not fighting against a hostile army but against a hostile population. Mao Ze-dong, in fact, did not discover that the guerrilla moves ''as fish in water''; he only offered a new formula for an old adage. To subjugate this population, one had to ''reach them through their crops, their flocks and their property,'' to quote the English colonel Callwell.[22] This leads directly to the rest of Bugeaud's strategic principles. He realized that the guerrillas' strength lay in their speed and mobility.

He therefore saw no reason to expand the existing system of fortifications. Instead he divided the French troops into lightly equipped mobile columns which could strike back quickly. His tactics were based primarily on the use of the infantry for fast raids. As the French historian Ch.-A. Julien very discretely put it: "Bugeaud n'était pas un sentimental."[23] Systematic annihilation was part of his approach, which was not directed toward victory over an opponent in the field but toward the subjugation of the population. These "procédés énergiques"[24] of Bugeaud were successful—not only against Abd el-Kader but also later in the even more difficult war against the Rif Kabyles. His well-known report *De la stratégie, de la tactique, des retraites et du passage des défilés dans les montagnes des Kabyles* was to remain a classic of French colonial war literature.[25]

The problems which Bugeaud encountered were the normal problems of the colonial war. His ideas were therefore adopted by many others. Faidherbe, for example, operated according to the same principle in Senegal.[26] Bugeaud's departure from the system of fortifications in preference to mobile columns was also to be seen during the Aceh War some 50 years later. There, in 1884, the "concentrated line" was established, a system of forts which resembled that found in Algeria before Bugeaud and which was just as ineffective. Like Bugeaud, Van Heutsz argued in his memorandums that mobile columns were to be preferred over a static defense.[27] Later as governor he indeed introduced this approach. The vigilance and the mobility of the Netherlands Indies Army were increased. The troops were divided into lightly equipped, mounted brigades and infantry patrols with no more than four or five days' rations per man.[28] In fact, Van Heutsz could also be commended with the words spoken in praise of Gallieni: "C'est du meilleur Bugeaud."[29]

There was, however, an essential difference between Van Heutsz and Bugeaud, namely, in their approaches to the native population. Not that Van Heutsz was "unsentimental," but he did forbid the burning of homes and kampongs.[30] In this respect Van Heutsz followed the French school of thought that was developed later on by Gallieni and Lyautey, who emphasized in particular the coordination of military operations with political and socioeconomic policies. In general, it can be stated that the theorists of the colonial war—who were very practical men who incorporated their own experiences in their directives and reports—could be separated into two schools of thought. The first consisted of those who viewed the colonial war as a purely military operation, the second included those who emphasized that the military activities were secondary to the political aims. The first could be called the English school, the second the French school.

TWO SCHOOLS OF COLONIAL WARFARE

In 1904 the English lawyer and amateur strategist T. Miller Maguire published a book entitled *Guerrilla or Partisan Warfare*.[31] Maguire was astonished that

British officers received no instruction whatsoever in guerrilla warfare, in spite of the fact that during the reign of Queen Victoria the British army had been involved in at least 82 military campaigns, almost all of which could be characterized as irregular wars.[32] He even stated that not one single book on this subject could be found in the London bookshops.[33] This, however, was a slight exaggeration, since a major survey of this type of war had been published in 1899: Colonel Callwell's *Small Wars. Their Principles and Practice*. This book was to be reprinted several times.[34] The most striking aspect of these books, certainly when compared with the papers written by Gallieni and Lyautey, is that they completely ignore the political side of the war. Callwell treats the colonial war as one of the forms of "small war." His definition of the latter is simple: "the war of a regular army against an irregular fighting force."[35] These wars are divided into three categories, depending upon the intended purpose: (1) conquest or annexation; (2) subjugation or pacification; and (3) discipline or punishment for frontier violations or insults.[36] Although the political significance of the three categories is very different, their strategic principle is always the same: "overawing the enemy by bold initiative and by resolute action."[37]

Still, the small war had its own problems because the objective of this bold initiative was not always immediately clear. In a normal war the goal is the monarch, the government, the capital, the occupation of populated areas, or victory over the enemy army. But what does one do if none of these exist? The answer was given by Sir Garnet Wolseley, an eminent soldier whose talent for organization was so great that "All Sir Garnet" was to become a slogan meaning "All is well."[38] Wolseley maintained that in a war against an "uncivilized nation" (that is, a population without a capital), "your first objective should be the capture of whatever they prize most."[39] For Callwell too this was the nucleus of the matter: "If the enemy cannot be touched in his patriotism or his honour, he can be touched through his pocket."[40] In such a case it is necessary to resort to stealing cattle and burning villages, "and the war assumes an aspect which may shock the humanitarian."[41]

Callwell's voluminous book consists mainly of a series of fairly precise descriptions of the most important colonial campaigns which he then uses as a basis for a number of practical suggestions for all types of problems, such as night attacks, fighting in the hills or woods, how to use cavalry, camels, or horses, and so on. More important, however, is what he says about the mental aspects of colonial warfare. Callwell's book is a plea for offensive warfare, directed toward breaking the morale of the opposition: "in small wars moral effect ranks almost before material gain."[42] This moral effect must be achieved through a combination of strength and bluff. The commanding officers must continually seek and hold the initiative. They must fight—not maneuver: "the enemy must not only be beaten, he must be beaten thoroughly."[43] In the end a colonial war is a psychological war which must take into account the character of the colored people: "This is the way to deal with Asiatics—to go for them and to cow them by sheer force of will."[44]

Callwell's views appear at first glance to be rather similar to those of the French school of thought, as expressed, in particular, by Gallieni in his "Principes de pacification et d'organisation"[45] and Lyautey in "Du rôle colonial de l'armée."[46] They have the same preference for initiative and attack. According to Lyautey these are, in fact, the "eternal principles of war." Included in these age-old principles are such simple adages as: "Attack is the best form of defense."[47] Moreover, in Gallieni's writings we also find Callwell's social-Darwinist views reflected in his stereotyped ideas about the races and their mutual relationships. Gallieni was in fact an admirer of Spencer, whom he found to be "strikingly objective."[48] He conveys, therefore, little or no respect for the doctrines, morals, and culture of the native populations. In this respect there is a marked contrast between Gallieni and Lyautey. Lyautey's approach to reality was more aesthetical, he loved the world because of its variety. In this connection Deschamps remarks on his "horror of uniformity and assimilation."[49] The resemblance between Gallieni and Lyautey, and the major differences with respect to Callwell lie, however, in their political approaches to the problem of pacification. More than most colonial commanders, the two Frenchmen were able to comprehend the background leading up to native resistance and they developed methods to help eliminate these sources of discontent.

The cooperation between Gallieni and Lyautey, which was to grow into a strong mutual admiration, began in Tonkin. Gallieni, who had served in Senegal under Faidherbe, was sent to Tonkin in 1892 to take charge of the pacification. Lyautey followed him in 1894 when, because of his controversial article "Du rôle social de l'officier,"[50] it appeared wiser to leave the motherland for a while. Two years later, in September 1896, Gallieni departed for Madagascar. A year later he asked Lyautey to join him there. Gallieni remained there until 1905, while Lyautey left for North Africa in 1902 where he was to win his greatest fame. In view of this prolonged cooperation and mutual influence, it is justifiable to speak of the Gallieni-Lyautey method—in spite of all their differences. Their method is characterized by a preference for the empirical approach, which is rather unusual for a Frenchman. Their basic ideas are that the individual is more important than the system, and experience more important than the rules. As Lyautey says: "I have no doctrine . . . I simply know men."[51] Adaptation and evolution are the watchwords. "Idées préconçues" and rigid organizations are disastrous.

Using this Anglo-Saxon approach, Lyautey and Gallieni attacked the problems they were facing. Because political and military activities must be coordinated, they argued that agreement among all authorities is essential. Initially, all power must be placed in the hands of the military commanders since that is when the military problems are the most important. (Not surprisingly, the desire for autonomy and the tendency toward insubordination by both of these generals was to become infamous!) But the military authorities should lose no time in treating the political problems. Pacification has two aspects, namely, the "action lente" and the "action vive."[52] The "action lente" or "occupation progressive,'' which is the better approach, consists of the establishment of permanent posts and the gradual purging of the area. During the course of this process it may be necessary to provide the native populations with weapons to protect themselves. The ''action lente'' was based on their experiences in Tonkin. Being unable to pursue and destroy the rebels, they opened up the area with roads and fortified posts. The method was, however, especially valuable in Madagascar and Morocco, while in Tonkin resistance was so marked that it was necessary to resort fairly often to ''action vive,'' the actual military operations. These were executed according to Bugeaud's method, that is, rapid attacks by lightly equipped mobile columns. But even if the ''action vive'' is directed toward the destruction of the opposition, it is essential to keep devastation to a minimum. Immediately after the operations the villages must be rebuilt, schools organized, and markets created. As one historian summarized the strategy: ''Fight if necessary, but fight as little as possible.''[53]

The purpose of colonial wars was, after all, different from that of European wars. It is not only victory over the enemy that counts; it is also essential to provoke as little hatred as possible and to kill as few people as possible.[54] This is why the military activities must be coordinated with the socioeconomic organization, with the construction of roads and development of telegraph communications, with the granting of concessions to Europeans and natives. It was in this context that Lyautey formulated his famous image of pacification as a drop of oil on the water: ''with pacification a great wave of civilization spreads out like an oil slick.''[55]

In comparison with the thundering artillery in Ernest Psichari's colonial-military novels,[56] the howling dervishes of Abu Klea, and the humming spears of the Zulus at Rorke's Drift, this obsession with telegraph poles and village schools with ''patient, unrewarding and obscure duties''[57] seems somewhat unrealistic. Were Gallieni and Lyautey then ''sentimental''? Of course not. The same passion for action, adventure, and responsibility which drove the *officiers soudanais* also motivated them to choose the colonial army. In this respect they were no different from the others. It can be stated, however, that they, with others, were not *sabreurs* but officers with an intellectual training and a social conscience. Certainly, within the framework of French colonial ideology, which was highly saturated with a passion for the *mission civilisatrice*, it was important that these two men added humanitarianism to the image of the colonial war as well as that of French officers, without destroying their image of romance and heroism. Thus, they contributed a great deal by enhancing the prestige of the officers and elevating public opinion of the army at a time when this was urgently needed, namely, after the Dreyfus affair.[58]

COLONIAL WAR AND ARMED PEACE: A BALANCE SHEET

This last comment brings us back to the problem with which we began, that is, the relationship between (colonial) wars and (armed) peace. The year 1894 marked the pacification of Tonkin, but also the Franco-Russian alliance; 1898 was the year of Fashoda, but also of the Dreyfus affair. The foreign, domestic, and colonial policies were not three isolated areas but were joined together in various ways. Colonial expansion—in any event for France and Germany—could be carried out thanks to armed peace; it existed in the margins of major politics and as far as the government and parliament were concerned, it remained a question of secondary importance. The public regarded it with "bienveillante indifférence,"[59] sometimes after a spectacular victory flaring into a collective but brief enthusiasm which was quickly doused by irritation over expenses and losses in these far-off places. Therefore, colonial warfare was left to the experts. The colonial armies developed their own style and *esprit de corps*. Control by the government and parliament was non-existent, organization was anarchic. Knowledge of the terrain and opposition of country and people was limited to a few rare experts so that there was little choice but to follow the compass of these *connaisseurs*, of whom it is a truism to say that "nothing succeeds like success." The secret of this success was, according to the best, from Bugeaud to Van Heutsz, forget what you have learned and start afresh. Thus, the theory was born that the colonial war was a war *sui generis* with its own laws and rules.

And yet this did not mean a total breach between these small wars and the great war which had already started to cast its shadow in 1905. Many of the well-known generals and colonels from the colonial wars, such as Kitchener, Gallieni, and Lyautey, were to assume positions of significance during the First World War. The French theorist of the "offensive à outrance," Colonel Grandmaison, had been Gallieni's adjutant in Tonkin.[60] Allenby and Wilson had studied under the English theorist of guerrilla warfare Miller Maguire.[61] Within the realm of military theory there was a clear relationship between the two types of war. This connection is reflected in particular in the theories of moral factors and offensive strategy.

The First World War was to be characterized by large-scale offensives accompanied by massive slaughter. This strategy was based primarily on the conviction that willpower and morale would be the decisive factors: "Victoire égale volonté," in the famous words of Foch.[62] This belief in the offensive, whereby the will of the enemy must be broken, depended upon several presumptions which were partly psychological and partly philosophical in nature.[63] But the theory was also supported by a series of analyses of recent conflicts. The most important studies concerned, of course, the two most recent great wars: the Boer War and the Russo-Japanese War. However, the colonial wars were also included in the general considerations and their influence on military thinking is self-evident. The "eternal principle" of the colonial war, according to Lyautey, that "passive defense can only lead to being overrun"[64] differs little from Foch's "principle of war" that "passive defense cannot avert defeat."[65] Callwell's statement on small wars, namely, that "moral effect ranks almost before material gain,"[66] is reflected in Grandmaison's comment: "factors of morale are not the most important; they are the only ones that matter in war."[67]

The colonial armies were accustomed—and often compelled—to attack continuously, irrespective of their chances of success, in order to sustain the image of European superiority. It is not difficult to discover the connection between this approach and the predominant mentality of 1914–1918, which focused sharply on willpower, morale, and holding the offensive. The infantry quickly discovered that machine guns and barbed wire are not as easily hypnotized as poorly armed Asiatics. But as Kiernan wrote: "Their generals in the rear, many of them with minds still farther away in the Asian or African campaigning grounds of their youth, could not be got to see the point."[68] Thus, for the French army the road from Sedan to Verdun passed through Tonkin.

However, the large and the small war are not only interwoven in the realm of military doctrine, but also in a more general sense. Colonial wars took place in a world of romance and heroism. The setting was exotic, the war hard, but rich in glory. The social-Darwinist concepts, which influenced the way many viewed the world, attributed a moral right to the strong, and therefore superior person to dominate the weak, and therefore inferior one. Thus, the colonial wars were not only exciting, they were also justified and necessary. And, possibly even more important, the colonial wars were almost always successful and the colonial armies were—almost by definition—triumphant armies. Of course, there were some exceptions such as Isandlwhana and Khartoum and, above all, the shame of Adowa; but these were only incidences which demanded revenge. As a rule the colonial army came, saw, conquered, and remained.

The colonial wars confirmed the military doctrine which maintained that the key to victory is willpower and the offensive; colonial military novels painted a scene that made it possible, 50 years after Solferino, to believe once again in the beauty of war. Thus, the small wars helped to create the conditions which led to the Great War.

Chapter 3

Knowledge Is Power: Some Remarks on Colonialism and Science

Tropical studies—or colonial studies, as they used to be called—have a long tradition in the Netherlands. From the very beginning, European expansion stimulated some forms of study of the East, its flora and fauna, its geography, and its topography. All the same, one might say that the systematic study of the East started only in the nineteenth century. This was obviously due to the expansion of colonialism. Colonial studies were introduced into some Dutch universities, especially in Leyden, where the training of colonial civil servants was incorporated in the University in 1877. Several relevant disciplines and subjects were developed: administration, colonial economy, "adat" law (customary law), Islamic studies, Chinese studies and, of course, linguistic and cultural studies of the peoples of the Indonesian archipelago.

Apart from the universities, other important institutes and societies were also founded in this period such as the Colonial Institute, the Institute of Linguistics, Geography and Ethnography of the Netherlands-Indies, and the Geographical Society.

The history of these studies and institutes, covering more than one hundred years, may illustrate a number of problems engendered by the relationship between colonialism and scientific studies, which I should like to discuss in this chapter. I will concentrate on two questions.

1. Was decolonization a rupture, and did development cooperation mark the beginning of a new era, or could one say that even during the colonial period a kind of development policy existed?
2. What were the advantages and disadvantages of these tropical studies? Should one praise them as a branch of pure science and as useful knowledge or reject them as an instrument of domination and a symptom of Western supremacy?

But before looking somewhat more closely at these questions, we should briefly overview the development of the East-West relations that form the background of these studies.

EAST-WEST RELATIONS IN PERSPECTIVE

When speaking of East-West relationships during the period that followed the end of the Second World War, one was usually referring to the antagonism between the Soviet Union and the North Atlantic Alliance. As far as the relations between Europe, Asia, and Africa are concerned, we no longer refer to them as East-West but as North-South relations. In this change of name, from East-West to North-South, the change in the relationship itself is reflected. Indeed, the current term, "North-South," is not a neutral one; it is the definition of a problem, the problem of economic hierarchy, of an economic balance of power: rich-poor, dominating-dominated, central-peripheral, developed-underdeveloped. The earlier term of East-West was different. The East obviously also implied to a certain extent underdevelopment and backwardness. The well-known lines: "Het daghet in den Oosten" (Day is breaking in the East), which also served as a motto for the Colonial Museum, illustrated this notion. The East still had to begin its development. It was still shrouded in darkness. It was the colonizer's task to kindle the light of modern civilization. But the East was not only darkness. There was also the rich, refined, mysterious East, the East of ancient high civilizations, even older than that of Europe. Once, the light of civilization had come from the East: "Ex oriente lux."

To a certain extent, the shift from East-West to North-South illustrates the depreciation and the decline in appreciation of most of Asia seen in recent history. Not so long ago, Asia was the ancient world; later, together with Africa, it formed the colonial world, and still later the "Third World." This is no promotion! Not so long ago, people were more aware of the recentness and fragility of Western development and supremacy; of the fact that not so long ago, the West had been the pupil of the East; that until the nineteenth century, the West had had hardly anything to offer and barely anything to teach to the East. The vessels of the Dutch East India Company returned from Asia with treasures from the East, but they sailed there in ballast. This was simply because Europe did not possess anything of any value to Asia, except for the gold with which the merchandise was bought. That, however, came largely from America.

How was it possible for this relationship to be changed so completely? The answer to this question may be found in the history of Western expansion. That history covers about five hundred years, which I will have to traverse in seven-league boots. It all started at the end of the fifteenth century with the great voyages of exploration. In 1492, Columbus discovered America and in 1498, Vasco da Gama sailed around the Cape of Good Hope and reached Asia. Columbus discovered America, we say. Nobody, however, will say that Vasco da Gama discovered Asia. One should realize that Asia was not really unknown in

Europe. It formed part of the same world, the old world. Within that world all kinds of contacts and exchanges had existed since time immemorial. For example, Alexander the Great had travelled to India. And when Vasco da Gama arrived in India, in Calicut, he was addressed in Portuguese, the lingua franca, the English of the sixteenth century. This was obviously not the case with America, not unjustly called the New World. This first phase of exploration was followed by a phase of expansion, of extending Europe's power, but initially on a modest scale only. For a long time, Europe's role in Asia was only marginal. This we tended to forget in the era of colonial triumphalism. However, as the great Dutch historian Van Leur pointed out as early as the 1930s—it would be absurd to assume that the arrival in 1596 of three small Dutch vessels at the roadstead of Bantam brought about a fundamental change in the history of Asia.[1]

And what applies to the Dutch naturally also applies to the Portuguese and the English. Such a world-historical turning point did not arrive until later, at the end of the eighteenth century, with the industrial revolution. At that juncture, the potential was created in Europe to sway the world, first from an economic point of view, later from a political one and a military one as well.

This time England led the way. Consequently, the nineteenth century was the Golden Age of the British Empire. The other European countries followed in the final quarter of the nineteenth century, when the great scramble for colonies started, which is known as modern imperialism. The distribution of the world was completed by 1900 and only then did the period of full colonialism start, the era of Europe's actual domination of the earth. As early as 1945 this era came to an end. In 1950 the decolonization of Asia was almost completed. In 1960 the decolonization of Africa was in full swing, and by 1975 the colonial era was over.

In this history the Netherlands played a fairly significant role. It participated in the exploration of Asia. In the seventeenth and eighteenth centuries, it enjoyed great commercial expansion through its trading companies, whose world stretched from the Cape of Good Hope to Japan, and from the Gold Coast to Brazil. After the Napoleonic times, the Dutch activities were restricted almost entirely to Indonesia or, more specifically, to Java.

The first phase of this new period, which lasted from 1815 to 1870, may therefore be called the "Java era." The Netherlands was very deeply involved in the administrative and economic exploitation of this garden of Eden—more deeply, it would seem, than any other colonial power in any other colony. The rest of the Archipelago, however, largely remained beyond its scope. With the rise of industrialization and modern imperialism, the Netherlands also altered its course. It followed the fluctuation of the world economy and world politics. As a result, the years 1870–1900 constituted a second phase, a period of transition. This was characterized by new economic exploitations, particularly on Sumatra, and an accelerated establishment of Dutch rule in what were called the "Buitengewesten" (Outer Districts). Around 1900 this process had been completed.

In 1899, the year in which Kipling published his famous poem on the White Man's Burden, on the occasion of the American conquest of the Philippines, Van Deventer published his well-known article in the Dutch review *De Gids*, entitled "Een Eereschuld" (A Debt of Honour), by which the so-called "ethical policy" was introduced. This policy was officially proclaimed in the 1901 "Troonrede" (Speech from the Throne) by Queen Wilhelmina.

This means that, for the Netherlands, the era of full colonialism also started around 1900. This third and final phase in actual fact lasted until the Japanese occupation of the Netherlands Indies in 1942. The spirit of this era was characterized by two things: unwavering self-confidence and belief in the colonial system, on the one hand, but, on the other hand, a new sense of responsibility, a new colonial ideology of education and development, in short: a clear conscience. In retrospect, it is strange to realize that the belief in the colonial system was never stronger and the conscience of the Europeans never clearer than at the time when the counterforces were already manifesting themselves. As early as in 1885 the Indian National Congress had been convened and in 1914, Gandhi returned to India and began his independence movement. In 1908 the Budi Utomo was established in the Netherlands Indies and in 1912 the Sarekat Islam, the cornerstones of the nationalist movement. It may seem a paradoxical phenomenon, a firm belief in colonialism with the rise of decolonization in sight, but in actual fact it is very natural. They form two aspects of the same issue, the development of the colony.

THE CONTINUITY OF ECONOMIC DEVELOPMENT

The colonial era came to an end with decolonization. Especially in the case of the Netherlands and Indonesia, there was a sharp caesura, a dramatic rupture. But if we look at the development side, the rupture is not quite so sharp there. The caesura of development does not lie around 1950, but rather around 1900, with the "Ethical Policy" and "The White Man's Burden," or in plain language, with modern colonization. There is a kind of continuity between the type of colonialism that was developed in the course of the twentieth century and development cooperation of a later date.[2]

To begin with, this continuity is to be found on the level of subjective experience. The memoirs of former colonial civil servants—whether written by Frenchmen, Englishmen, or Dutchmen, about either Asia or Africa—all express the same sentiment, the feeling that they have been in the avant-garde of development work. They indicate a strong sense of having been called, of being responsible for the indigenous population, and the feeling that they contributed to a difficult but important process: the lifting up, as it was called at first, the edification, as it was called later, the development as we call it today, of the overseas territories. That was what the famous French author Sarraut, in 1931, called the colonial grandeur and servitude in his book by the same name, *Grandeur et servitude coloniales*.[3] And isn't it interesting to note that the Dutch business world considered the colonial civil servants educated in Leyden such ethicists, such friends of the indigenous population, and so heedless of the interests of the business world, that it started its own school at the University of Utrecht in 1925?

One can also find continuity in the line of argument. Summing up the amounts in favor of development aid, this is first and foremost propagated as a matter of duty—Christian or humanitarian duty, but in any case duty—a moral obligation, an expression of solidarity, of altruism. At the same time, as theorists and politicians will add, it is a matter of well-understood self-interest. Without this aid, the wretched of the earth would come to take what we refuse to give them.

Let us now listen to Lord Lugard, the famous governor of Northern Nigeria. With him, we find word-for-word the same line of argument: not only philanthropy, but also gains. According to him we should not believe that European penetration into Africa was taking place only to bring civilization, peace, and "good government" there. "However greatly such objects may weigh with a large and powerful section of the nation," he wrote, "I do not believe that in these days our national policy is based on motives of philanthropy only." And he continued: "It is well, then, to realize that it is for our advantage—and not alone at the dictates of duty—that we have undertaken responsibilities in East Africa."[4] Please note the phrases "not only" and "not alone." Who would believe today that colonialism had philanthropy as its sole motive?

"Capitalism dressed up like Christianity," was the sharp criticism of the "Ethical Policy." But Furnivall, the famous colonial author, who admits that this might have been true, also points out that one need not doubt the good intentions.[5] And how can anyone who does not for a moment believe in those good intentions indeed believe in the altruism of our own development cooperation? At a later stage, this will probably be criticized as "Capitalism dressed up like humanitarianism." After all, we are no better than our ancestors—at least, there is no reason to assume this a priori. Neither were these enlightened colonialists like Lugard, Sarraut, and Van Deventer any better than their predecessors—the difference simply was the result of a change in the situation, of the structural change in Western expansion, which I indicated by the term "full colonialism." And this brings us to the third kind of continuity: apart from subjective feelings and political argumentation, we finally come to the development activities themselves. Let us have a look at the current activities of the Royal Tropical Institute in Amsterdam. "Rural development, regional development, tropical hygiene, food and agriculture" are the areas in which the Institute has gained know-how and experience. A thick, triumphant book with reviews on the Netherlands Indies appeared in Amsterdam in the gloomy war year of 1941, entitled *Daar werd wat groots verricht* (Great Achievements Overseas). One of its co-editors was the economist Tinbergen, the first Nobel prize winner in economics and a specialist in the field of development studies. The areas of achievement referred to in this book are: local agriculture, health care and nutrition, welfare, and so on. The wording is different and so is the tone, but the theme is the same: development.

The notion that the act of colonizing was identical with that of developing was an idea that gradually took hold, but not without being challenged either, because then, too, people realized that development also implied change, interference with a society, disturbing the existing order. Two of England's most famous imperialists, Winston Churchill and Joseph Chamberlain, formulated this dilemma concisely. Churchill wondered why one should not allow Africans to keep their strange habits. On the occasion of a punitive expedition in Nigeria, he wrote: "I see no reason why savage tribes should not be allowed to eat each other without restraint."[6] But that was not the policy of the day. Certainly, not under the Colonial Secretary, Joseph Chamberlain, who thought that Africa needed the same things as Birmingham, the city he had been mayor of, namely, a proper administration and sound drinking water. Even the ever-enthusiastic "Joe," however, had his hours of disillusion, just like any developer. "I sometimes feel," he wrote, "that we force our civilization and hygiene too much upon the backward nations. If they like bad water or insufficient water, it might be as well to let them find it out for themselves."[7]

Such doubts, however, could not put a stop to the course of events. After 1900, development had become a household term.[8] The Netherlands joined in this game with conviction and with success. Even at an early stage, the Netherlands administration of Java was seen as an example to others. As early as the nineteenth century, French and English authors praised the Netherlands for the prosperity and profitability of its colonies and told their own governments to follow this example.[9] Later on, because of the cultivation system, the Netherlands would also be faced with international criticism, but this system had disappeared by 1870 and played no role in the great discussion on the development issue after 1900. In the twentieth century, the Netherlands met with international recognition as an exemplary colonizer, in particular of its scientific and technological activities. Later on, however, the very same factors were criticized. All these development activities, the critics said, served Western colonialism. The whole scientific business, they also said, was merely another form of colonialism, an instrument of colonial domination and an ideological justification of it. And this brings us to our main subject, the relationship between knowledge and power.

SOME PARADOXES OF TROPICAL STUDIES

In today's world, we maintain an uncomfortable relationship with science. On the one hand, we realize only too well that we owe all our prosperity and some of our well-being to science and technology, that the future of mankind depends upon them. On the other hand, we know that this knowledge carries problems with it as well. Knowledge in itself is not a boon. The point is that it has to be used in a sensible way. This was formulated in a typically Dutch manner by the poet Nicolaas Beets:

> Be knowledge power; no power is well disposed
> if wisdom not be juxta- or superimposed.

We might even go further than that and state that to many people knowledge and science contain something dangerous, even diabolical. Coining a syllogism, one might say: Knowledge is power. Power corrupts. Knowledge corrupts.

Science evokes forces it no longer can control. The scholar is not only learned, but dangerous as well. This is one of the Western views on science. It is one of the leitmotifs in the well-known Faust saga, the notion that all human knowledge is inspired by the devil. Still, we do not need to ascend to such great cultural heights. This idea is also to be found in the very familiar Dutch comic strip of ''Tom Poes en Heer Bommel'' (Tom Puss and Mr. Bumble). Here, science is personified by the sinister Professor Sickbock, in his white coat, staring into his flasks and retorts. His counterpart in these adventures is the innocent, awkward, but good-natured Professor Prlwitskowsky. In itself, it is remarkable enough that the Dutch image of science is determined by two stereotypes, the absentminded professor and the depraved professor. But it is true, Prlwitskowsky represents the other movement in Western science, not that of useful knowledge, but that of pure science; not Dr. Faust, but Archimedes of Syracuse who, when he was stabbed by a Roman soldier, merely asked him not to ruin his circles: ''Noli turbare circulos meos.'' In practice, however, this difference cannot often be maintained, because even pure science may lead to practical results. This will become apparent if we now turn to the role of knowledge in East-West relations.

Let us first turn back to the dilemma we already mentioned, the great dilemma of colonialism: develop or not, interfere or not, impose Western values as universal truths or respect indigenous values? Here we should realize that this debate, which is still going on, is an old one. The British in India in the eighteenth century already wondered: What are we doing here? How should we act? What right do we have to meddle with this society, to interfere with this culture? We are all familiar with the outcome of the debate. Colonialism followed its own inner dynamics. Economy, science, and technology collaborated in the exploitation of the overseas territories. Knowledge about the East was absorbed and systematized in Western science. In this way, disciplines came into being, like: tropical hygiene and tropical medicine, tropical agriculture and silviculture—in short, studies relevant to development.

What is interesting, however, is that at a very early stage this debate led to a different reaction as well. That reaction was: whether we wish to change or rather respect those societies, in either case we shall have to know what they are like. Thus, another form of tropical studies arose, focused on cultures and societies overseas. Its oldest branch is mainly concerned with Asia and is known as oriental studies. A later shoot of this stem, which flourished chiefly, but not exclusively in Africa, is called anthropology, or, by an earlier name, ethnology.

Let us now look at how this knowledge was acquired. Right from the beginning, European expansion contributed to knowledge and science. Originally, of course, the need for knowledge included the weather and climate, the geography and topography of the Eastern world, indispensable knowledge to shipping and exploration. Next, obviously, scientific concern turned toward the flora and fauna of the tropical world, another understandable field of interest. After all, everything revolved around spices!

Rumphius, the author of the *Herbarium Amboinense* (Flora of the Moluccas), was so famous that he was called the "Pliny of the Indies."[10] These interests continued to exist. The ancient cartographers were succeeded by the famous topographical service of the Netherlands Indies. Rumphius's work was continued in the famous botanical gardens in Buitenzorg of the legendary Treub, the richest gardens in the world, in a financial sense too, because their budget exceeded even that of the Royal Gardens at Kew.

But in addition—and this to us is more to the point—there was an interest in Eastern culture and society, both in the material sense of products and artifacts, and in the immaterial sense of language, customs, and traditions. This interest also existed right from the beginning, but it has increased considerably since the eighteenth century. There were four successive movements to provide it with strong impulses: the Enlightenment in the eighteenth century, the geographical movement in the nineteenth century, and colonialism and development cooperation in our own century. The Enlightenment gave the first impetus to the formation of numerous learned societies, among which the "Hollandsche Maatschappij der Wetenschappen" (Dutch Scientific Society, founded in 1752) occupies an important position. One of the branches of this society founded the Colonial Museum in Haarlem in 1864, the first colonial museum in the world. The Enlightenment also gave birth to another learned society, relevant to our subject, namely, the "Bataviaasch Genootschap van Kunsten en Wetenschappen" (Batavian Society of Arts and Sciences), which likewise was the first of its kind, for it was the first learned society in Asia. It was founded in 1778 and is therefore slightly older than the Asiatic Society of Bengal, founded in 1784 by the famous British orientalist Sir William Jones.

The Enlightenment gave many impulses for collecting objects and gathering knowledge about the East. This interest chiefly concerned Asian civilizations whose past was held in great respect. The eighteenth century did not know a developed West as against an undeveloped East, and consequently did not have the feeling of superiority that was so characteristic of nineteenth-century Europeans. On the contrary, it often found something superior in civilizations overseas.

This outlook changes completely in the nineteenth century in which we find the proud and superior European. The most typical example of this phenomenon was created by Jules Verne, in his *Journey Around the World in Eighty Days*, in the figure of Phileas Fogg, the English gentleman, member of the Reform Club, who travels around the world with his servant and his umbrella, for a wager, while *en passant* combatting barbaric customs like the burning of widows in India.

Travels, and particularly exploratory journeys, were the great passion of people in the nineteenth century and this also explains the increased interest in geography. In the years between 1820 and 1830, geographical societies were founded in most European countries, whereas this did not happen in the Netherlands until 1873. Still, it should be noted that the "Koninklijk Instituut voor Taal-, Land- en Volkenkunde van Nederlands Indië" (Royal Institute of Linguistics, Geography and Ethnography of the Netherlands Indies) had been founded earlier, in 1851. This was a very active institute, but the Netherlands hardly participated in the major adventure of exploration. That was the work of Stanley and Livingstone, of Brazza and Sven Hedin, and of so many more explorers, but none of them was Dutch. This was a source of irritation to the enthusiastic chairman of the "Nederlands Aardrijkskundig Genootschap" (Dutch Geographical Society), P.J. Veth. Thanks to Veth, a Dutch expedition was finally organized to Angola, which was led by his son, Daniël Veth. It ended in a terrible disaster, however, and his son lost his life in it.

Veth had pursued theological studies and lectured on biblical exegesis in Franeker. This did not prevent him from becoming a professor of geography and ethnology in Leiden, from 1864 onward at the "Rijksinstelling voor de Opleiding van Indische Ambtenaren" (National Institute for the Training of Colonial Civil Servants), and later, from 1877 onward at the university. Here we see a significant result of the geographical movement and the journeys of exploration. The discovery of all those primitive peoples, together with the scientific urge to systematize, led to a great boom in ethnology. The museum that forms part of the Royal Tropical Institute therefore used to have and still has a fine ethnographical collection. This was also the reason why a department of ethnology was established there, and an anthropologist appointed, "in order to study the physical and psychological racial characteristics of certain ethnic groups."[11] Needless to say, these words, which today have such a sinister ring to them, were quite normal at the time.

Ethnology had two branches: the physical one which tried to arrive at a systematic classification and description of the races by means of measuring skulls, and so on, and the cultural branch, which wanted to compile an inventory of the differences in "the social state of development." This enthusiasm for historism and systematization was quite understandable. Geology had provided new insights into the length of the earth's existence; prehistory had brought new facts to light about human life on earth; and then—the most important novelty of the nineteenth century—there was biology, which in the Darwinian pattern of evolution offered a concept to distinguish between levels of development. No wonder that anthropology also adopted this evolutionary perspective and, on the basis of the current situation, divided mankind into higher and lower races or—a milder variety—into peoples at different levels of development. In this manner, anthropology produced an ideological justification of colonialism, because it legitimized the existing power relations as being based upon objectively perceptible differences. It was science that turned the other person into a stranger, an object, to paraphrase Sartre. Here I should like to add, immediately, that it was anthropology, too, which later on produced entirely different insights.

The third great impulse for scientific studies of the world overseas was engendered by the colonial system itself. An increasing degree of involvement necessitated knowledge in all kinds of areas. It dawned on people that "every form of government should be based on sound knowledge."[12] If one was to respect the indigenous society, one would have to get to know it first. This explains the flourishing studies of adat law (customary law). On the other hand, the same rule also applied if one was to develop this society. Consequently, the training of colonial civil servants had to become more scientific and was incorporated in the university, to become the discipline of indology. This is how, at the beginning of the twentieth century, the colonial studies and all that they entailed—or, as Lord Salisbury said, "the necessary furniture of Empire"—came into being: colonial institutes in Amsterdam, but also in Brussels and Paris; academies of colonial sciences; international colonial conferences; societies for colonial sociology; and finally, the "Institut Colonial International" which, within a short space of time, published some 40 books on subjects like labor law, administration, landownership, irrigation systems, legislation, education, and so on. All this may be summed up in one term: social engineering. And here, too, we will find continuity.

After decolonization had set in, De Kat Angelino wrote, in his brochure on the change from Colonial to Tropical Institute, that with each attempt at opening up a tropical country it would be necessary "to conduct a preliminary study to be followed by regularly continued studies of the local society, the nature and customs of the population, labour relations and the labour reserve, and agricultural legal relationships." There is a striking similarity to the program of the "Institut Colonial International."

And thus, on the threshold of the present, we are about to draw our conclusion, and this conclusion poses yet another question, in a sense even the most important question. We have seen how in the course of the five centuries of Western expansion, East-West relations have changed drastically. On the other hand, we have also noticed that since the beginning of the twentieth century, a marked continuity in economic development has manifested itself. And finally, we have seen how important a part was played by knowledge and science in these relationships and in this development. But what is the outcome of it all? Did knowledge and science produce good or evil? Needless to say, this question has been answered in various ways, depending on the place and the time. Initially praised as benefactors and scientists, after decolonization these scholars and researchers were often attacked as accomplices of colonialism. The Vietnam War and the disputed role of the social sciences in it formed an occasion to critically review the past on that score, too. Snouck Hurgronje, one of the leading figures in Dutch oriental studies, was depicted by some as an agent of Dutch imperialism, because he was an advisor to the government during the Aceh War. And this war, it was argued, in fact did not fundamentally differ from that other war, a century later, in Vietnam.

Today, people rarely take up such extreme positions, but the problem of the relationship between knowledge and power is still there. There are two aspects to it: the transfer of Western knowledge to the East, and the transfer of knowledge of the East to the West. Each of these has met with very high and with very low moral appreciation. Technicians and development workers have been considered as propagators of salvation, of economic growth, health, and wealth, but also as agents of change and uprooting, of subjugation to the Western capitalist system. The orientalists, on the other hand, have been considered as sublime representatives of Western science, but also as ideologists advocating a semiscientific racism and as instruments of colonial domination. Although colonialism is over and many things have changed, this issue is as alive today as it was in the past. Thus, the relationship between knowledge and power continues to be what it always has been: a problem.

Chapter 4

The Netherlands as a Colonial Model

I should like to conjure up two historical scenes. The first took place in September 1862, in the palace of the Duke of Brabant in Brussels. The Duke of Brabant was the Belgian successor to the throne and was to enjoy wider fame under the name of Leopold II of Belgium. Already in his younger years, Leopold was a fervent colonialist and, for that matter, one of the most primitive kind. In fact, his way of thinking resembled more that of a buccaneer or a Mafia leader. For example, in 1859 he wrote in a letter: ''In Japan there are incredible riches. The treasure of the Emperor is immense and *poorly guarded,*'' in which he underlined the last words![1] Leopold was to try to acquire, buy, or conquer a colony practically everywhere in the world. But in this he had a special preference for the regions in the Indian Ocean. The reason for this was that as a young man he had been impressed by the riches of the Dutch possessions. This lay at the root of his colonial belief, his colonial vocation. Shortly before the moment when this story begins, his belief had been strengthened by reading a book that had received wide attention. It was the book by Money: *Java, or How to Manage a Colony.* As Jean Stengers has convincingly demonstrated, this eulogy of Dutch colonialism supplied the future king with the definite proof for his faith in the importance of colonies.[2]

Now, in September of 1862, he received two visitors who were of great importance to him, namely, Sir James Brooke, the white rajah of Sarawak, and his closest collaborator Spenser St. John. These visitors were important because, in his indefatigable search for a colony, Leopold had just come across Sarawak. He had learned that the sultan was looking for a European protector or even a European purchaser. With his usual eagerness he had immediately put himself forward as such, and these contacts had finally led to the conversation in Brussels. Although the duke underlined his colonial ambitions with great emphasis, the meeting ended unsuccessfully—as happened so often with Leopold's plans. The ideas he expressed on colonization shocked his visitors. Spenser St. John wrote about it:

I found that the Duke had been reading Money's book on *Java, or how to govern a colony* [sic, W.] and was enamoured of the Dutch system and talked of doing the same in Sarawak. I assured him that it would be perfectly impracticable . . . I confess I am greatly disappointed in him. I found no enlarged views, no liberality of sentiment, he thought of nothing but how he could squeeze money out of the people. . . . He laughed at the idea of respecting the rights of the natives, and talked of having a garrison to coerce them into paying revenue.[3]

Before examining this text and the remarkable colonial ideas of Leopold more closely, we will first consider another, and a very different scene.

For this we must move forward many years, 36 to be exact, to the year of 1898. The place is the French provincial town of Rouen in Normandy. In a meeting hall—probably a small one—a less illustrious but still notable company has gathered. It is the Normandy Geographical Society. It is not without satisfaction that the president introduces the speaker of the evening, who has taken the trouble to travel to the province for this meeting. There is certainly good reason for that satisfaction, because the speaker is a well-known gentleman, even though the secretary does not get his name right in the minutes. His name is Joseph Chailley-Bert, and he is 44 years old at that time. He is the grandson of the famous economist Jean-Baptiste Say and the son-in-law of a man even more famous at that time, Paul Bert. Paul Bert was one of the founding fathers of the Third French Republic, a former minister of education, who had been tucked away as a governor-general because of his anti-clericalist views in Indochina. After his marriage to Paul Bert's daughter, Joseph Chailley had, not without a sense for publicity, added the famous republican name to his own, and had followed Bert to Indochina. By then his colonial interest had been aroused for good, and he gradually became one of the most renowned colonialists in France.[4]

In 1898, Chailley-Bert had just returned from an extended study-tour to India, Indochina, and Indonesia. It was thus with understandable pride that the chairman introduced him. Chailley-Bert will speak about Java: "He wants to instruct us by means of examples, and for us it is a pleasure to become pupils again with such a great teacher. We shall learn how a people that is less rich, less well equipped than we are, has managed to make profitable a country which was most unfavourable to Europeans, to make it healthy, to bring about development and to create a market there of the utmost importance to the mother country."[5] But it is time to let the speaker himself begin. Chailley-Bert tells about the work of the Dutch in Java. He is not wholly uncritical. The Dutch, he says, have not always done well. They had been "hard, severe and merciless"; but that was before, in the times of the Cultivation System, which he called a "terrible system." And yet, his words betray a certain awe in telling—

with some exaggeration—about how this system has yielded ''incredible riches'' to the Dutch: ''All the railroads, all the canals, all the dykes, all the great public works which one sees in Holland have been accomplished thanks to the capitals drawn from the island of Java.''[6] However, this is not what Chailley-Bert praises in the Dutch. He is in favor of ''modern colonization,'' to apply the term of the famous colonial economist Paul Leroy-Beaulieu; that is, of an exploitation and ''mise en valeur,'' based on free enterprise and private capitals.[7] He is also an enlightened spirit who regards the interest of the colonizers and of those colonized as being in perfect harmony, as is apparent from the following words: ''There can be no other policy than that which consists, not of impoverishing or robbing the natives, but of enriching them and enriching oneself at the same time. That is the policy which I went to study in Java.''[8]

These two accounts are, at first sight, very different. They took place at different times, in different countries, and in a different setting. Also the lines of the two protagonists are very different. For one, Leopold, the point is exploitation, the cultivation system, surplus revenues, and the transfer of profits to the treasury of the colonizing power. To him, Java is a gold mine and this gold mine is an incentive to hunt for colonial possessions. Chailley-Bert's words were spoken almost 40 years later when France had all but completed its great expansion. Thus, to him the point is not the acquisition of colonial territory, but the question of what to do with the already acquired lands. He pleads for the imitation of the Dutch exploitation by free enterprise. To him, Java is a Garden of the Hesperides, or if one prefers, a Garden of Eden. But the similarities are equally clear: both of them are grasped, grasped for good even, by the example of Java, by what one might call the Dutch colonial model. And in this, they did not stand alone. Far from it. Attention, admiration and, most of all, imitation of the Dutch colonial example were frequent themes in imperialistic Europe. It is this influence of the Dutch colonial model that I will try to discuss here.

A COLONIAL EXAMPLE?

At first sight, it does not seem to testify to good taste to speak of the Netherlands as a colonial example or model. It will, however, be clear that no value judgement is implied in these terms. They are solely intended as technical terms, that is, to describe how the imperialist powers in their zest for expansion mirrored themselves in this example and used it as a model for orientation in their own exploitation systems. For this is the question I especially want to deal with. What was the influence of what was generally regarded as the Dutch colonial successes on the European imperialist expansion process and on the colonial administration and exploitation?

This way of putting the question does, of course, imply an almost Hegelian *a priori*, that is, that the history of European expansion has generally been ''rational.'' It would evidently be foolish to deny the role of coincidence and misunderstanding, or of what Schumpeter has called ''atavistic'' and Seillière ''mystic'' factors.[9] But ultimately, imperialism was definitely built on a conviction, if not a ''grand design,'' namely, the conviction that colonies were, in one way or another, useful. The words of the famous English historian Sir John Seeley do appear to be somewhat exaggerated. In his *The Expansion of England* he wrote: ''We . . . seem as it were, to have conquered and peopled half the world in a fit of absence of mind.''[10] If it was madness, then, as in Hamlet's, there was ''method in it.''

What exactly the factors were which brought about modern imperialism, is, as is well-known, a point of argument among historians. There are great differences in interpretation. Some authors stress political motives (power, greatness), others economic (riches, profits), still others social motives (order, stability). I will not enter into that discussion here. But all agree that a certain reassessment of colonial property lay at the root of the general spreading of imperialistic ambitions. This reassessment was mainly based on a phenomenon which escaped few interested observers, namely, that the two great colonial powers, England and the Netherlands, combined an enviable level of prosperity with a remarkable degree of political and social stability. The connectedness of these two qualities with the overseas possessions was a conviction to be found in many authors. Hence their attention to these examples. It would be worthwhile to examine more closely the image of Britain and the British Empire with German and French historians, essayists, political scientists, sociologists, and so on, in the late nineteenth century. In France, for example, we see in conjunction with an evident dislike, fear, and hatred of the perfidious Albion, a continuous tenor of admiring analyses of the British Empire. Such well-known names as Renan, Taine, and Pierre de Coubertin, the founder of the Olympic games, illustrate French interest in the question, which was worded at its most arresting in the title of a French book of 1899, Edmond Démolins' *A quoi tient la supériorité des Anglo-Saxons?* In Germany we find ideas of a similar kind.[11]

We will, however, restrict ourselves here to the Netherlands, a restriction which moreover has the advantage of presenting the colonial model in a purer form. For in the Anglo-Saxon analysis racial ideas play a part as well. Admiration for the British Empire is inseparably bound up with admiration for Anglo-Saxon empiricism, education, sense of enterprise, and so on. There was a long-standing tradition in this respect. But in connection with the Netherlands, of course, these considerations hardly played a role. Few people would even have been aware of the existence of the little kingdom on the North Sea if they had not been reminded of it by its immense colonial empire. Furthermore, no small number of authors maintained that England possessed a more powerful empire, but that the Dutch accomplishments were the more remarkable, the Dutch system sounder, and the economic successes greater.[12] Therefore, the colonial model is here to be found in its purest form. In dealing with the Dutch colonial example and its impact on others, mention would have to be made of Spain and Portugal, but I shall limit myself to the countries that have played the leading parts in the new imperialism, namely, England, Germany, France, and Belgium; although, in this last instance it would be better to speak not of Belgium but of the Belgian King Leopold II, as he truly presented a "one-man show."

ENGLAND

Interest and admiration for the Dutch colonial empire were born in England. The groundwork for it can be found in a book of 1861, Money's aforementioned great two-volume work *Java, or How to Manage a Colony, Showing a Practical Solution of the Questions Now Affecting British India.* As the second part of the title indicates, it was not so much an academic work as a committed tract. Money, a British lawyer, travelled to Java in 1850 after a four-year stay in Calcutta, because he had heard that it was a beautiful island "with a fine climate, easy travelling and an opera," and because a change of air was desirable for the sake of his wife's health.[13] It was not his intention to make a study of the colonial administration. But, impressed by the results of the Dutch colonial system, he soon decided to study it and write a book to enlighten his fellow countrymen. For, according to Money, Java had been in an even worse position around 1830 than was India in his own time. Then came the change. "It pleased God, in mercy to a suffering people to inspire the King of Holland with confidence in apparently the wildest schemer of his realm."[14] This "wildest schemer" was the "great statesman General van den Bosch," to whose memory this learned, pious writer dedicated his book. And the beneficial system was the Cultivation System, which had changed Java as if by magic into the model colony that it then was.

Money was not a wholly uncritical admirer of Dutch colonialism, but in any case, he found it infinitely superior to the British rule in India. He greatly praised the material and moral results of the Cultivation System and was particularly impressed by the surplus profits. Moreover, Money argued not only that Holland was a successful colonizer, but also that it could be an example for others. "Surely with the Dutch example under analogous circumstances so perfectly successful as that will seem to have been, England, officina gentium, can do for India what Holland has done for Java."[15] Moreover, Money was certainly not the only English writer enthusiastic about the Dutch colonial system. In 1869, the English traveller and biologist Alfred Russell Wallace published *The Malay Archipelago*, a voluminous, widely read, and often reprinted account of a journey completed in 1861. Although he dedicated his work not to Van den Bosch but to Charles Darwin, Wallace is no less enthusiastic than Money, to whose "excellent and interesting work" he repeatedly refers. He, too, considered the Dutch system "the very best that can be adopted," whenever a European country acquired a country inhabited by "an industrious but semi-barbarous people."[16] These adjectives are rather surprising, as generally the opposite opinion was voiced: the populace is civilized but lazy. According to Wallace, the Dutch pattern rested above all on two principles: Indirect Rule and the Cultivation

System. He would not permit any criticism of this. *Max Havelaar* by Multatuli, that well-known critique of the abuses in the Dutch colonial rule, had been translated into English a short time previously, "and with our usual one-sidedness in all relating to the Dutch colonial system, this work has been excessively praised." Wallace did not agree with this at all. It was "a very tedious and long-winded story," a very unfair criticism.[17]

From this material—and there is more—it appears that there was a clear appreciation of and attention to the Dutch system in English circles. The practical influence of all these theoretical writings appears, by the way, to have been small. It is true that in 1875 the first governor of the Fiji Islands, Sir Arthur Gordon, carried with him a copy of Money's book to his new post with the intention of introducing the Cultivation System there.[18] He was, indeed, not the only one to foster schemes of that kind; the French government thought along similar lines with respect to Cochin-China and, in 1864, consulted the former Governor-General Rochussen about this matter.[19] Spain, finally, copied the Cultivation System in the tobacco cultures on the Phillipines, but in the end all these attempts did not amount to much.[20]

BELGIUM

One of the most enthusiastic and illustrious readers of Money's book has already been mentioned, namely, the Belgian King Leopold. Jean Stengers, the Belgian historian on whose work this paragraph is mainly based, has convincingly demonstrated the importance of Money's book for Leopold's colonial ideas.[21] It was, however, not their primary source. As a young man, Leopold had been persuaded of the importance of colonies. This conviction was, obviously, above all based on what he had seen in Holland. As is well-known, his belief in this was not shared by his subjects; far from it. Belgian public opinion was decidedly anti-colonial and would not hear of his majesty's wild schemes. He was quite soon forced to give up his attempts to overcome this resistance, and decided to go it alone. But for a certain time he attempted to change the Belgian outlook and—for Leopold could be a serious man at times—we find him zealously ordering whole libraries or, to put it in modern terms, true databases on colonial systems. This information was, by the way, not so much intended to form his opinion or to put his ideas to the test, but rather to supply him with facts with which to prove the rightness of his preconceived ideas. That is why Money's book was a truly heaven-sent gift to young Leopold.

The imperialistic conceptions of Leopold II do indeed appear rather old-fashioned. It is true that his colonialism was strongly inspired by economic motives. He speaks about colonies being above all markets for products from the motherland, as suppliers of raw materials, as stimuli for trade, as sources of employment for the young, and as a basis for a capital market. But yet, all these modern, imperialistic arguments were only of secondary importance to him. His views were fundamentally old-fashioned colonialistic. To Leopold, overseas possessions were colonies in the Roman sense of the word, objects for exploitation which should transfer profits to the treasury of the motherland. For example, he formulated these commercial ideas in his typical lapidary manner, in a letter to Major Brialmont in 1863, where he wrote: "India and Java are inexhaustible mines. The question can be summarised as follows: is it profitable to possess gold-mines?"[22] But in his later views, Java above all constitutes the true ideal for Leopold. What he wants to imitate is the Dutch system in Java: state exploitation, forced labor, and surplus profits. To this "Java-pattern," as Stengers has named it, he remained faithful his whole life, and it lies at the root of the policy he was eventually to follow in the Congo. The two essential characteristics of this policy were both inspired by the Dutch example, that is, the "domanial system" and the way of spending the profits. The domanial system does differ in many aspects from the Cultivation System, but there is the essential similarity that the harvesting is organized by the state, which also regulates the selling of the products. The colonial profits made in this way (a consequence of the mounting rubber prices) Leopold used mainly for the contracting of great public works, being also inspired in this respect by the Dutch way of using surplus profits.

GERMANY

Much more could be said about the attention given by other other Belgians, such as Jooris, Collet, and others, to Dutch colonization.[23] But suffice it to say in conclusion that the Belgian colonial outlook was a very commercial, or if you will, realistic one. In this respect they resembled not only their northern, but also their eastern neighbors. Henri Brunschwig did not unjustly call the Germans and the Belgians the most realistic colonizers: "They did not disguise the fact that their main desire was to extract large profits from their colonies as quickly as possible. The example to which they referred most often was that of Java. Their ideal was to succeed in Africa as the Dutch had done in Indonesia."[24]

In the 1880s there was an extensive discussion in Germany about the question formulated in the title of a book by Friedrich Fabri, one of the leading figures in the debate, which runs: *Bedarf Deutschland der Colonien?* (Does Germany Need Colonies?). The answer of the author is in the affirmative. Fabri—and in this he was not the only one in Germany—was much impressed by the great riches of the Netherlands. In his elaborate study, illustrated with countless statistics, he argues that this wealth is relatively the greatest in the world. The explanation of this phenomenon, depicted by him not without a certain envy, is to be found, he says, in Dutch trading and particularly in "the exploitation of its rich colonies."[25] These colonies make it possible for the Netherlands, after allowance for all the costs, to transfer very considerable net profits to its own treasury.[26] To the author, this is convincing evidence for his opinion that Germany, too, should embark upon the colonialist course. With another author,

Hübbe-Schleiden, a similar line of thought is to be found, be it with an even stronger orientation toward the Netherlands than Fabri's, who also paid much attention to England. Hübbe-Schleiden argues that the Dutch results in Indonesia were considerably better than those of the British in India and Africa. They demonstrate "that the British, in the art of management, have by far not reached the mastery of the Dutch."[27] For the French theories about the civilizing and humanitarian task of the West he has nothing but contempt. They offer a ridiculous contrast to the skillful and realistic colonial approach of the Dutch.[28]

These few passages show sufficiently that the Dutch example has been a factor in the revaluation of colonial possessions which is apparent from German literature as well. It is much less clear, however, to what degree this revaluation has influenced political decision-making. The German political system had a strongly authoritarian character and it is well-known that the chancellors were not born colonialists. Did not Bismarck openly declare: "I am not a colonial man"? And his successor Caprivi, in an amusing speech in the Reichstag, openly poked fun at the budding colonial enthusiasm: "They believe that, if we had colonies, and bought ourselves an atlas, and coloured Africa blue all over, then we would be respectable people."[29]

Nevertheless, Germany too, albeit late and with little success, was to try to get its place at the table where Africa was divided up. The explanation for this change of course, however, is not generally sought by historians in an intrinsic, authentic colonial conversion, but for different motives, namely, those of a sociopolitical or diplomatic nature.[30] It would lead too far to enter upon that discussion here, but in any case it can be argued that the riches and the sociopolitical stability of colonial powers like Britain and the Netherlands have, in the aforementioned treatises and arguments, played an important part.

FRANCE

A Great Debate

Nevertheless, it can be said that the Dutch colonial model received the greatest attention in France. This was related to the peculiar position of French imperialism. In contrast to Germany, where colonial expansion was a late and marginal concern, France had a long-standing maritime and colonial tradition and had acquired an empire which was exceeded in extent and significance only by the British. On the other hand, unlike in Britain, there existed no genuine colonial consensus, nor clear commercial, demographic, or political motives. Thus, the extensive and costly empire remained a permanent object of discussion. Moreover, contrary to the straightforward commercial approach of Germans, Belgians, and Dutchmen, the last-named only just beginning to be troubled by ethical problems, there were forever voices which were concerned with the dissemination of French ideals, of European civilization, and of the belief in humanity and progress.

So, an extensive discussion arose on the question as to how the colonial lands should be developed to the greatest advantage both to themselves and to the motherland. The Dutch colonial experience played an important role in this matter.[31] French attention to the question appeared from time to time, in general, political, and cultural journals, but naturally the specialized colonial papers were far more important. Before 1870 two colonial journals already existed, the *Revue du Monde Colonial* and the *Revue Coloniale et Maritime*, and between 1875 and 1880 a few more were introduced. The great increase in such publications came after 1890. Practically every year between 1890 and 1905 a bulletin, revue, or a periodical with another label appeared (see Table 4.1). Naturally, not all these papers were equally serious, but many gave detailed information on various colonial questions. Thus, they also provide a picture of the nature of contemporary colonial interest at the time. From this it appears that it was more concerned with questions of exploitation and the development of agriculture, education, and administration than of expansion and acquisition. Of course, not all of them discussed issues of the Dutch East Indies. For instance, in the current affairs section of the *Bulletin du Comité de l'Afrique Française*, which gave much attention to England, Germany, and Belgium, interest in the Netherlands is completely lacking. The situation was different in the *Bulletin du Comité de l'Asie Française*, set up ten years later; in the *Quinzaine Coloniale*, the paper of the ''Union Coloniale Française'' (a society inspired by Chailley-Bert); in the *Bulletin de la Société des Etudes Coloniales*; and in the *Revue Coloniale* (later *Revue Maritime et Coloniale*), both of an older date, which all regularly contained contributions on the Indies, as well as the *Revue des Cultures Coloniales* of 1897, in which Chailley-Bert again played a role.

In general, not very much attention was given to political questions, although there was an exception on the question of international rivalry. The disparity between the small, politically and militarily insignificant Netherlands and its immense and thriving colonial empire obviously aroused wonder. How was it possible for the Netherlands to keep this treasure out of the jealous and grasping claws of England, Germany, and above all, Japan? This was a question that greatly occupied French writers.[32] Predominantly, however, it was the problem of exploitation and administration, of the ''mise en valeur'' in short, which attracted attention. The *Quinzaine Coloniale* had a separate heading in which can be found varied bits of news about railways, tobacco, rubber, cocoa, and other crops. Agricultural questions were often prominent and botanical gardens, agricultural colleges, and those sorts of things were held up as examples for the French.

An important illustration of the interest in Dutch colonial affairs is also provided by the reports of the study trips to the Dutch East Indies, which can be found in the collection ''Missions,'' of the Archives Nationales, Section Outre-Mer. About twenty of the enormous number of missions are devoted to Dutch affairs, obviously not an important proportion but an indication of a lasting interest in what was happening. Despite the limitations of the material here, too,

Table 4.1
The Rise of French Colonial Interest, as Mirrored in the Periodicals

Year of founding	*Title*
1891	Bulletin du Comité de l'Afrique Française
1893	Revue Indochinoise Illustrée
1893	Bulletin de l'Exposition Permanente des Colonies (continued after 1895 as: Revue Coloniale)
1894	Bulletin de l'Union Coloniale Française (continued after 1897 as: La Quinzaine Coloniale)
1894	Revue Tunisienne
1895	Revue Coloniale
1895	Revue des Colonies et des Pays de Protectorat
1896	Dépêche Coloniale
1897	Revue Diplomatique et Coloniale (continued after 1902 as: Questions Diplomatiques et Coloniales)
1897	Revue des Cultures Coloniales
1901	Bulletin de l'Ecole Française de l'Extrême-Orient
1901	Bulletin de la Société des Elèves et des Anciens Elèves de l'Ecole Coloniale
1902	Bulletin de l'Académie Malgache
1903	Annales Coloniales
1904	Bulletin de l'Océanie Française

the fact is illustrated that colonial interest began to develop particularly after 1890. Before then, there were only one or two missions sent out, but thereafter, in the period up to 1914, there was a journey almost every year to study some aspect or other of the colonial system (see Table 4.2). The objects of study manifest the same sort of interest as in the colonial journals. The missions were concerned with agrarian matters; with the development of cultivation, irrigation, railways, rice, textiles, and medical care; as well as with administration, edu-

Table 4.2
French Interest in the Dutch Colonial System as Mirrored in the "Missions"

Year	*Name*	*Profession*	*Object*
1890	Ricard		administration of Dutch East Indies
1890	Thillard	agriculturist	agriculture in Java
1890	Greslau	agriculturist	trading possibilities
1891	Petyt	railways inspector	railways in Java
1892	Chailley-Bert	publicist, politician	colonial training in Holland
1896	Prud'homme	agriculturist	agriculture in Java
1896-1897	Raoul	pharmaceutical chemist	gutta-plantations
1897	Chailley-Bert	publicist, politician	administration of Java
1899	Vigoureux		colonial methods in Dutch East Indies
1899-1900	Bernard	officer	irrigation, railways, military equipment (Java-Sumatra)
1900	Mengeot and Delmas	businessmen	colonial museums in Holland and Belgium
1901	Spire	agriculturist	agriculture in Java
1904	Alexandre Cohen	journalist	landowning system in Java
1905	Mercier		colonial education in Holland
1905	Rondet-Saint		economy and tourism in Dutch East Indies
1905	Vieillard	inspector of agriculture	rice culture
1906	Hardouin	Indochina government official	immigration of workers
1906	Lazare	officer	waterworks and sanitary problems in Java
1911	Hautefeuille	agriculturist	textile congress in Java
1912	Froideveaux	teacher	colonial education in Holland and Belgium
1913	Schaefer	agriculturist	professional training in Java
1913	Loisel		agriculture in Java
1914	Fauchère	inspector of agriculture	agriculture in Java

cation, and the training of officials, colonial museums, and other academic aspects of colonial rule.

An examination of publications on the Dutch colonial system gives the same result as that produced with regard to the missions and the journals. Before 1890, there was only incidental consideration, mainly in the form of travel descriptions, but after that year the larger works and more serious studies and reports, about ten in all, began to appear.[33] These facts of chronology are important because they imply two things. First, the Dutch example did not play a role in the sense that Dutch colonial profits provided an incentive or an argument for colonial expansion as, for example, was so clearly the case with Leopold of Belgium. The colonies were in large measure already acquired and there is no indication that the major expansionists had the Dutch profits from colonization particularly in mind. Second, these writings appeared in a period during which the Dutch colonial system had itself undergone radical changes. The Cultivation System and the surplus profits, those twin hobby horses so fervently ridden by Leopold with regard to the old Dutch colonial system, had already disappeared.

Opinions on the Cultivation System

The French theoreticians thus began to examine the Dutch example at a time when the latter had undergone radical changes and in which liberal colonial ideas had triumphed internationally. Consequently, the Cultivation System did not play such a great part in their consideration and was seldom an object of esteem or admiration. On the other hand, it must be said that the opinion of Clive Day, that the French were always independent and critical in their judgement of the Cultivation System, does not quite hold for the older literature.[34] A report of 1843 by Captain Dubouzet spoke of the "most enlightened administration of General Vandenburch [*sic*]" which replaced the unproductive land-rent by the "work tax"; even if it was also said that the task of civilizing, the only way in which the author could justify conquest, was greatly neglected by the Dutch.[35] Also noteworthy is a major article of 1863 by Emile Cardon in which Holland is expressly set as an example. According to the author, the colonies have often been a scourge for France, but just how profitable colonies could be could be learned from Holland. The article is above all notable for the author's lack of knowledge not only of the Dutch colonies themselves (Malacca is considered as one) but also of the colonial system. The author defined this as a sort of peculiar mixture of the Cultivation System and the system of Free Labour, said to have been introduced by General Van den Bosch and called "a system of free cultivation."[36]

Generally, appreciation was considerable in the other literature. Jonquières spoke of "the affection of the natives for Holland's light yoke" and of a "magnificent prosperity"[37]; Jules Itier described "a perfect order," an "immense model farm," and an administration that should serve as "a model for all colonies."[38] But criticism was not wholly absent. Early on there was criticism of the absence of free trade and the bad consequences of the system for the Javanese. The Count de Beauvoir, who made a journey in Java in 1866 and produced an extended report on it, illustrates clearly these mixed feelings. The colonial achievement was prodigious for a small country like Holland, so he argued, and a proof of Dutch genius. The administration was excellent and the Dutch officials were the best in the world. But he could not hide his criticism of the system. Although he called Van den Bosch "a man sent by providence" and called his ideas "sweeping and fertile," he was not blind to the obverse of the picture and spoke of "violent methods which are fit for a time of peril and rescue, but which become immoral and perfidious when the rescue operation has been completed." He pointed to three main drawbacks: (1) The reprehensible forced labor edicts; (2) the dominant idea of disguised slavery; and (3) the wide open door for illegal actions and abuses.[39]

It is clear that the writer was not only an enlightened man, but was also a convinced liberal and a kindred spirit of the Dutch liberal-colonial lobby. His sharpest complaints were against the moral humiliation that the system produced, the "humility" and "lethargy" which prevailed and which had destroyed the intelligent, mild, industrious Javanese race. The liberation and uplifting of the population was the only permissible task of modern colonization. The Javanese must be led out of "intellectual and moral darkness into the wider domains of liberty, christianity and civilisation."[40]

Similar opinions can be found in the few writings of the 1870s and 1880s. There is a travel report of 1874 by Th. Duret which still manifests mixed feelings about the Dutch scheme of things. The Van den Bosch system was called a "singular" one because of the overly great state influence in it, but on the other hand, it is conceded that prosperity was greatly augmented by it. The system was despotic, but "relatively pleasant and in any case enlightened." Dutch rule was a great improvement and a "veritable benefit" for the population, but it agreed so little with contemporary principles that it could only work in special conditions and had no lasting future. Indeed, that was seen in Holland, too: "it is thus reasonable to hope that the day is approaching when a regime of freedom of labour and trade will have replaced that of administrative control and monopoly on Java."[41]

A certain degree of ambiguity can also be found in Leroy-Beaulieu. As a liberal and a propagandist for modern colonization (namely, that of capital export), naturally he saw the system of state exploitation as a blot. Thus, his judgement on the Cultivation System was predominantly critical. "Sèche et dure," he called the rule of the Dutch.[42] The Van den Bosch system ("the famous system") could only be right if the only task of a colony was to send funds to the motherland's exchequer. In that perspective, he recognized that the system was an advantage for the Netherlands. For Holland, Java was "a milk-cow whose udder is carefully squeezed by the Dutch government."[43] But however attractive it appeared, it would finally lead to "expense and prodigality."[44] Luckily, the system which had in fact brought a certain increase in prosperity was gradually disappearing to make way for free enterprise, which contributed greatly to Dutch prosperity and prestige, and also there was now a greater awareness of the moral and civilizing task. "Colonisation cannot simply be exploitative. A colony cannot remain a farm for ever. Alongside the material production, a colonising people has a social duty, a moral duty, to accomplish."[45]

On the other hand, undisguised defense of the Cultivation System can be found in a few descriptions of later date, as it was in a major series of articles in 1891 by Victor de Ternant. No system, so the writer began, had been so severely criticized as the Dutch, nor so unfairly. Most critiques were based on ignorance or on absurd egalitarian ideologies. The Dutch were happily free of these. As a serious and dogged people, they sought simply their own benefit from the colonies and were wary of ''sentimental theories'' or ridiculous ideas about mission and vocation. As can be seen from the following quotation, the writer was obviously a great friend of the Dutch: ''it has been said that they are the most civilised people in Europe, and an intimate and virtually perfect acquaintance with the Netherlands leads me to believe that this is a true assessment.''[46] As to the Malays, he was succinct: ''In one word, they belong to an inferior race.''[47] Criticism of Dutch colonial methods was to be attributed to jealousy, so he said. The Cultivation System was outstanding because it was a ''heroic remedy for evils which no one dares to tackle.''[48] The same outlook also pervaded the most detailed and seriously intended work on the Dutch colonization in Java, Pierre Gonnaud's 1905 doctoral dissertation (603 pages long) *La colonisation hollandaise à Java*. The writer is full of praise for Van den Bosch, ''a man of genius,'' and for ''the marvellous system to which he lent his name.''[49] The doctor-to-be explicitly attacked the liberal theoretical criticism of the system. ''The very people who condemn from first principles all attempts at state colonisation and all forms of monopoly, recognised the value of the powerful system of government set up by General Van den Bosch.''[50] All criticism paled in the light of the great riches that Java provided for its inhabitants and for the motherland.[51]

However, these incidental voices on Java from an overt racist and an enthusiastic examinee are not representative of the opinions of French writers on the Cultivation System. As was mentioned above, most publications on Java stem from a period in which the Cultivation System virtually no longer existed in practice and the theory of ''modern colonisation,'' to use Leroy-Beaulieu's terms, had triumphed. On the other hand, the Dutch profits gave French theorists an important argument against the opposition which claimed that colonies could only cost money. The Dutch example proved the contrary! But, against this stood the fact that the concept of exploitation as the sole aim of colonial possession was not very popular in France, at least not as an officially espoused goal.

Thus, feelings about the Cultivation System were generally very mixed. On the one hand, there was respect for the colonial profits it had delivered; on the other, criticism of its narrow aims and above all of the abuses to which it had led. But the conclusion generally was that the Cultivation System had been really quite sensible in its time; that it had led to new possibilities for private enterprise, increased prosperity, and had made population growth possible.[52]

The Dutch Example and the "Mise en valeur"

When we turn from these almost historical appreciations of the Cultivation System to look at the opinions held on Dutch colonialism in general, as it had developed in these writers' own times, then the conclusions are much more positive. The realization of a social or humanitarian mission did not play such a great role in this. Colonial circles of this time were primarily interested in the commercial possibilities of the colonies and not so much in their political or humanitarian aspects. They looked to the Dutch above all as a people concerned first and foremost with making money and doing business and not with evangelization or political aspirations.

Praise for the results of Dutch colonialism was generally overwhelming. The Netherlands were often set up as an example. Words such as "model, example, imitation, lesson, instruction" were heard all the time. No other people, so one constantly reads, had made such a success of its colonies as Holland, both for itself and for its inhabitants.[53] According to many, England no doubt had a larger empire, but it was not so prosperous and profitable as the Dutch.[54] This was often ascribed to Dutch business sense, industriousness, stubbornness, diligence,[55] and so on, but also to Dutch realism, to a hard-headed and realistic scientific approach, to the renouncing of theories and preconceived notions.[56] Java was depicted as an ideal colony where peace and prosperity reigned; an earthly paradise full of contented inhabitants, a model farm, an example of enlightened government. That the population was content was generally demonstrated by the fact that the Netherlands spent so little on the army and the police, although often also the patience and tractability of the Javanese, with their tradition of serfdom, were pointed out as important factors.[57]

In all these eulogies two themes come continually to the fore; namely, the good apparatus of government and the level of agricultural growth. This is not surprising. Holland was and is a small country, but it succeeded in ruling a very large empire. For French colonial propagandists, who knew very well that there could be no question of massive emigration and who wanted to keep the costs of bureaucracy as low as possible, this was a splendid object lesson. On the other hand, it is logical that the theoreticians of the "mise en valeur," who had, in the years between 1880 and 1895, seen France acquire immense territories with a very poor population, should wonder how in the world to create the famous export markets which it was all about. It was not only Chailley-Bert who stressed that the agrarian question was the kernel of the colonial question.[58] Thus followed the second great interest, the agricultural problems of Java.

The interest in the Dutch administrative system cannot be separated from the great debate in French colonial circles at the time on the questions of assimilation and association. France had a strong tradition of administrative centralism, which had been carried over to Algeria. The question which became ever more pressing with the annexation of large overseas areas between 1880 and 1895 was whether the old administrative system was suited to these newly acquired regions. The critics of French colonial policy, who were continually becoming more influential, said that it was not. They argued that France must not treat the overseas areas as if they were part of the motherland, but must design a special policy for them.

This discussion about assimilation and association in French colonial theory has been competently dealt with in Betts's well-known work, and does not need to be summarized here.[59] But in so far as the Dutch system played a role in this, it cannot be wholly ignored, for in that discussion both practical and theoretical problems played a part. First, there was the question as to whether colored people had a special character which had to be respected. This central problem of "colonial sociology" and psychology attracted much attention. The names of Gustave Le Bon, Léopold de Saussure, and Joseph Harmand are closely connected with it.[60] These writers based their opinions on the racist and social-Darwinist ideas of such men as Gobineau, Darwin, Virchov, and Taine, and stressed the inequality of the races and the consequential impossibility of a policy of assimilation. Obviously, English and Dutch methods were praised, because these countries had never pursued such a policy. Saussure, for example, wrote that the French were blind to their colonial mistakes, because these were "characteristic of their race," while a Dutchman or an Englishman would immediately recognize them.[61] Harmand went further and declared that only the Dutch were successful colonists.[62] These ideas were put forward in such establishments as the Institut Colonial International, at colonial congresses, and in conferences on "colonial sociology."

But there was also a practical motive for their discussions, namely, the problem of costs. Gustave Le Bon argued: "as well as all our nice humanitarian ideas, we need 60,000 soldiers to keep the peace in Algeria."[63] Harmand, an important writer on these matters, therefore differentiated, in his *Domination et colonisation*, between settler colonies, to which white civilization was introduced, and possessions, in which indigenous society was left as intact as possible, with Europeans having only a supervisory and paternal task. In this connection, it made sense to refer to the Dutch East Indies. "Only the Netherlands know how to go about things attuned to and conforming with natural conditions, and this explains and justifies their success. Except for those mistakes common to all peoples and for certain abuses which they have corrected, they can serve (with regard to agricultural matters and relations with the natives) as a model for all countries, even including Great Britain."[64] Generally, there was approval for the system of Indirect Rule, in which the population was to a large extent under the authority of the traditional native elite, who, as "regents," carried out the actual administration under the supervision of a very limited Dutch governmental apparatus. This form of rule was admired for its efficiency and its respect for indigenous society.[65] However, there were critics. Lamothe, a "gouverneur des colonies," who made an official trip to the Dutch East Indies in 1905, declared in his report that "I do not believe that we can find many examples to be followed as regards political orientation and administration."[66] He called the regime "almost paternal," criticized the sharp division between Europeans and natives and the bad educational system, and considered the Dutch future uncertain, partly because of the lack of sympathy toward them among the native population. Like many writers at the time of the Russo-Japanese War, he considered Japan to be the greatest menace to the Dutch position.[67]

The training system for Dutch colonial officials, however, was a common object of appreciation. In virtually all reports and writings, their high standard was praised. According to Dassier, the administration was "a perfectly balanced edifice and of an impeccable structure."[68] Leclercq called it "perhaps the most perfect colonial staff in the world."[69] Many writers commented on the outstanding education, the good wages, and the high social prestige of the government officials, which also appeared from the great number of patrician names.[70] As the French had no tradition in training colonial officials, they were prepared to accept inspiration from foreign examples. Indeed, it can be said that here the Dutch model had a direct practical significance.

The question became acute late in the 1880s when it was becoming clearer that something had to be done about education for the colonial service. The noted Republican politician and anti-clerical Minister of Education Paul Bert, who had been tucked away as Governor-General of Tonkin, first proposed the setting up of a special state school.[71] In view of the French tradition of such state schools this was a rather logical step to take. Etienne, the Colonial Under-Secretary who made a start with this Ecole Coloniale in 1889, declared explicitly that it was based on the Dutch example.[72] The "Colo's" beginnings were not trouble-free or without opposition; for colonial courses of a sort had already been set up at the private (but very influential) Ecole (Libre) des Sciences Politiques. This school, founded after 1870, had become in practice the more or less regular apprenticeship for high political and diplomatic posts. Moreover, it was an establishment in which there was much interest in colonies and overseas expansion. It is not surprising that its director, Emile Boutmy, was worried that an important job outlet for his ex-pupils might disappear. The very critical pamphlet on *Le recrutement des administrateurs coloniaux*, which he published in 1895, thus cannot be called disinterested or non-partisan. But for our theme what is important is that the Dutch example was so authoritative on the question that Boutmy devoted numerous pages to showing that Etienne had completely misunderstood it.[73]

If Paul Bert succeeded on one point with the setting up of the Ecole Coloniale, he lost another when he simultaneously suggested the appointment of his son-in-law, Joseph Chailley-Bert, as its director. That was too much, even for Etienne. But even if Chailley-Bert did not get that job, he remained one of the most important colonial activists and publicists. More than anyone else, he stimulated comparative colonial studies and advocated following the Dutch example on many points. Thus, it is worth going somewhat further into his career and ideas.

Chailley-Bert and Dutch Colonialism

Joseph Chailley-Bert, a grandson of the noted liberal and anti-colonial economist Jean-Baptiste Say, was born on 4 March 1854 at Saint Florentin in the department of the Yonne, where he attended secondary school prior to going to

Paris to study law. After this he became a teacher at the Ecole des Sciences Politiques and developed into an active publicist. He was editorial secretary of the *Economiste Français*, and editor of such authoritative organs as the *Journal des Débats* and the *Revue des Deux Mondes*. When he married Paul Bert's daughter his keen sense for publicity prompted him to add this celebrated Republican name to his own, and he followed Bert into service on his appointment as Governor General to Tonkin. Chailley-Bert's interest in colonial matters was thereby definitively awakened, and he became one of the best-known colonialists. In 1893, he founded the Institut Colonial International, a sign of his interest for comparative research on colonial matters, and in 1894 he started the important pressure group L'Union Coloniale Française, whose *Bulletin*, later *La Quinzaine Coloniale*, he would for a long time edit. As a close friend of the influential colonial parliamentary group of Delcassé, Bourde, and Etienne, he also chose a parliamentary career. After an unsuccessful attempt in 1902, he took his seat in 1906. He remained in the House until 1914, and played an important role as a maritime, colonial and socioeconomic specialist. He introduced several bills, was appointed Rapporteur du budget and put forward many oral questions.[74]

But Chailley-Bert was above all an organizer and animator and an authoritative publicist. He was a clear example of the new orientation and interest in colonial matters to be found after 1890. The Union Coloniale Française had a rather different orientation from such older groups as the Comités and l'Afrique et de l'Asie Françaises. The Union was above all a mouthpiece for commercial groups. Its committee included representatives of the Chambers of Commerce and of business circles and banks, especially from Marseilles, Lyons, and Le Havre. They had much bigger funds at their disposal than the other organizations and their aims were purely commercial; at issue was the defense of mercantile interests in the colonies.[75]

Chailley-Bert was the authoritative speaker and the most important theoretician of this group. He had influential relations and published widely. Chailley-Bert's firm opinion was that colonialism in France still had a clean sheet and that the most important phase, that of the *mise en valeur*, was opening. He believed that this "mise en valeur" presented a general problem which must be studied internationally. France should thus learn from more experienced and more successful colonists. That Chailley-Bert took this seriously is seen from the foundation of the Institut Colonial International, a successful body which survived a long time and published numerous comparative studies. It also appears from his study trips and missions. In 1892, he travelled with an official mandate to Holland to study the training of colonial officials and published *La Hollande et les fonctionnaires des Indes Néerlandaises* on the subject. In 1897, he made a long study trip to India, Indochina, and Java and this trip, about which he held many lectures, led, in 1900, to his great book *Java et ses habitants*. He also visited the English possessions and published about that *La colonisation de l'Indochine. L'expérience anglaise en Inde britannique*. He was interested in every aspect of the "mise en valeur," in railways, in tariffs, in government and administration, but above all in agricultural matters, as appears from his *L'Age de l'agriculture*.[76] Chailley-Bert was a man of the second generation of French imperialists, of the group which was primarily interested in the commercial exploitation of the new French Empire, as is evident from his intensive study of and admiration for Dutch colonialism.

This admiration naturally was not for the Cultivation System. Chailley-Bert was a man of the modern school, an advocate of attracting private capital and free enterprise to achieve economic development. The state had only a servicing and supporting task, in such fields as legislation, administration, and so on. His great work, *Java et ses habitants*, was thus dedicated to "Monsieur J.-S. Fransen van de Putte, the reforming Dutch Minister for the Colonies, by his pupil, admirer and friend, Joseph Chailley-Bert."[77] Fransen van de Putte had become very rich in a short time in the Indies as the holder of a sugar contract and, thereafter, became a prominent colonial specialist as a liberal member of the Dutch parliament. He was a strong proponent of the deployment of private trade and industry in the Indies and thus was an adversary of the state-directed Cultivation System.[78] As Minister for the Colonies in the liberal second Thorbecke administration (2 February 1863 to 30 May 1866), he issued a number of regulations along these lines, including the abolition of various forms of forced cultivation and monopolies, the lowering of import duties, and the granting of a railway concession to private enterprise. These are precisely the areas (tariffs, railways, agriculture) which attracted the attention of Chailley-Bert and the Union Coloniale Française. It is thus understandable that Chailley-Bert admired Fransen van de Putte and associated with him in the direction of the Institut Colonial International.

Chailley-Bert did not pay much attention to the Cultivation System. He spoke in general terms of the "regrettable errors" and "painful gropings" of the past of the English and Dutch colonies.[79] However, as to the significance of the system itself ("système terrible"), he was very decided and wrote "that this exploitation of the natives was unjust and even impolitic, was obvious to everyone from the beginning."[80] This would have sounded strange to Multatuli, Fransen van de Putte, Van Hoëvell, and the others who had fought against it for 30 years! Chailley-Bert's interest was concentrated, rather, on later developments. With his Indochinese background it is understandable that his concern was above all with the English in Burma and the Dutch in Java. However, he thought that the developments in Java were not only important for Indochina. "Javanese conditions are like those in most of our colonies; it is a tropical country, the native population is numerous, so that manpower is readily available."[81] That was his argument in various speeches. Thus, it was wise to study closely the lessons of Java. The Dutch were successful colonists, he said, because of their distaste for systems and principles, and because of their practicality, based on empirical data and directed to change within the traditions. Here he echoed the admiration for Anglo-Saxon empiricism which could be heard so often in France at that time. According to Chailley-Bert, the key to the Dutch success lay in their conception that the goal of colonial government was "understanding native interest, respecting it, and then reconciling it with European interests."[82] No doubt, for Chailley-Bert the latter was the primary consideration, even if he excessively valued the new spirit of humanism, kindness, and sympathy which had recently become widespread among Dutchmen. "There is more than a new policy there; it stems from the heart. Interests seem to be kept in check by kindness; but interests always get something out of that."[83]

All the same, the point of departure for the Dutch had not been especially favorable. The Dutch were not richer or better equipped for colonization than the French.[84] Certainly, the officials were excellently trained, active, diligent, and conscientious but, as the reporter of a speech by Chailley-Bert summarized it, they lacked "the skill of 'penetrating' the natives, a skill which he [Chailley-Bert], attributed to our compatriots, who are particularly suited to guiding inferior races."[85] Apart from the training and education of officials, which Chailley-Bert had studied in an official capacity, and which he recommended as a model for France,[86] there were two aspects which received his particular admiration: the systems of administration and of agrarian exploitation. The Dutch system of Indirect Rule, which Chailley-Bert also advocated for Algeria, had been particularly salutary for the Dutch East Indies: "Nowhere has the protectorate system produced better results."[87] But he was afraid that the system would develop too much in the direction of direct rule. "Java is over-governed"; so ran his warning conclusion.[88] Too little was done to educate the people and to prepare them for the necessary development toward increased self-government. Chailley-Bert thus pleaded for a greater delegation of power and for the establishment of a native council chosen from the general population as a counterweight to the aristocracy, as Paul Bert had arranged matters in Tonkin. Thus, the example was sometimes reversed.[89]

In the field of exploitation, however, the writer had no criticisms. As the reporter summarized it, "above all from the point of view of economic exploitation, the Dutch have shown themselves to be truly masters. On this head, M. Chailley-Bert gave unreserved praise."[90] In a lecture to the Société Normande de Géographie, Chailley-Bert claimed that the heart of the colonial question was agriculture. This may seem strange, because the colonies were praised above all as export markets for industrial production, and thus furthering of the commerce of the metropolis should have been the central point. Chailley-Bert understood this. "I would much prefer to come and tell you: 'commerce is what matters.' But it is not true, for at this moment there is only one basic question: that of colonial agriculture."[91] What could be expected of an export market, if there was no purchasing power or demand? The natives had no money with which to buy goods and so the only solution is for them first to make some. And so the speaker resorted to the old physiocratic dogma: all riches come out of the ground. What must first take place is the development of all sorts of tropical cash crops: tea, coffee, tobacco. "There can be no other policy than that, not of impoverishing or despoiling the natives, but of enriching them, and at the same time enriching yourself. That is the policy which I went to study in Java.''[92]

He gave a lyrical picture of the results of Dutch agriculture in Java. There was no more beautiful sight than a coffee plantation in full bloom and no better life than that of a coffee planter. ''No mode of life gives an equal satisfaction or, I may add, equal rewards.''[93] Incomes of *f*70,000 were not exceptional, profits of 25 percent (as opposed to the norm of 3 percent) were made. How had this paradise come about? The answer ran: ''through an alliance of capital and labour.''[94] Here we run up against the nut of the French colonial problem. Like many in the Union Coloniale Française, Chailley-Bert was very well aware of the unwillingness of French capitalists to invest in the colonial empire.[95] This was the great point on which every attempt at economic exploitation and ''mise en valeur'' turned. Now, in his opinion, this unwillingness stemmed from the lack of competent colonists who could do something useful with the capital. And this lack was due to the absence of schooling and experience. Thus, the precondition for any successful approach was colonial agricultural training. ''The colonial problem can be reduced to a question of education, and there is no more important problem facing us at this moment.''[96] And here again, the Dutch were advanced as an example. They came to Java with a good agrarian education, ''fully prepared for their tasks,'' while young Frenchmen going out trusted to their hands and their energy ''to shift for themselves.''[97] In the writings of Chailley-Bert the problems and the remedies of the propagandists of the ''mise en valeur'' clearly came to the fore. Thus, they are a good illustration of what Dutch colonialism on Java had to tell the modern French colonials of this period. The significance and the limits of the Netherlands as a colonial model appear very clearly in his work.

CONCLUSION

Our conclusion can be brief. The purpose of this chapter was to demonstrate how great the interest and the admiration have been in imperialistic Europe for what was regarded as the remarkable successes of Dutch colonialism in Indonesia. This appreciation was motivated in different ways. First, it stemmed from an old-fashioned conception of colonial exploitation, then, from a striving for modern capitalistic exploitation. But in both cases the admiration was great and criticism minor. This interest did not only have theoretical significance, for in several cases it formed a clear incentive for the exercising of a policy of colonial expansion. In other cases, it served as an inspiration for the setting up of an administrative and economic system. In general, one might say that Dutch colonialism has contributed to the revaluation of colonial possessions which formed the basis for the flood of European imperialism. This new imperialism, partly inspired by the Netherlands' example, gradually became menacing to the Netherlands' hegemony in Indonesia and endangered its commercial interests in other parts of the world, such as Africa. This is one of the countless paradoxes that characterize the history of European expansion.

Part II

Imperialism

Chapter 5

The Debate on French Imperialism, 1960–1975

MYTHS AND REALITIES

In 1960 there appeared a small book with an arresting title, *Mythes et réalités de l'impérialisme colonial français, 1871–1914*.[1] Its author, Henri Brunschwig, who in previous studies had already been concerned with French and German colonial expansion, provided here an interpretative essay. And his interpretation was clear enough. The "myths" were the attempts to find an economic explanation for French imperialism. The reality was different. In fact, French colonial expansion was the consequence of a traditional policy of *grandeur*, strengthened by the virulent nationalism of the late nineteenth century and, in France, colored in a particular way by the defeat of 1870.

In retrospect, Brunschwig's book can be accepted as a significant part of the historiographical developments of the 1960s, in which an important debate about the nature and the causes of modern imperialism took place. In 1961, just one year after Brunschwig's book came out, there appeared the important article by D.K. Fieldhouse, "Imperialism: A historiographical revision," and in the same year Ronald Robinson and Jack Gallagher published *Africa and the Victorians. The Official Mind of Imperialism*.[2] In these studies, which were concerned more with British imperialism, criticism of the economic interpretation was also a main theme. Similar debates followed in other countries.

Given the specific intellectual climate that existed in France in the 1950s and 1960s and in which Marxism played such an important role, it was to be expected that Brunschwig's book would lead to vivid controversy. And it most certainly did. But even the Marxists could hardly deny the fact that there was little capitalist interest in the French colonial empire. In order to rescue the imperialist concept in its Marxist interpretation they therefore argued that French imperialism should be sought elsewhere, not in the colonial empire but in the European periphery, the Russian and Ottoman empires in particular. Thus, the French Marxists came to the somewhat paradoxical conclusion that French colonialism was not imperialist and French imperialism was not colonial.

In 1984 the important study by Jacques Marseille, based on an extensive data bank of French colonial trade, settled the question.[3] Following this study, and due to the change in the intellectual climate in the 1980s, the debate has become far more empirical. In the last five years or so a number of important works of synthesis on the French colonial history as a whole have been published.[4]

Looking back on these historiographical developments one can conclude that Henri Brunschwig started an important dicussion by asking fundamental questions about the most important aspects of French imperialism. Many of them are still at the center of present-day historical interest. The aim here is to look back to the origins of this debate and to reconsider the issues that were at stake.

PROTECTIONISM AND IMPERIALISM

It is not surprising that one of the most important chapters in Brunschwig's book is the one he called "The legend of protectionism." In the economic interpretation of modern imperialism, protectionism is an important factor. A well-known line of thought holds that with the end of free trade and the closing of the international markets, the race for the colonies began. Colonies acted as providers of raw materials for the expanding European industries and, above all, as markets for their products. Rivalry between the industrialized countries led to protection and overproduction and these, in their turn, to colonial expansion. It was Jules Ferry, the founder of the second French colonial empire, who in elaborate treatises gave this explanation (to him, a defense) of imperialism. On such occasions he waxed lyrical over the immensity of the Chinese markets and proceeded, no less poetically, to call colonial policy the daughter of industrial policy.[5]

However, it must be admitted that this explanation of French imperialism has never been regarded as exhaustive. It has never been customary to explain French colonialism purely on commercial or mercantile grounds. An interesting example of the official view of French historical writing before the Second World War is Hanotaux's opinion in 1933 on the occupation of Algiers: "En occupant Alger, la France remplissait la mission que la Providence et l'Histoire lui avaient confiée. . . . Et ce fut, de nouveau, une de ces belles aventures à la française: l'attirance de l'inconnu, la joie du risque, du sacrifice, le déploiement du courage individuel, le désinteressement dans le dévouement, l'élan de la création généreuse et éducatrice." [By occupying Algeria France fulfilled the mission that History and Providence had entrusted it with . . . and this was, once more, one of those beautiful French adventures: the attraction of the unknown, the pleasures of taking risks, of sacrifice, of showing individual courage, disinterestness and devotion, the elan of generous and educative creation.].[6] Naturally, this need not be taken too seriously and, anyway, it is concerned with an earlier period, but other, more laconic historians, like the Americans Th.F. Power on Tunis and J.F. Cady on Indochina, have explained French imperialism in these regions above all in terms of political and, earlier, dynastic motives: pride, prestige, influence.[7]

Brunschwig resolutely puts himself in this tradition: "Ce fut un mythe puissant que celui de l'influence du protectionnisme sur l'expansion coloniale mais ce ne fut qu'un mythe" [It was a powerful myth, the one of the impact of protectionism on colonial expansion. But it was a myth all the same.].[8] His attack on the link between protectionism and imperialism rests on two arguments: no chronological connection or quantitative relationship has been established between the two. This is to say that some countries, Germany, for example, followed a protectionist policy before they had an imperialist one, while others, like France, did not become protectionist until long after the expansion process. Moreover (and this is the qualitative relationship, or rather the lack of it), he argues that the trade balance between France and the colonies gives no reflection of the influence of protectionist laws. That is, there is no noticeable growth in the trade between France and the colonies after the introduction of the Méline protectionist tariff in 1892. However, as Marcel Emerit has shown, this argument is not very strong, as a serious intervention occurred much earlier with the customs reform of 1884 in Algeria, which had a preponderate place in the total trade.[9]

But the chronological relationship deserves closer study. The system of bilateral treaties introduced in France in 1860 had a strong free trade character. The defeat of 1870–1871 and the loss of the industrially important province of Lorraine contributed to the revival of protectionist ideas after 1870. Particularly in agricultural circles, these were strengthened by the great depression of 1873 (which occurred much later in France than elsewhere), but for some time without success. Only in 1881 was there a general tariff review, in which limited protection was introduced for industrial products.[10] This tariff, imposed by the Chamber, was meant as a basis for negotiations, but the government was more inclined to free trade than was the Chamber and generally took a liberal stand at the bilateral negotiations. The export crisis of 1882, however, strengthened the fear and conservatism of French industry, which was not very vital and was traditionally inclined to protectionism. The protectionist movement gradually gained momentum. In 1887, the large ports of Bordeaux and Marseilles came round to this way of thinking.[11] Meanwhile, a protectionist lobby for industrial and agrarian products had been formed in the Chamber, acting very carefully in the face of liberal public opinion and the fear of "dear bread." Its leader was Méline, a former under-secretary in the 1881 cabinet of Ferry, whom he had already (in 1882) converted from support to free trade.[12] In 1892, Méline achieved great success with the introduction of the very heavy tariff named after him.

The chronological correlation between imperialism and protectionism is thus not as simple as Brunschwig claims. Before the breaking of the strike in 1892, there was a gradual adjustment of tariffs, with a slow retreat from free trade ideas and the reemergence of old protectionist thinking. This process occurred simultaneously with, and in part even before, colonial expansion. Of course, this is not to say that a causal connection between the two can be proved. Rather, it may be presumed that various economic factors, such as the loss of Alsace-Lorraine, the stagnation of population growth, and the economic crises of 1873 and 1881, contributed to a revaluation of colonial possessions, also from an economic point of view. In this connection it is important to remember that mere fear of protection—even if unjustified—may have had some influence. It is generally recognized that English anxiety over the French protectionist tradition with regard to the colonies was often a motive for the propounding of territorial claims. Did not Salisbury tell the French that they would not find England so covetous if they themselves were not so protectionist?[13] Similarly, in France there was concern over the growing weight of German protectionism and therefore an effort to find prior protection through the acquisition of colonial possessions. One of the most notable aspects of imperialism was precisely its ''preemptive'' character. It was governed by anxiety and ''by pegging out claims for the future,'' by annexations without need or clear purpose, with no other goal than to be first.[14]

"GROUPE COLONIAL" AND "PARTI COLONIAL"

One of the heuristic similarities between the historian and the detective is their shared assumption that, in order to find out ''who's done it,'' one has to start from an investigation of motives. To discover who prompted imperialism, one must look at those to whom it was of importance. This reasoning, which limits itself to the consideration of results, is, of course, not watertight, because men can be impelled by the expectation of profit—and thus by economic motives—which are not justified by the results (a phenomenon that is not unknown, for example, among gold prospectors). The starting point, however, is sufficiently interesting, because it puts the question of the profitability and thus the economic motivation of colonialism in another way. For the question is not simply ''profit or loss'' but rather ''profit for whom and loss for whom.'' Even if there is no ''credit balance'' from the macroeconomic accounting of profit and loss, it is still possible that colonial expansion was initiated by particular groups who had an interest in it. Or—even worse—they took the profits and let the government cover the costs. This train of thought stems from a number of presuppositions, namely, that there were certain economic interest groups, that they exercised pressure on governments, and that the latter were influenced by them. Let us have a closer look at these interest groups.

One of the most remarkable phenomena of French imperialism is the enormous difference between the fine theory and the meagre practice. This holds true in the economic field as well. It was a French economist, Paul Leroy-

Beaulieu, who was the prophet of "modern colonisation" being distinguished not by settlements but by capital investment.[15] The reality was different. The distaste of Frenchmen for colonial investment was one of the permanent problems of the French colonies.[16] This is not to say that there were no economic interests in the colonies at all. In particular, in such trading and industrial cities as Lyons, Bordeaux, and Marseilles (and to a lesser extent in Lille, Roubaix, and Rouen), there was appreciation of their commercial possibilities. Lyons was concerned above all with Asia because of the silk industry, which was threatened from 1855 by the silkworm disease. Already by 1865, this trade with Indochina was of vital importance for the industrial activities of Lyons. Various expeditions were the consequence of this. By 1895, Lyons had thus become an important center for imperialist activities and in 1895 its Chamber of Commerce was proudly described by its vice president as the most colonial in France.[17] A contributary factor was that Lyons was the headquarters of the French branch of the Propaganda Fide, and thus the center of French missionary activities. Besides religious mission, the "mission civilisatrice" also played a role. The typical Lyonnais variant of this was formulated by the president of its Chamber of Commerce in a striking way: "Civiliser les peuples au sens que les modernes donnent à ce mot, c'est leur apprendre à travailler pour pouvoir acquérir, depenser, échanger" [Civilizing peoples in the modern sense of the word means: to teach them how to work, in order to be able to buy, to spend, and to trade.].[18]

Marseilles was another city which played an important role in colonial expansion. The Banque Franco-Égyptienne, based there, under Jules Ferry's brother, was substantially involved in the financial penetration of Tunisia, which preceded the establishment of the protectorate under the Ferry Cabinet of 1881.[19] The Marseilles banking and business world maintained an interest in the economic perspectives of the colonies, particularly in North Africa. A typical figure from this milieu was Maurice Rouvier. This somewhat shadowy figure was a powerful man in French politics around the turn of the century. He was many times a minister and also became premier. He is the prototype of the "politicien affairiste," a typical example of the close intertwining of politics and the business world.[20] Thus, he maintained close relations with the Banque de Paris et des Pays Bas, of which he had been president and which in Morocco closely cooperated with a German bank, but he was opposed in this by Delcassé, for whom France's political interests were paramount. As premier during the first Moroccan crisis, in 1905, he actively contributed to the fall of Delcassé. The Banque de Paris et des Pays Bas afterward (as a reward?) received half of a lucrative Moroccan government loan, via a German bank.[21]

Just as the legendary riches of Yunnan in South China played a role in the Lyonnais interest in Indochina, so there was a similar legend in the background of French exploration in the Sudan. Bahr-el-Ghazal, in this region, also aroused the interest of Leopold II and strengthened his honestly confessed desire to acquire a sizeable slice of the "magnifique gâteau africain."[22] Stengers has shown that this myth of a new Eldorado had a persistent life and could still be found in 1904 when it was accepted by a serious author like Leroy-Beaulieu.[23] That the expectation would, however, not be fulfilled was propounded in poetical form by Hilaire Belloc as early as 1894.

> Oh Africa, mysterious land
> Surrounded by a lot of sand . . .
> Far land of Ophir! Mined for gold
> By lordly Solomon of old,
> Who sailing northward to Perim
> Took all the gold away with him . . . [24]

Financial and business interest groups were thus certainly in existence, but it is striking that they were not dominant within the French colonial groups and committees.

Brunschwig has made a first survey of this microcosm, about which more is now becoming better known. The main activity of most of these colonial committees was the issuing of colonial propaganda. To this end, they organized lectures and congresses, but above all, banquets. Not for nothing was the colonial group known as "le parti où l'on dîne."[25]

By far the most serious committee was the Comité de l'Afrique Française, which in addition to propaganda, also devoted itself to colonial expeditions. It was supported financially by banks, but, remarkably enough, mainly by bankers who had no interests in Africa but who were personal friends of members of the committee.[26] The committee derived its influence above all from the outstanding relations that many of its members had with government circles. Also influential was its offshoot, the Comité du Maroc. Here, too, the interest was above all of a political rather than an economic nature, although a few members had financial concerns. The main motive was the nationalist-imperialist dream of a French Mediterranean empire with an African hinterland, in which Morocco naturally played an important part. The undoubted leader of these committees—and of many more—was Eugène Etienne, "le guide, le chef, le maître, l'ami." "You will lead me, you will give me orders, you will command me, and I shall obey" wrote the colonial expert Chailley-Bert in an open letter to Etienne, with all the reverence and humility due to this "Notre Dame des Coloniaux."[27] These groups and committees attempted to influence government directly, with a certain amount of success, but also, in an indirect but no less efficient way, through Parliament.

In 1892, 28 deputies formed the Groupe Colonial de la Chambre. This group—naturally, it was not a genuine party—grew fast in the following years, and at its zenith in 1902 numbered 200 members. In 1898, a Groupe Colonial du Sénat was also formed, and meetings between the two groups often took place. It is difficult to establish the political character of the first group, because it included almost all shades of French political life, with a certain preponderance of *Modérés*, and, later, of Radicals.[28] The group was linked to the colonial committees by close personal ties and, naturally, its leader was Etienne. Although the group was thus of very heterogeneous composition and also included many purely nominal members, it was able to exercise considerable influence in matters of foreign policy. This occurred not only because of good personal relations with the ministers of the colonies and foreign affairs but also because of structural factors, such as the French governmental system. Ministerial instability and the weak position of the executive offered pressure groups many chances to influence events. Also, there was no question of interdepartmental cooperation and ministers were independent from and frequently opposed to each other.[29]

Thus, undoubtedly, at the beginning of this century there was a close intertwining of politics and business. However, it would be wrong to suppose that politicians were just puppets of the world of business. The reality was more complicated. Ministers as often attempted to manipulate and make use of financial forces for political ends as the reverse—with varying success. The problem was that national political interests did not always run parallel with the commercial interests of particular groups, which, moreover, often had a strong international connection.[30] French business circles were very pleased with the English takeover in Egypt because this established law and order, even though the Egyptian question brought England and France into conflict more than anything else.[31] The English and the French conducted a long prestige battle over the construction of a railway in Southern China, finally won by the French, after which English business took most of the profits therefrom.[32] When, in 1905, France and Germany were deeply at odds over Morocco, the German firm Krupp was cooperating there with the French Schneider-Creuzot group against their German steel competitors Mannesmann and the powerful French Banque de Paris et des Pays Bas.[33]

If a theory of governmental incitement by steel barons and arms dealers must be rejected as being too simplistic, the relations between politicians and businessmen do present a genuine and complicated problem. The same social stratum, the same ''classe dirigeante'' set the tone of politics and business and, in their modern approach to the national interest, politics and economics could scarcely be separated. The true interrelation between politics and the business world must thus be explained not so much in terms of irresistible pressure from the latter, or of a confusion of private and political interests, but rather of the common social identity evident among the leading figures.[34]

IMPERIALISM AND NATIONALISM

Brunschwig wrote that ''C'est dans la poussée de fièvre nationaliste consécutive aux événements de 1870–71 qu'il faut rechercher la vraie cause de l'expansion'' [The true cause of French colonial expension is to be found in the nationalist fever that followed after the war of 1870–1871.].[35] In his opinion, imperialism is thus essentially nationalist ''grandeur'' politics, stimulated by the humiliation of 1870–1871. This argument resembles the traditional explanations of French colonialism during the Restoration and the Second Empire as well as in the Third Republic. Princes and ministers thus sought expansion to gain standing. The defeat of 1870 had left behind a legacy of heightened sensibility for national glory and military successes which was expressed overseas. Did not Gambetta write to Ferry, after the latter's establishment of the French protectorate over Tunisia, that he had recovered for France its place as a great power?[36]

The relationship between nationalism and imperialism is a complicated one in the sense that nationalism certainly did not automatically lead to imperialism. On the contrary, the most fierce patriots after 1870 strongly opposed the policy of colonial expansion which they considered to imply an acceptance of the new order and a deviation from the main task of *Revanche* and the reconquest of the lost provinces. It was Ferry's archenemy, Georges Clemenceau, who declared that ''Quant à moi . . . mon patriotisme est en France'' [As far as I am concerned, my patriotism is in France.].[37] What can be seen here is the contradiction, evident in French nationalism immediately after the defeat, between the directions of ''rétraction continentale'' and ''expansion mondiale.''[38] It is questionable, however, whether this contradiction was so deep-seated. The champions of colonial expansion also considered it, in a certain sense, as a *pis aller*. But because the relations of power in Europe could not be tampered with, it was necessary to seek the French revival elsewhere, that is to say, overseas. This, however, did not mean that the final goal was lost from sight, as their opponents complained. The difference was not so much in the ends as in the means, because the policy of imperialism can also be understood as a form of *Revanche* politics.

The relationship between the two could even be very concrete, such as in exchange plans which existed from the beginning. Already in the Franco-German War of 1870 there was a French proposal to trade all the then colonies for the retention of Alsace-Lorraine, which Bismarck, of course, rejected. There were similar suggestions later by many others (Gambetta, Ferry, Combes, Delcassé, etc.).[39] In particular the Asian possessions were considered suitable for trading.

In a different way the first colonial literature of the time introduced a concept of national renewal or rejuvenation. The thought ran that France would rediscover itself overseas. ''La colonisation, école d'énergie''; such was a conviction with metaphysical, even mystical implications, which from the beginning existed in manifold obscure forms.[40] In this connection, Raymond Betts has spoken of a ''frontier'' function. The colonies were alleged to be for the French what the West was for the United States, namely, a space for the unfurling of action, energy, and national devotion. The at once Arcadian and Spartan colonies were the antithesis of a ramshackle and sick metropolis. Such writers as Joseph Peyre, Ernest Psichari, and Robert Randau described colonization as a great epic, preferably acted out on the wide stage of the immense desert or in the darkness of the jungle. Here, too, great, empty, primitive Africa was clearly the favorite.[41]

Many ideas of this kind existed, but one cannot say that there was an imperial sentiment that propelled expansion. A colonially conscious public opinion only developed at the end of the century in the form of pride in the "empire" acquired, thus clearly an imperialism ex post facto. The Chamber, too, was not really interested in the colonies, but there, and also in the press, considerable surges of national sentiment can be observed in times of colonial perils. The first example of this occurred with the ratification by the Chamber of the Brazza-Makoko treaties in 1882. With this agreement, an African chief, the Makoko of the Bateke, handed over the sovereignty of large areas of the Congo to France. A contested point remains whether the Makoko fully understood the meaning of this decision. Anyway, after his return to France, Brazza carried on a successful advertising campaign. The press depicted the enormous potentialities and the riches in raw materials of this area, which was praised as "une terre vierge, grasse, vigoreuse et féconde,"[42] a surprising combination of qualities. The propaganda did not fail in its object. The debates in the Chamber were no less lyrical and the proposals for ratification were adopted unanimously in a flood of patriotic elation. The Chamber had been, so *Le Temps* wrote, "vraiment française."[43]

Brunschwig and Stengers make much of this event and describe it as the beginning of the "Scramble for Africa." The initiative for the scramble is thus given to France and can be dated to 1882 by this treaty and by the introduction of a protectorate policy in West Africa in January of the following year. As against the well-known view, put forward by Robinson and Gallagher, that the "Scramble for Africa" was only a sequel triggered by the Egyptian question, Brunschwig and Stengers argue that the partition of Africa was an independent process. The true cause lay in the fact that the French ministers of foreign affairs, who were not initially expansionists and scarcely interested in Africa, began to support a forward policy. This new departure can first be noticed with Duclerc in November 1882 and was a consequence of the pressure of public opinion, aroused by concessions to Britain.[44]

Newbury and Kanya-Forstner also think along these lines, but they put the beginning earlier and elsewhere, in 1879 rather than in 1882, and in West Africa rather than in the Congo. Nor do they consider the Minister of Foreign Affairs responsible, but rather, the Minister of the Navy, Admiral Jauréguiberry. He and the Prime Minister, Freycinet, arrived at a reevaluation of the role of the state in colonial expansion that amounted to a revolution in French policy on Africa. Like Brunschwig and Stengers, Newbury and Kanya-Forstner thus place the most influential moves and the decisive responsibility for the "Scramble for Africa" with France. For England it may be true, as Robinson and Gallagher would have us believe, that imperialism was a sequel, a consequence of the partition of Africa and of the Egyptian question. This does not hold for France, which started the process. So, Newbury and Kanya-Forstner attribute a decisive influence to the "official mind," to the plans, ideas, and conceptions of the ministers, junior ministers, and officials; Delcassé, Etienne, Freycinet, Lebon, and so on who made the plans for Africa. That expansion in West Africa was popular is, so they claim, true, but of little importance, because the actors were not under the influence of public opinion but, rather, worked according to a plan of many years' standing.[45]

Rather than seeing the pressure of an imperialist public opinion, we thus see the reverse process; first a reevaluation of colonial possessions from the point of view of international politics in governmental and official circles, followed by a gradual decrease in the anti-colonial spirit of the Chamber, and finally followed by a certain degree of colonial enthusiasm in wider circles. This was, however, not the case until after the great partition treaties of the 1890s, which established the division of Africa. This enthusiasm was above all marked by a nationalistic pride in the newly acquired empire and by an evaluation of colonial possessions in terms of European rivalries. A high point was reached in the years 1894–1896, when the Chamber supported such risky expeditions as that of Marchand. At that time there was truly political pressure from the Chamber and from officials on a moderate Minister of Foreign Affairs like Hanotaux, who could not resist it.[46]

The new phenomenon, apparent in the last decade of the nineteenth century, was that the great powers increasingly wished to demonstrate their position in the world by their colonial possessions. In 1890 still, Caprivi could make fun of these ideas.[47] Yet, the process was irresistible, and there seemed to be no rest until the whole atlas was colored accordingly. There were annexations without clear reason or intention and even, as Stengers observed, without enthusiasm.[48] This policy, driven on by anxiety and greed, cannot possibly be quite explained on rational grounds. It is clear that the minds of European statesmen of this era were to a large extent governed by the social-Darwinist viewpoint that relations between states, too, were ruled by the survival of the fittest.[49]

COLONISTS AND COLONIALS

"On gouverne de loin, mais on ne peut, de loin, que se borner à gouverner" [We administer from far away but, being far away, administering is the only thing we are able to do.].[50] This dictum of a French colonial official was a striking description of the situation. For the problem remains as to how far imperialism can be understood through studying the plans and activities of ministers and others in authority, in short, understanding the "official mind." To begin with, their plans were dependent on the information they received from elsewhere. If only for this reason, the impressions and interpretations of the men on the spot were of great importance. What is more, the officials were largely dependent on the latter for the execution of policy. In many cases the initiatives were taken locally and Paris could do little more than adjust a bit, and more or less wholeheartedly, follow. The picture of an imperialist policy developed in sovereign autonomy in ministries and chancelleries is certainly false. Some authors have gone so far as to see the whole of imperialism as just a sequel, a consequence of positions laid down earlier which were accepted rather reluctantly. With the collision between old and new authority, old and new culture, existing structures collapsed and a sort of power vacuum was created into which men were helplessly sucked.[51]

This argument would seem to go too far, at least for France. Colonial and imperialist policies were definitely conceived and executed in France, but they were indeed very largely influenced by the holders of local power. Newbury considered "a steady devolution of executive power from Paris to administrators abroad" to be the most important development of the 1880s.[52] This was first and foremost true of the military administrators. More than any other group the military stimulated French expansion. As Sanderson wrote in relation to the Sudanese officers, they conquered a subcontinent "while ministers protested and businessmen placed their investments elsewhere."[53]

French colonial history has often been described as a military epic, with Bugeaud in Algeria during the Restoration, Faidherbe in the Sudan under the Second Empire, and Gallieni in Indochina and Lyautey in Morocco during the Third Republic. In 1897, Lanessan, Governor-General of Indochina, already formulated a sort of "theory of employment" when he declared that France was forced into colonial expansion by the need to create jobs for the army and navy.[54] While Algeria was the "chasse gardée" for the army, Indochina was explored by navy officers. The navy, which until 1893 was included with the colonies in one ministry, was a nursery for nationalism and imperialism.[55] Doudart de Lagrée and Francis Garnier organized the Mekong Expedition in Indochina in the 1860s, acting purely on their own initiative, impelled by the dream of a great empire that would realize the promises of Dupleix.[56] Later, the "troupes coloniales" developed. Nominally under the supervision of inspector-generals, in practice they operated virtually autonomously and without paying much attention to orders. There was a long tradition of this, dating back to General Bugeaud, under whose rule in Algeria "military insubordination was raised to the level of an art."[57] Particularly in the Sudan was this art carried out to perfection.[58]

Of course, the concern with a successful career played an important role in the choice of a colonial vocation, military as well as civilian.[59] But there were certainly other factors. The need for action, adventure, and a dynamic way of life which could not be satisfied by a garrison life in metropolitan France must have been a major inducement for the military. The historian Gottmann recorded the saying of a colonial expert that the French empire was conquered by "bored officers looking for excitement."[60] The colonial army offered chances for a varied and responsible existence, and for the exercising of the whole range of soldierly functions. There was a wide colonial military literature which described and glorified this life. It was all smothered in nationalist sauce, in which the ideas of the French vocation and of "la plus grande France" were the most prominent ingredients, all strongly spiced with dislike for perfidious Albion.[61]

Understandably, the relations between these men holding power locally and their nominal superiors in Paris were frequently rather tense. Ambitious ministers who wanted to get a grip on things came swiftly into conflict with no less ambitious and self-willed generals. One well-known example of this is the quarrel between Delcassé and Lyautey in the years 1903–1905 over the Algerian-Moroccan border, which was decided by Lyautey to his own advantage.[62] Such a victory was naturally not unimportant, because it stimulated other commanders to take similar action. Imperial history is thus full of altercations between the metropolis and the periphery. Consequently, not only the ''official mind'' but also the ''military mind'' and above all the relations between the two are of significance for the study of the motives of French imperialism.

CONCLUSION

The investigation of the regional and peripheral aspects of the process of colonial expansion is an important contribution to the history of modern imperialism. The excessively theoretical and dogmatic approach that only looked for the causes in European problems and concerns has given way to a more rounded vision, which alternately focuses attention on the various scenes. It would clearly be wrong to go to the other extreme and to undervalue or even dismiss the role of the metropolis.[63] Every event that became a historical fact was actually a chain of events—and thus a chain of causes—which ran from the homeland to the colonies and back and, like all chains, was as strong as its weakest link. Every decision was in fact a series of decisions taken at various times and on various levels. The military appetite for expansion, the pressure of colonial committees, ministerial rivalries, parliamentary and journalistic opinions, and many other factors form a tangle that is difficult to unravel. The course of the process of expansion was more complicated and the colonial panorama more richly variegated than was supposed in the older literature. That is the prevailing impression received from an overview of the discussion in the past decade and a half.

Chapter 6

The Giant That Was a Dwarf or: The Strange Case of Dutch Imperialism

> "What a pity that you could not stay in the Indies, isn't it, Otto?"
> "Oh no grandmama. It is the most miserable, the meanest, the dirtiest country I know. We should sell those colonies to England. Otherwise they will take them from us one day or another."
>
> Louis Couperus, *The Small Souls*

The words that serve as a motto for this chapter are taken from the finest novel about Dutch *fin de siècle* society and indeed, in my opinion, the finest novel in Dutch literature, Louis Couperus's *De Boeken der Kleine Zielen* (The Books of the Small Souls). They form part of a dialogue between the widow of a former governor-general of the Netherlands Indies and her, obviously, very disappointed grandson, a young colonial civil servant at the beginning of his career.

Couperus knew the Indies well. He had lived there for some time and both he and his wife, Elizabeth Baud, belonged to important Dutch "Indian families." The dialogue reveals various aspects of Dutch colonialism. On the one hand, the pride and grandeur represented by the widow of the Viceroy at Buitenzorg. On the other hand, the very mixed feelings of the young civil servant: fatigue and disappointment, the awareness of being involved in something too big for Holland's limited possibilities, and consequently, of doom and danger. Of course, the strong *fin de siècle* undertone of the book is a rather special aspect of Couperus's work and not typical for all of Dutch colonialism of that time. But the text is nevertheless revealing for some of the ambiguities of Dutch imperialism and maybe of imperialism in general.

THE QUESTION OF IMPERIALISM

After a century of use, the meaning of the word ''imperialism'' seems to have become more confused than ever. ''Imperialism is not a word for scholars,'' Sir Keith Hancock remarked quite correctly, and a long time ago.[1] But what choice do scholars have? Either they can give up the word entirely, which is unrealistic as it will be used anyway, or they can try to agree on a specific meaning, which is even less realistic because with every debate the concept has become less rather than more clear. Not much choice thus, or shall we say, Hobson's choice?

Indeed, the whole problem about imperialism started with Hobson. Not that Hobson invented the word—it had already been in use as a political term for quite some time—but he was the first to develop something like a theory of imperialism, and to believe that this was a useful thing to do. As is well-known, Hobson, a Radical, was deeply impressed by the South African War. What he had in mind when he wrote about imperialism was ''the recent expansion of Great Britain and the chief continental Powers.''[2] For him ''expansion'' meant the fact that over ''the last thirty years . . . a number of European nations, Great Britain being first and foremost, have annexed or otherwise asserted political sway over vast portions of Africa and Asia, and over numerous islands in the Pacific and elsewhere.''[3] Thus, Hobson was not at all vague about imperialism: it was the establishment of political control. Nor was he vague about where imperialism came from: from the financial milieu in the mother country. Other persons, statesmen, soldiers, missionaries, and the like, might play some role, ''but the final determination rests with the financial power.''[4] Thus, Hobson gives us a definition, a periodization, and an explanation.

Unfortunately, it can hardly be said that the many authors after Hobson who used the same word and took over part of his argument were equally clear. Soon a great conceptual confusion came into being, above all under Marxist influence. However, in the historical literature before the Second World War a certain consensus existed about the principal facts. Imperialism was the extension of empire. At the end of the nineteenth century a great and sudden extension of empire had taken place. This was the consequence of certain developments in the European economy and society.

This consensus broke down after the Second World War under the influence of two major political developments: the end of empire, that is to say decolonization, and the rise of two new empires, those of the United States and the Soviet Union. The new world political situation had an impact on the theory of imperialism. The rise of the American hegemony inspired two Cambridge historians to rethink nineteenth-century British imperialism. In their well-known article ''The imperialism of free trade,'' Jack Gallagher and Ronald Robinson developed the concept of ''informal empire.''[5] They argued that the real heyday of British imperialism was not during the spectacular scramble of the late nineteenth century but rather during the mid-Victorian period of economic and commercial hegemony. What mattered was not the struggle for political control but the quiet exercise of economic power: not formal but informal empire. For Gallagher and Robinson informal empire was not so much another type of expansion as a certain stage in imperialism. It was imperialism before empire.

Thus, in the case of Britain, the "age of imperialism" disappeared to make way for the concept of an "imperial century." This century began with the Napoleonic wars, climaxed in the early days of Queen Victoria's rule and was already marked by gloom and decline in the decades around her famous Diamond Jubilee. In more recent interpretations the heyday of the British Empire has been moved forward to ever earlier days. With this continuous antedating of the climax of empire corresponded an equally permanent antedating of its decline—and one could ask oneself the question, which of the two tendencies in post-Thatcherite Britain is psychologically the more interesting one?

In the same years other theorists discovered imperialism after empire. This resulted not so much from a reflection on the rise of the American empire but from a reassessment of decolonization. The hope that the end of empire had opened up a new stage in the development of the overseas world had not materialized. Independence had not brought an end to social problems nor to economic dependency. Some of the new states became more involved in and dependent on the Western-dominated world system than they had been under colonial rule. Neocolonialism was the new word and dependency the new theory. For many people it became increasingly clear that the end of empire was not the end of imperialism. The good old days of Hobson's definition and periodization were over. According to these new theories, imperialism was not only the extension of political control, nor was it limited to a certain period. Other forms of dominance were also labelled imperialist. Empire was only one form of imperialism, one stage in the history of Western dominance, sandwiched between informal empire before and neocolonialism afterward. The idea of an "age of imperialism," 1880–1914, was abandoned. It did not make sense within the new conceptual framework of imperialism.

However, why one form of imperialism was replaced by another remained a question. Hobson's—and thus the traditional—answer to this question had been in terms of economic transformations in the mother country. This answer was also to be questioned and it was again Gallagher and Robinson who ventured a new theory. They argued that changes in the periphery, in the overseas world rather than in the mother countries, were responsible for the changes in the forms of imperialist control. Imperialism is to be considered as a system of collaboration between European and non-European forces. The changing forms of imperialism are in fact changing forms of collaboration that result from changes in the bargaining positions of the two parties. These so-called periphery and collaborationist theories contributed greatly to our understanding of both British and general imperialism.[6]

Since Hobson, many theories have been presented as theories about imperialism in general that are in fact theories about British imperialism. This is perfectly understandable. After all, Britain was the imperial power par excellence.

But for that very reason Britain was not the most typical imperial power. Rather it was atypical. Therefore, theories about British imperialism cannot by simple extrapolation be transformed into general theories of imperialism, and therefore the discussions in other European countries on imperialism have followed different lines and focused on different questions.

In France, Henri Brunschwig's *Mythes et réalités de l'impérialisme colonial français, 1871–1914*, which appeared in 1960, just one year before *Africa and the Victorians*, set the tone for the debate on French imperialism.[7] Brunschwig does accept that, in the case of France, there has been a definite "imperialist" period: roughly 1880–1914. Indeed, this could hardly be denied. But while traditional in this respect, he is original in his interpretation of this phenomenon. According to Brunschwig, the causes of French imperialism are to be found in the rising tide of nationalism in the French Republic deeply wounded by the defeat of 1870. Thus, his book is basically a refutation of the economic theory of imperialism.[8]

H.-U. Wehler's theory of German imperialism follows a rather different train of thought.[9] Although he stresses the economic background of imperialism, he agrees that for Germany, too, the empire was not very profitable. In his view, the link between economics and empire must be sought on a different level. He emphasizes the economic problems of the new Reich (with its rapid and unbalanced economic growth) as well as its social problems (its lack of legitimation because of its creation *von oben*, by force). He considers Bismarck's bid for colonies as a shrewd political move intended both as part of a general, more or less anti-cyclical, economic policy, and of a social policy seeking to unite the Germans around issues of foreign policy and thus to overcome internal tensions. Wehler's emphasis on the domestic rather than on the diplomatic motives of German imperialism—that is, in German historiographical jargon, on the *Primat der Innenpolitik*—and on the continuity of German history forms part of the general debate on the course of German history since 1870. Therefore, the historiography on German imperialism has a character very much its own, dominated by political issues and characterized by an almost exclusively Eurocentric approach.

Italian imperialism was also studied from a special perspective, that of the "new imperialism" of the fascist era. Jean-Louis Miège, in a general survey, emphasizes its political and ideological dimensions, comparing it in this respect to Spanish imperialism (*Hispanadad* and *Italianità*).[10] The interpretation of Portuguese imperialism was dominated for a considerable time by Hammond's theory of an "uneconomic imperialism."[11] Gervase Clarence-Smith has recently challenged this view and made a strong case for an economic interpretation of Portuguese imperialism.[12] Jean Stengers has described the extraordinary case of Belgium, where imperialism was the one-man show of King Leopold II, and analyzed the singular nature of the king's imperialism.[13] Thus, since the 1960s, we find new theories, revisions, and debates on imperialism in all the European countries involved, but not in the Netherlands. Let us now see how this silence is to be explained.

DUTCH COLONIAL POLICY

The absence of the Dutch in the international debate on imperialism is striking. Until very recently there was no discussion at all of the Dutch case. In the many volumes on comparative imperialism and on the theory of imperialism, and indeed, even in most of the international bibliographies, we do not find any discussion of it. What is even more surprising is that the same is true for Dutch historiography. Of course, there are scores of studies on Dutch expansion and Dutch colonial policy but none of the authors discusses this subject within the conceptual framework of imperialism.

How is this to be explained? To a certain extent, ideological factors may have played a role in this. The traditional self-image of the Dutch makes it very difficult for them to consider themselves as an imperialist nation. From the nineteenth century onward the Dutch have made a sharp distinction between the great powers, on the one hand, and on the other hand, their abject but inevitable game of power politics and their own small and peaceful nation cultivating a policy of neutrality, mutual respect, and the promotion of trade and progress. In this context it was possible and even logical to distinguish between Dutch colonial and European imperialist policies. Thus, the prime minister who presided over the final stage of the Aceh War, Abraham Kuyper, found it "an utter absurdity" to call the Dutch policy in Indonesia imperialist. That was a contradiction in terms as imperialism was by definition a monopoly of the great powers.[14] Now Kuyper was a man of the Right, but even Dutch Marxist authors and politicians have also argued that the economic preconditions for imperialism required by their theory were, in the Dutch case, not fulfilled, and thus that Dutch imperialism could not and did not exist.[15] It was not so much ideological reasons but rather conceptual problems that made Dutch politicians and political analysts hesitate to speak of a Dutch imperialism.

The fact that the Netherlands was not discussed in the historical debate on imperialism may, however, have a different explanation. There are two particular contributory factors. The first is a rather practical one. From its very beginning up to the present, the debate on imperialism has first and foremost been a debate on the partition of Africa. As is well-known, the Netherlands was practically the only West European power not to take part in the scramble for Africa. Instead, in 1872 it sold its last possessions on the Gold Coast to England. As they did not play a role in the scramble the Dutch have received little mention in the debate.

The second reason is of a conceptual nature. However exactly it is defined, the concept of imperialism has strong associations with the idea of expansion and territorial aggrandizement. Historically, it is also closely connected with the concept of an "age of imperialism." According to this there was one period in

European history (1880–1914) in which this expansion took a very spectacular form. This is, of course, rather obvious in the case of France, Germany, Italy, and Belgium; but the British advocates of continuity and informal empire also could not and did not deny that during the ''age of imperialism'' a huge formal empire was acquired by the British. In the Dutch case, however, the general pattern of the nineteenth century is not one of expansion but of contraction.

The Dutch seaborne empire had its heyday in the seventeenth century. By the eighteenth century it had already lost its paramountcy in Asia to the British. The great days of the British East India Company came and those of the Dutch East India Company (VOC) were over. In 1799 the once so glorious Company was dissolved. Shortly after this, the Netherlands became part of the French imperial system, and during the days of Napoleon all Dutch possessions were taken over by the British. When, finally, peace was restored, the Dutch regained some of their former possessions, essentially those in Indonesia.

When in 1816 the Indies reverted to the Netherlands, Dutch domination was virtually restricted to Java. Even on that island, as the long and bloody Java War of 1825–1830 demonstrated, their mastery did not go undisputed. Moreover, Dutch influence on the economy was limited, since trade was entirely dominated by Britain, whose Industrial Revolution allowed it to exchange textiles for tropical products. Holland had no such industry at that time and thus Dutch ships frequently sailed for the East in ballast. In order to change this, a trading company, the Nederlandse Handel Maatschappij, was founded in 1824 with the support of the dynamic King William I. Improvement in the financial position of the colony, however, did not come about until 1830, when Governor-General Van den Bosch introduced the Cultivation System. This brought great economic changes to Java and put an end to the financial burden the colony placed on the Netherlands because of the deficit in its finances.

The Cultivation System was in fact a tax in kind: the population had to devote a proportion of its time to the colonial government and to cultivate a proportion of its land—in principle, one-fifth—with products suitable for export to Europe, above all, coffee, tea, sugar, and indigo. These had to be delivered to the government. For this labor the population received a certain wage, the so-called *plantloon*, which was unilaterally determined by the government and bore no relation to the value of the products. Nevertheless, it was sufficient to allow the land-rent to be paid. The land-rent had been inherited from the era of British rule under Raffles. The original intention of Van den Bosch had been to replace it entirely by the Cultivation System, but this was found impracticable.

The Cultivation System flourished until 1870, and although thereafter it became steadily less important, it remained in existence until the last remnants were dismantled in 1915. This system had made Java an important producer and exporter of tropical produce and was initially an object of international praise and admiration, although it was not to last very long. As early as the 1840s criticism of this system, so out-of-tune with the liberal spirit of the times, had begun. It became steadily more insistent and reached its peak in 1859 in the famous novel by "Multatuli" about the abuses of the Cultivation System, *Max Havelaar*. This book was to influence public opinion decisively. When in 1860 the liberals came to power, the system was gradually demolished to make way for a system of free labor and private enterprise made possible by the 1870 Agrarian Law of Minister De Waal. By an irony of history in those years, the conservatives (in principle, supporters of the system) also had their criticisms of the excesses of the Cultivation System, whose proceeds reached their highest point as a result of price rises on the European market. The liberal theoreticians argued that private entrepreneurs would take over the task, but this argument proved false as these entrepreneurs preferred the protection of the government above truly free enterprise, for which in Java the social conditions were not as yet present. Equally, Dutch capitalists preferred to invest in American railways or Russian bonds rather than Netherlands Indies enterprises, which they found too risky. Thus, the frequently repeated theory that the Cultivation System was obsolete and disappeared spontaneously, as it were, because entrepreneurs took over its function was a myth of liberal historiography, as C. Fasseur has demonstrated.[16] Rather it was the victim of liberal ideological criticism and repeated complaints and scandals about nepotism or favouritism in the awarding of the very lucrative sugar contracts. In other words, the explanation of its disappearance has to be sought from among political, not economic, factors.

In 1870 there began a new period of economic development and territorial expansion as a consequence of the opening of the Suez Canal and of De Waal's Agrarian Law, which allowed the settlement of European planters in Indonesia. However, there were many economic problems, arising not least from the impact of the "Great Depression" of 1873–1896. In the same years there was also the bloody struggle over territorial expansion in Aceh (north Sumatra). Expansion in the form of punitive expeditions and administrative extension was a constant feature of Dutch colonialism in the nineteenth century, but the Aceh War was different because of its scale and intensity. It lasted for a very long time—from 1873 to 1903—and the number of casualties, at approximately 100,000, is unmatched in Dutch military history. What, then, were the causes of this long conflict? Was it an act of jingoistic imperialism? Certainly not. The war was very unpopular, as much with the ever-prudent Dutch government as with the protesting Dutch taxpayers and the public at large. Nor can the reasons be found in economic motivation. There was no need of markets or raw materials, let alone capital investments on these far-away shores. Some historians have smelled petroleum behind the drawn-out conflict. But this penetrating odor cannot be traced before about 1895 when the war had already been long under way.

The causes of the Aceh War lay in diplomatic factors. Fear of American intervention and later of England, Germany, and Japan forced the Dutch government to plant the flag and to have it respected in areas which they would rather have left alone. As a small country with limited abilities to react, the Netherlands could not permit dangerous vacuums to exist on the fringes of its colonial belongings, but on the other hand, could not allow the onset of major military operations either. Therefore, the war dragged on for about 30 years until General Van Heutsz brought it to an end in 1903. No wonder the conqueror of Aceh was received in Holland as a hero in 1904. The reception of this Dutch Kitchener can be seen as the first clear demonstration of an imperialist mentality in Holland. Widespread criticism of the Boer War (1899–1902), which was seen as a struggle by those of Dutch stock, was in no way alien to this mood.

The introduction of the *Korte Verklaring* (''Short Declaration'') in 1901 by the colonial government of Batavia is a clear indication of a systematic policy of effective occupation. This declaration—to be signed by almost all regional Indonesian rulers and princes—meant a legalized and uniform objection to Dutch colonial rule. In the same year, too, a new colonial policy was introduced that became renowned as the ''Ethical Policy.'' Its background is to be found in a famous article by C.Th. van Deventer in the journal *De Gids* of 1899. Van Deventer claimed that the Netherlands had a ''Debt of Honour''—the article's title—to the Indies. He calculated the debt at 187 million guilders, the sum that Holland had earned from the Cultivation System. Van Deventer's idea that the millions should be given back was not taken up in this form, but it was accepted that an active policy had to be followed to increase the prosperity and improve the position of the Indonesians. This policy was officially introduced in the 1901 ''Speech from the Throne,'' in which was stressed the ''moral duty'' which the Netherlands, as a Christian nation, had toward Indonesia. This policy was manifested in the improvement of education, public health, and agriculture and the appointment of Indonesians to local administrative bodies. This happened for the most part simultaneously with a more active interest in the Netherlands Indies on the part of the Dutch business community.

By 1904, a period of economic growth had begun that lasted until the crisis of the 1930s. Important parts of the so-called ''Outer Possessions,'' such as Sumatra's east coast, southern Borneo, and tin islands like Banka and Biliton, were integrated into the economic system. Minerals such as tin and petroleum became increasingly important. Nevertheless, until the Second World War, although the proportions of individual commodities changed, three-quarters of the export trade consisted of agricultural products. Tobacco growing expanded, coffee became less significant, and rubber took up a major place. In these years the idea arose that the Netherlands was permanently bound to its overseas empire and its prosperity could not exist without it. B.C. de Jonge, Governor-General from 1931 to 1936, declared, ''We have worked here in the Indies for three hundred years and we will need another three hundred years before the Indies might possibly be ready for some form of self-government.''[17] It was thus very quickly forgotten that the Dutch had only entered most of the areas just 30 years previously, let alone ruled them. These later developments, interesting as they are, are not of so much importance for the question of whether or not there was in Dutch colonial history, as in other countries, ''an age of imperialism'' between approximately 1880 and 1914.

COLONIAL EXPANSION

What we do see in this period is the expansion of Dutch authority in the Archipelago. But the nature of this phenomenon is open to debate. It can be interpreted as the consolidation of what had hitherto been a tenuous colonial authority. Certainly, this process was a protracted one which continued throughout the century and was far from new in the 1880s. Such continuity contradicts the concept of an "age of imperialism," with its implications of novelty or innovation. These are probably the main reasons why implicitly or, in some cases, explicitly historians have hesitated to speak of a Dutch imperialism.[18]

Only very recently has it been argued that the Dutch case is, after all, roughly analogous to others, that the Netherlands followed more or less the general pattern, and that a Dutch imperialism can be incorporated into the general debate on imperialism. The Utrecht historian Maarten Kuitenbrouwer has developed this argument in an interesting and well-documented book.[19] In this treatment he not only pays attention to the development of Dutch colonial policy, but also deals with Dutch international policy in general (for example, its diplomacy with regard to the partition of Africa) and Dutch public opinion (for example, the agitation about the South African Wars of 1881 and 1899–1902). On the basis of a rich documentation he offers a fine analysis of the interaction between domestic, foreign, and colonial policy. What interests us most here, however, are his conclusions.

Kuitenbrouwer argues that the Netherlands was definitely an imperialist power and that its behavior did not differ much from the general European pattern of imperialism. The first argument is, of course, essentially a matter of definition. According to the two definitions of imperialism Kuitenbrouwer offers, Dutch imperialism already existed in the seventeenth century.[20] More important is his conclusion that the Netherlands followed the general European pattern. Dutch actions in the period 1880–1914 were comparable with those of other powers during this age of imperialism. Kuitenbrouwer follows in his argument the suggestion made by Raymond Betts in his book *The False Dawn* that the age of imperialism was characterized by two elements, "contiguity" and "preemption."[21]

In general, these are not very useful concepts, nor do they illuminate our understanding of Dutch expansion in particular. "Contiguity" is supposed to signify that power expanded from existing possessions to neighboring territories. In such a very general form this is, of course, a truism, applicable to all forms of expansion of power in all periods of history. What is much more characteristic of the age of imperialism, however, is that often expansion did *not* follow this pattern; instead, quite unconnected and most unexpected territories were annexed. After all, what contiguity brought the French to Madagascar, the British to Egypt, the Germans to New Guinea, or the Italians to Adowa? Generally speaking, contiguity was both much more a characteristic of the previous period, and was indeed characteristic of the Dutch in Indonesia in the period of imperialism, 1880–1914. That, however, does not make the Dutch case a replica of the others, but rather illustrates how different it was from them.

The second characteristic according to Betts (and Kuitenbrouwer) is ''preemption.'' Betts, following William Langer, understands by this what in imperial Britain was called ''pegging out claims for the future'' and in Germany was known as the *Torschlusspanik*: that is to say, the claiming of territories without any real need to have them and only in order to prevent others from taking them. Here Betts is surely right. This often irrational behavior is indeed typical of the imperialist period, and this explains, incidentally, why there often was no contiguity. But I do not think Kuitenbrouwer is correct in arguing that this was also typical of the Dutch. What Kuitenbrouwer calls the preemptive aspect of the Dutch expansion is something very different. His understanding of this is the introduction of effective occupation in areas that belonged to the Dutch sphere of influence in the Archipelago but where its authority was not actually present. This was done with the aim of removing from the other powers all excuses or pretexts for intervention.

To any devotee of bridge-playing this use of the term appears quite appropriate, more so than the way in which it is employed by Betts and Langer. In bridge, the term ''preemptive'' is used for actions that are tactically aggressive but strategically defensive. That is indeed what the Dutch expansion in the Archipelago amounted to and therefore, in this case, the term ''preemptive imperialism'' is very suitable. But it does not make Dutch behavior more like that of the others; on the contrary. The confusion comes from the fact that the term is used in two different senses. ''Consolidation of the existing,'' as Kuitenbrouwer calls the Dutch form of preemption, is a policy of the ''haves.'' It is something very different from the *Torschlusspanik* or annexation-fever of the colonial ''have nots'' that was so typical of most of the other imperialists.

Thus, the question remains whether in Dutch colonial history we can distinguish an imperialist period, different in nature from previous and/or later periods. Was the late nineteenth century such a period? Do we see a new colonial policy, new incentives, new results?

A new policy there was not. The imperialist ambition was more openly confessed and public opinion was more aware of the importance of empire, but it was essentially the same policy as in previous periods and the ambitions were not aimed at securing any larger territory than before. Nor do we find in the Netherlands new incentives for colonialism. There were no new economic or political problems that demanded novel forms of imperialism. An imperialist ideology and mentality came only after 1900, and this as the result, not as the cause, of imperialism. The same colonial policy was indeed executed with more energy and thus there was a greater amount of imperialist activity. Yet this had nothing to do with changes in Holland: it was associated with the changing international situation.

Imperialist activities could be initiated at various levels. They could come from private initiatives, local government officials, the colonial government, an imperialist pressure group, the cabinet, and elsewhere. Imperialist actions, however, were always the result of a chain of decisions and that, like every other chain, was only as strong as its weakest link. That is to say, imperialist actions could be initiated but they could also be stopped or they could misfire at any level. As Fasseur has demonstrated, in the case of the Netherlands Indies the chain consisted of three links: the man on the spot, the Governor-General at Batavia and the Ministry at The Hague.[22] In general, imperialist ambitions slackened with every step to a higher level. Traditionally, The Hague frustrated imperialist ambitions in the East. There was only one exception to this rule, which was when lack of action could create an unclear situation offering to other states the possibilities or a pretext for intervention. Then, for a short moment, prudence and parsimony had to give way to "affirmative action." The novelty in the last quarter of the nineteenth century was that there were more of these situations, or at least there was more fear of the possibility of them arising. Thus, if Dutch imperialist activity increased in this period it was the result of changing circumstances, not changing policies. Dutch imperialism was not a matter of action but of reaction. It was—and this seems to be unique—almost exclusively a function of international politics. In short, the only reason for Dutch imperialism was the imperialism of others.

Did this result in new acquisitions or annexations? Was the age of imperialism one of territorial expansion in the Archipelago? This is a delicate and difficult matter because the answer to the question as to whether new possessions were acquired depends on what are considered to have been already-existing possessions. There is, of course, no doubt that in 1914 the Dutch effectively controlled a much greater part of the Archipelago than they had done, for example, in 1815. This extension of effective control was a continuous process that went on from the very beginning right to the end of the colonial period. The question is whether this was a form of territorial expansion. Effective control was something much debated in theory but very difficult to assess in practice. In any case, it was not the real criterion in the definition of what were colonial possessions. Much more important was the official or silent recognition by the other powers.

It is debatable whether the entire Archipelago was accepted as a Dutch sphere of influence. There was no international official recognition of its exact borders. The Treaty of London was open for discussion on a few points and, of course, the other powers were not party to this. On the other hand, the protection of England, the *arbiter mundi*, was an important asset and in actual practice the other powers never questioned the right of the Dutch to pacify or punish whatever part of the Archipelago they wished, as long as other powers' ambitions and claims were reasonably discussed and respected. This the Dutch were always willing to do, as the treaties with Britain, Germany, and Portugal demonstrate. There were no great disputes about this. As a matter of fact, one finds in Dutch colonial history quite a few respectable statesmen, cabinet ministers, and governors-general who suggested selling or giving away huge parts of the Archipelago, like Borneo or New Guinea—or, indeed, everything but Java and

Sumatra—to some foreign power. This never happened, but it is also true that in 1914—after a century of "imperialism"—the Dutch colonial possessions in Indonesia did not exceed the limits of the Dutch sphere of influence of 1815. Nor did they when the Dutch left in 1949. If the same had happened in the case of France, England, or Germany, Hobson would never have published *Imperialism: A Study*, and historians would not be discussing the subject today.

CONCLUSION

What conclusion should be drawn from this? Let me say first that in my opinion the important question is not whether we should or should not speak of Dutch imperialism. As there are so many definitions of imperialism this would be purely a matter of semantics. Some definitions include Dutch colonialism and some do not. Nor do I subscribe to the idea that if Dutch policy cannot be properly called "imperialist" it would then by any standard be better or morally superior. Imperialism by any other name would be as bad. Nor, finally, am I arguing that we should do away with the term altogether. Imperialism is here to stay—at least as a concept.

In fact, the word "imperialism" is used more often than ever, not only by historians but also, and maybe even more so, by students of international relations. This leaves us with two possibilities. We can either consider it as a historical concept applicable to a specific period in the history of the expansion of Europe, or we can define it in such a way that it becomes an analytical tool in the study of international relations in general or of power politics *tout court*. The latest theory of imperialism put forward by Ronald Robinson, the so-called "excentric theory" of imperialism or the "Robinson model Mark IV" (because there are three previous ones), belongs to the last category. In this model imperialism is conceived of in "terms of the play of international economic and political markets in which degrees of monopoly and competition in relations at world, metropolitan and local levels decide its necessity and profitability."[23] While older Robinsonian models, like the "imperialism of free trade," the "periphery," and the "collaborationist" theories, explained several aspects of the transition from imperialism to empire, then to independence, the new model is a convertible: it can be used both to explain some specific problems of the history of European expansion and as a universal theory. It analyzes imperialism in terms of a struggle between big and little brothers, of asymmetry of power, and of changing terms of collaboration.

Thus, formulated history becomes a rather abstract thing. All power relations have some asymmetry and all history is the history of collaboration—as well as of conflict—between human beings. Perhaps it is better, therefore, to reserve the term for one particular episode in world history: that of the expansion of Europe. Then the concept of imperialism can be used as an analytical tool to distinguish specific periods in the history of European expansion and specific forms of interaction between European and non-European factors.

What do the British and the Dutch cases tell us about this? The first question, then, is the old one of periodization. Is it useful to distinguish a specific stage in European expansion, the last quarter of the nineteenth century, and label it imperialist? Both the Dutch and the British cases seem to suggest that this is not true. Continuity is much more important. In the case of Britain, however, there is the undeniable fact that, for whatever reasons, a very considerable and even extraordinary territorial expansion took place in that period. Therefore, for Britain one can still defend the thesis of an ''age of imperialism.'' This was not the case in Holland. In Dutch colonial history the main transition was the one from old to new colonialism that took place around 1900. It was this new colonialism characterized by a systematic *mise en valeur* and an active role on the part of the state that brought a new dimension to Dutch colonialism.

This was not an exclusively or uniquely Dutch phenomenon. The new colonialism that came into being around the turn of the century was something of a rather more general nature. The only difference was that in the other European countries it received less attention because by that time they were still fully engaged in the territorial partition of the world that was going on and continued until 1914. Holland was not so engaged. Then came the Great War in which most European powers were involved. Again Holland did not participate, with the result that 1914–1918 is not such a watershed in Dutch history as it is in other countries. Only after 1918 did it become clear that a new period had begun, that of full colonialism. For this reason Thomas August has argued that the 1920s and 1930s should be considered as the real age of imperialism.[24] It would surely be very unhelpful to do this, because it would make the term even more confusing, but one can agree with the idea that the heyday of colonial rule was not in the nineteenth but in the first half of the twentieth century. Economically, socially, and administratively, colonialism was only then fully established while at the ideological level a colonial consciousness also came into being.

The interesting thing is that, due to its particular position, in the case of the Netherlands this transition became visible round about 1900. There are indications that in France and Germany as well the transition to ''the highest stage of colonialism''—if not of capitalism—took place around this time. It would be interesting to look more deeply into this and to consider whether the traditional caesura of 1880 should not be replaced by one around 1900.

So much for periodization. The other issue is the one of typology or morphology. What general patterns and what specific national articulations can be found in European imperialism? What similarities and dissimilarities can be distinguished? Here it seems that although there were, of course, many important and obvious differences between Britain and the Netherlands, there is an essential similarity between their respective attitudes toward the new imperialism. Both were essentially displeased with what was happening. In their own and very different ways, both were happy with the world as it was and would have preferred things to stay as they were. In other words, as far as the overseas world was concerned, both were satisfied powers. This explains why their reaction to the new imperialism was ambiguous. On the one hand, they showed a very real imperialism in the sense of a more systematic and officially accepted policy of economic exploitation. On the other hand, for them the new world of imperialism was also full of new problems, of growing competition and possible conflicts. The age of imperialism was an age of new possibilities but also, and more importantly, of new dangers. It was not an age to be welcomed; but it could not be evaded. In their attitude toward the new imperialism no two powers showed greater similarities than Britain and the Netherlands: defensive rather than offensive, reluctant rather than enthusiastic. In short, their attitude was one of reaction rather than action. In both cases there was more continuity than discontinuity, and what discontinuity there was derived from a change in circumstances, not in policy. The famous words from the Cambridge *Book of Proverbs*, "informal if possible, formal if necessary," seem applicable to the Netherlands, too.[25]

There was, of course, the important difference that has already been mentioned. The British—reluctantly or not—acquired an immense new empire. The Dutch did not even think about it. Their sole concern was to keep what they had, which was a great deal. No colonial empire was considered to be more attractive, profitable, and worthwhile than the Indies. From Germany to Japan the Indies were looked at avariciously. Yet the Netherlands was one of the smallest and most vulnerable states of Europe. This makes the position of the Netherlands unique: it was a colonial giant but a political dwarf. Therefore, Dutch imperialism was, after all, *sui generis*. It followed to some extent the general pattern of European imperialism, introducing a more active and systematic colonial policy after 1900 than before. It was comparable to a large extent with Britain insofar as its attitude toward imperialism was concerned. Yet, due to its unique position, it had to follow a very specific policy. In the colonial field it protected its sphere of influence, demonstrated great *souplesse* vis à vis its neighbors, developed the economy of the Indies and, all importantly, kept them open to foreign trade and investment. In international politics it followed a policy of strict neutrality and almost perfect aloofness.

As the age of imperialism proceeded, diplomacy became a subject of mass politics and also of the mass media. The tone of the public debate changed, in the Netherlands as elsewhere. Racist attitudes toward the Indonesians were openly admitted, a brutal policy of mass extermination of the Achinese was publicly advocated. Jingoistic feelings of hatred against the British because of the South African War were vigorously demonstrated. Many a Dutchman felt humiliated by his country's lack of power and brooded upon its glorious past in the seventeenth century. Nevertheless, in practice none of this influenced Dutch foreign policy at all. Diplomacy remained in the hands of the "establishment" which knew all too well that in a world full of dangers a small nation can only walk on tiptoe. It is in this realism that there lies the answer to a question perhaps even more puzzling than the one posed by Paul Kennedy: Why did the *Dutch* Empire last so long?[26]

Chapter 7

The Berlin Conference of 1884–1885: Myths and Realities

In the historical imagination of Africa an important place is given to the Berlin Conference of 1884–1885. In his book *The Challenge of the Congo*, from 1967, the former president of Ghana Kwame Nkrumah wrote that "The original carve-up of Africa [was] arranged at the Berlin Conference of 1884."[1] This is a myth. It is a persistent myth, to be found even today, but it is a myth all the same. There was no carving or dividing up of the black continent in Berlin. This is not to say, however, that the conference was not of historical significance; on the contrary. The conference was both practically as well as symbolically of great significance; practically, because some decisions taken at or during the conference were to influence the history of the partition of Africa and symbolically, because the fact that representatives from virtually all European countries came to Berlin to discuss the future of Africa was a clear indication of the interest that Africa had gained in the eyes of European politicians and diplomats. Twenty or even ten years earlier this would have been unthinkable. It is therefore still worthwhile to study the Conference of Berlin and the events that led to its coming together.

THE ORIGINS OF THE PARTITION

To all practical purposes the history of the partition of Africa began in 1881 with the French occupation of Tunisia. To be sure, some historians have argued that the revival of French expansionism after the defeat of 1870 took place somewhat earlier, with the introduction of a new forward policy in the Western Sudan. But this should not bother us here. Whatever happened in West Africa somewhat earlier, the foundation of a French protectorate over Tunisia in 1881 was the first clear official demonstration of a new French policy in matters overseas, and it was recognized as such. A few days after the event, Gambetta, the parliamentary leader of the Liberal Party, wrote to Jules Ferry, the Liberal Prime Minister who was responsible for the occupation, saying that "France has resumed her status as a great power."[2] A year later the Gambetta Note was presented to the Egyptian government by the short-lived ministry of Gambetta, but this government fell before anything had been done and the new French government procrastinated. Thus, Britain had to go it alone. On 11 July 1882 the British navy bombarded Alexandria. A few days later they landed an expeditionary force, then built up an army, defeated Arabi Pasha, and became the new masters of Egypt, a role which they would continue to play until well after the Second World War. Although the French had only themselves to blame for this blatant demonstration of instability and impotence, they did not blame themselves but the British, and for more than twenty years Anglo-French rivalry formed the background of the partition of Africa. This rivalry, which reached its climax with the Fashoda Crisis of 1898, came to an end only with the Entente Cordiale of 1904. But by that time the partition was nearly over.

Anglo-French antagonism and the French frustration over what they considered as the "loss of Egypt" were to influence developments in other parts of Africa as well, as soon was to be demonstrated. In the late 1870s a French naval officer of Italian extraction by the name of Pierre Savorgnan de Brazza had been pioneering in the Upper Congo area and, all on his own initiative, closing treaties with local chiefs. In these treaties the chiefs transferred their sovereignty to France. In 1882, Brazza returned to Paris, orchestrated a promotion, press, and public relations campaign for his new occupations and managed to convince the French Parliament and the French government of the necessity to have them ratified.[3]

The ratification of the Brazza treaties triggered other imperialist operations in the Congo area. King Leopold II of Belgium sent the famous traveller Henry Morton Stanley—the man who found Livingstone—to the Congo. His mission was to induce the Congolese to sign similar treaties with King Leopold and his Congo Association as Brazza had had them signing with him. The Portuguese who, as nearly everywhere, also had the oldest rights in the Congo Basin became nervous and found support from their traditional ally, Britain. This cooperation resulted in the Anglo-Portuguese Treaty of February 1884. The signing of this treaty, however, led to such tumultuous reactions in England and Europe that it never was ratified. Under French and German pressure the British accepted that these matters should be discussed at an international conference: the famous Berlin Conference that ran from 15 November 1884 to 28 February of the following year.

THE BERLIN CONFERENCE

Of course, it was only due to some coincidence that the Conference took place on the banks of the Spree and not of the Seine. Or rather, it was due to

French prudence that suggested keeping a rather low profile at what was supposed to become an anti-British manifestation.[4] All the same, the place of the Conference, Berlin, seems to have a certain symbolic meaning. The city was the center of power politics and world diplomacy at that time. President of the Conference was none other than Bismarck himself, *Realpolitiker par excellence*, master of diplomacy, connoisseur of power politics, architect of the German empire, father of coalitions, partitions, and wars. Thus, the words "Berlin Conference" have historical connotations. They suggest something in the tradition of the great diplomatic congresses of the nineteenth century, comparable to the congresses of Vienna, Paris, and Berlin 1878. The very name Berlin conjures up the idea that something important happened.

But as soon as we start reading the Berlin Act and Protocols we know that we are in a very different world. This was not a conference like the Congress of 1878 or the Paris Conference of 1856. This was not the past but the future. It reminds one of the Peace Conference of The Hague, or the League of Nations or the United Nations. The political discourse was not that of power politics but of international law. The pros and cons of every word and sentence were discussed. The delegates carped at everything. Paragraphs were written and rewritten a dozen times. It was like the drafting of the resolutions of the United Nations. This was not the spirit of Machiavelli but of Hugo Grotius. One is reminded not of Otto von Bismarck but of Woodrow Wilson. To put it very briefly, it is immediately obvious that something very unimportant and something very unreal was going on.

What makes it even more unreal, of course, is that we all know that if ever there was a period of power politics, this was it. This period was to end with the Great War of 1914. This Conference took place while a major international crisis was going on, the Anglo-Russian conflict in Afghanistan, that was to come to a climax only a few weeks after the Conference and threatened to develop into the greatest war since the Crimean. The tragedy of Gordon at Khartoum had just taken place. For Britain, it was a desperate situation. As Lord Milner wrote: "Everything, yes absolutely everything, seemed bent upon going wrong at one and the same time."[5] Or, in the words of Granville, the Foreign Secretary, it was "dreadful, jumping from one nightmare into another."[6] The French government also had serious problems. There was a stalemate in Madagascar and a difficult war was going on with China. The defeat of Langson was about to take place. A few months later both the Gladstone and the Ferry cabinets would fall. Yet here we see these people seriously, slowly, and peacefully discussing matters of international law, codes of conduct, navigation acts, and postal unions. One should not be surprised that Bismarck lost all interest in the Conference, right from the start. His only role was to open and close it. Apart from that he was nowhere to be seen, an intention which he made clear in the opening session.

Of course, another Berlin Conference was going on at the same time, not in the conference room but in the lobby. And here a different language was spoken—that of *Realpolitik*—and matters of practical importance were discussed. The Congo Free State got its international recognition and its boundaries were fixed, albeit in a somewhat provisional way. When we discuss the meaning of the Berlin Conference, this side of it should, of course, be taken into account as well. But let us first return to the Conference itself and have a closer look at the diplomacy.

All the participating powers came to the Conference not only with aims concerning the official points of discussion as mentioned in the agenda, but also with considerations of wider imperial interest and of international politics in general. These considerations formed, as it were, three concentric circles of three different layers of interests, in order of importance. The African interest was subordinated to the imperial interest and that again to general diplomatic interests. This hierarchy of values is very clearly illustrated by the Dutch diplomacy at the Conference, a subject not further discussed here but elsewhere.[7]

These three levels of interest are to be found with each power that had an interest at stake in the Conference. (There were, of course, nations represented in whose case it is difficult to find such interests at all; for example, Sweden or Russia.) For Britain there was the Congo itself—the British had a trading interest there. But more important was the Niger, which was to be protected as a British sphere of interest. Even more important were the imperial problems: Egypt, the Canal, and so on. Above all there was the international situation at large, the danger of a united German-French front, of a none-too-splendid isolation at a moment of deteriorating relations with Russia.

For France there was the Congo itself—Brazza's acquisitions had become a subject of national pride and grandeur. The greater interest of imperial strategy was dominated by France's desire to reopen the Egyptian question with the help of Germany. Finally, there were considerations of international relations, the dilemma between continental and overseas priorities, the choice between Alsace-Lorraine and the colonies, or, as the popular poet and nationalist Paul Déroulède put it, between "two lost sisters and twenty servants."[8]

For Germany the priorities were even more obvious: even in his "colonial year" (1884) Bismarck did not for a single moment forget that, as he said, his "map of Africa was in Europe,"[9] that the empire would never be more than of very marginal interest to Germany. His colonial conversion has been discussed very many times. In essence the explanation seems to be quite simple and was perfectly formulated by Bismarck himself in a speech to the Reichstag of 26 January 1899, when he said of the German colonists: "They cannot prove that it is useful for the Reich. I, however, cannot prove that it is harmful to it, either."[10] In such a situation the policy to follow is not difficult: grab what one can get at the lowest possible price and as long as it does not harm major political interests.

Thus, we see that general strategic considerations rather than African interests determined the African policy of all the powers. This is what is so beautifully analyzed and demonstrated for the British case by Gallagher and Robinson in

Africa and the Victorians.[11] At the level of the official mind one sees the weighing of various interests. In this process, the general political interests of the nation as seen by the decision-makers are what counts. Perhaps it is not a surprising conclusion, because this is, after all, what foreign secretaries and cabinet ministers are supposed to do: formulate the national interest and act accordingly. But it explains to a certain extent one of the most remarkable aspects of the Berlin Conference, that it seems to have been one of those rare things in world history, a competition with only winners, a lottery without blanks. Germany was satisfied. It had an interest in free trade in the Congo and that was guaranteed. It wanted to be taken seriously as a colonial power. That had been the cause of the friction with England in 1884 when the British had originally refused to do so. Now it got Britain's recognition. And even more: it received Gladstone's personal blessing. On 12 March 1885, he said in the Commons: "If Germany is to become a colonising power, all I say is 'God speed her!' She becomes our ally and partner in the execution of the great purposes of Providence for the advantage of mankind."[12] Bismarck was not very impressed: he liked Gladstone about as much as Helmut Schmidt admired Jimmy Carter and must have fully agreed with Queen Victoria's judgement that he was "an old, wild and incomprehensible man."[13]

For France the Conference was a success. Brazza's new colonial acquisitions—a source of great French pride—had been secured. The preemptive right on the Free State's territories opened more possibilities for the future. Its nuisance value vis-à-vis Britain had been demonstrated. Its relation with Germany was improved, not fundamentally, but at least as far as possible.

Britain, of course, was the country against which the Conference was originally arranged. But it did very well and survived without great problems. Britain had nothing against free trade in the Congo. It was much more interested in the Niger and it had succeeded right from the beginning in obtaining an agreement that this river was not to be the subject of internationalization but considered part of the British sphere of interest. It had fought hard on the issue of effective occupation and the protectorate system. This issue was explicitly meant to be turned into a weapon against the supposed pretentions of a British Monroe Doctrine for Africa. Even this fight it had won, and it had demonstrated that insofar as Africa was concerned, Germany had many more interests in common with Britain than with France. An anti-British Continental League had become very improbable.

The Conference was perhaps the greatest triumph for a state that was not even officially present there, the Congo Free State. It gained its recognition and reached agreements on its boundaries with France and Portugal, as well as territorial recognition by Germany. Its existence was welcomed at the final session as a great step in the history of human civilization.

There *was*, of course, a loser at the Conference, namely, Portugal. But there was nothing unusual in that. It would be hard to find any colonial success for Portugal in the entire nineteenth, or for that matter even the eighteenth century.

The history of Portuguese colonization since the seventeenth century is essentially a history of decline.

How was this possible? How was it possible that a conference was a success for practically everybody? There are various reasons. In the first place, much of what was considered to be a success was a success only in the supposition that the Berlin Act would be applied in actual practice. As is well-known, this was not to be the case. Many of the arrangements were to be violated, particularly those concerning free trade and freedom of navigation. The Dutch traders, for example, were soon to find out that what they had welcomed and praised as a triumph for free trade was, in fact, a defeat of their trading interests. After that, they were no longer all that happy with the Berlin Conference. The second reason was that the various nations approached the African problems in different terms and therefore had different definitions of what was a success. Where the French were, generally speaking, more interested in political concepts, the British approach was a more commercial one. This made it possible to make bargains which both parties considered to be successes. This was the case not only in Berlin, but also with regard to later agreements; for example, the one between France and Britain on West Africa in 1898.[14]

But there was another and more fundamental factor at work, one that was characteristic of the partition of Africa in general, namely, the simple fact that there was indeed something for everybody. This is perhaps the most curious and unique aspect of the partition and of this stage of imperialism in general. There were, of course, fights and negotiations, bargains and deals. This was necessary if only for domestic reasons: one could not give away the national interest without a fight. But when all was said and done, there really was something for everybody. King Leopold's comparison of Africa with a ''magnificent cake''[15] was a very appropriate one, because it illustrated two important aspects of it at the same time. In the first place, there was no serious problem as long as there was a piece of cake for everybody. In the second place, the fight was about a cake, that is to say, about a luxury, not a vital need. This was an essential element of the Berlin Conference and of partition in general: these were not vital issues. Africa was not the Balkans, let alone Alsace-Lorraine. In his memoirs Bismarck devotes a full chapter to the Berlin Congress of 1878. He does not even mention the Conference of 1884.

Thus, there was satisfaction for everybody, but was there really reason to be so satisfied? Here again we enter a world of paradoxes. Most of the decisions that were taken were not respected and the one proposal that was rejected was to have a certain impact after all. The Conference decided to guarantee freedom of trade in an immense region, the so-called Conventional Congo Basin. This was never implemented. Leopold promised to create a state without customs. The Congo State, however, was to become a state of monopolies and exclusive rights under the domanial system. There was to be freedom of navigation on the Congo and Niger rivers. This was never realized, neither on the Congo nor on the Niger where Sir George Goldie's Royal Niger Company had exclusive rights. There were long debates and high-spirited speeches about humanitarian ideals. The results, however, were disappointing. Maybe the image of the Free State is dominated too much by pictures of amputated hands and feet. But it could hardly be considered as a triumph of humanitarian ideals, either. And then, of course, there was the famous fight about effective occupation. Here the text was so much watered down, by restricting it to *new* requisitions—thus not to old ones—to the *coasts* only—thus not to the interior—and to *occupations*—thus not to protectorates—that, in fact, it became meaningless. But the ultimate paradox is that although the principle was rejected, it nevertheless acquired some influence, because the principle of effective occupation was to gain a certain exemplary value, a normative meaning.[16] The British victory on this issue was very much a Pyrrhic victory.

THE SIGNIFICANCE OF THE BERLIN CONFERENCE

What then was the significance of the Berlin Conference? What role did it play in the partition? These are questions to which many answers have been given, of which I shall discuss only a few.

The first answer is a simple one: the Berlin Conference partitioned Africa; it drew the boundaries of the various European possessions. This is the vision as expressed by Kwame Nkrumah in the words that are quoted in the introduction of this chapter. But it is, as I said, a myth. The Conference itself drew only one boundary, that of the Free Trading Zone. Some of the bilateral treaties between the powers and the Free State were signed during, though not actually at, the Conference. But there was only one—that with Germany, which had already been signed before the Conference—that was accompanied by a map indicating the territory of the Free State and there were only two—the French and Portuguese treaties—which described the boundaries between their possessions and those of the Free State. There was no "carve-up" at the Berlin Conference.

The second theory is that of the hinterland, a story still to be found in many textbooks; for example, in the otherwise excellent book by R.R. Palmer, *A History of the Modern World*. Palmer writes that "a European power with holdings on the coasts had prior rights in the back country."[17] Nothing of this is to be found in the Berlin Act, but this again is a very persistent myth. Jean Stengers has tried to trace back the origin of this theory. He found the first mention of it in a French textbook of 1918.[18] But there are even older mentions. The original source of it might be a popular German textbook of 1907, D. Schäfer's *Weltgeschichte der Neuzeit*.[19] This exercise in historiography, interesting though it is, should not occupy us here.

The next theory is that the Berlin Conference laid down the "ground rules" for the scramble, or formulated the "code of conduct" for the partition. It is true that the Berlin Act laid down a few general principles: two articles out of the thirty-eight of the General Act are devoted to them. These articles, however, are not directives for partition, but diplomatic precautions to avoid international problems. Another very popular metaphor is that the Berlin Conference "fired the starting gun for the partition." These kinds of literary formulations are always rather flexible, but if this was a start it was a false one, because most of the runners were already well under way. If the Conference tried to do anything it was rather to call back the competitors. It was, to use Wolfgang Mommsen's phrase, a "holding operation." But it was a holding operation that failed.[20]

Thus, our conclusion is that the Conference did not partition Africa, nor did it want to do so. We might even agree that the Conference was not such an important thing after all. Quite a few modern historians have argued along these lines. It is an attitude of unusual modesty, because normally, when historians discuss a topic—whether it be the battles of Napoleon or the fertility of fishermen's wives in seventeenth-century Britanny—they tend to believe that their subject is the single most important problem in world history.

There is, however, something that is not completely satisfactory in all this playing down of the importance of the Berlin Conference. Politics are not only about facts but also about the perception of facts. To give just one example, politically speaking, the important question is not whether Britain really wanted to keep France out of Africa but whether France thought so and acted accordingly. When the Conference was convened, politicians and public opinion expected something important to happen. The partition was supposed to be on the agenda. A Dutch newspaper made a comparison between Bismarck and the pope who, in the fifteenth century, divided the world and gave away whole continents. In the same way, the journal continued, "Bismarck is carving up a continent and in a fair manner gives away empires and states."[21] In a literal sense, this was not true. But what was true was that the partition was taking place at high speed and under the supervision of the European heads of state and government. The misunderstanding was that people thought the partition took place at Berlin. In fact, it took place on the shores of Africa, but under the instructions of the same statesmen who instructed their representatives in Berlin. Politically speaking, the role of the Berlin Conference was not to do the partitioning itself, but to draw the attention of the world to this process and to legitimize it. Historically speaking, the meaning of the Berlin Conference is that it represents the partition in a symbolic form.

In this respect it could be compared with another conference and another partition that was also commemorated in February 1985, the Yalta Conference of 1945 and the partition of Germany and Europe. Here we find the theory that the present division of Europe was planned and agreed upon at the Yalta Conference. This is also a myth, and again a persistent one. The powers did not agree on partition; it was a result of power politics and military developments, not of Yalta. But Yalta did not stop this process, and Berlin did not stop the partition; indeed, rather, it accelerated it. Berlin and Yalta brought about a new awareness of what was going on: a continent was divided by powers that did not belong to it. For this reason they have symbolic value. "Yalta" became shorthand for the cold war and the division of Europe; "Berlin" for imperialism and the partition of Africa. Historical imagination and narration need such symbols.

What then is the meaning of the events of 1884–1885? In retrospect they seem very much to be a turning point, a watershed in the history of British imperialism and that of the partition of Africa. They mark the end of an era that could be labelled "the post-Napoleonic era." It is amazing how much the history of Britain's paramountcy in the nineteenth century reminds one of the United States in the twentieth. Both were based on economic superiority. Both supremacies only became manifest after wars to which, originally, they had not been a party. Both used the instruments of naval power and informal empire. Both preferred informal to formal empire. Both originally profited from the absence of serious competition: before 1870 Germany did not exist, nor did Italy. Austria and Russia were essentially continental powers and they were haunted by domestic problems. France had no naval power of any importance. As for the United States, after 1945 Japan and Germany were defeated, Russia was victorious but badly wounded, Europe was a shambles. By 1980 the picture was very different for the United States: the Soviet Union had become a major power, Europe was restored, Japan had become more of a rival than it had ever been. The same was true of Britain in the 1880s: the United States, Japan, and especially Germany had become economic rivals; Russia was a danger. In 1885 a "naval scare" went through England. The very basis of its empire was threatened. Finally, British imperialism was to be badly damaged by a war that was more of a domestic and political crisis than a military one. In this respect the Vietnam War can be compared to the South African War of 1899–1902. In 1914 the bell tolled for the British Empire. But in 1885 the writing was already on the wall.

The year 1885 was also a turning point in the history of the partition of Africa. Here, of course, we enter a great debate, the one about the causes and the chronology of the scramble. This debate essentially comes down to two questions: why did the scramble take place when it did, and in the way it did?[22] But there is a preliminary question: when did the scramble take place? Here the discussion is about the beginning. That the scramble was over by about 1900 is no matter for discussion. But its beginning is a far more complicated issue. Historians have taken different positions on this. Many years and events have been suggested: 1884, because of the Anglo-Portuguese treaty; the ratification of the Brazza-Makoko treaties in November 1882; the British occupation of Egypt earlier that year; the French occupation of Tunisia in 1881 or the forward policy introduced in French West Africa in 1879. The importance of this debate does not lie in the finding of the exact date, but in the fact that every date implies a certain theory about the causes of or the responsibility for the scramble.

I do not deny that these are important problems and debates, but I would also suggest that their significance should not be overestimated. It is perhaps possible to find out what was the very first beginning of the scramble but that does not mean that we have also found its *prima causa*. In mechanics one can indicate the first shock—and all that follows is predictable and can be traced back to it. But history is not like mechanics. Even if we find original initiatives, these say very little about what has followed. Imperialist acquisitions were not the result of one decision but of a chain of decisions, a chain with at least three links: the local activities and possibilities, the actions and reactions of the government, and the attitudes of public opinion, press, and parliament. Between these three factors there was a permanent interaction and feedback. One element was useless without the others and, as with all chains, the chain was only as strong as its weakest link. That is to say, the partitioning process could begin, but also be stopped, at every level. Cameron annexed the Congo for the British government in 1874. The only reaction of the Foreign Office was: ''an interesting proposal but of no practical use for our generation.''[23] That was the end of it. Maybe a few years later the French government would have liked to treat Brazza's annexation of the Congo for France in the same way, but by that time public opinion and the Parliament in France would not have accepted such an attitude. Neither the local nor the metropolitan factor alone was decisive—their interaction was.

Many imperialist operations originated in local initiatives, in local crises, subimperialisms, protonationalisms, and what have you. But this does not mean that these initiatives automatically developed into imperialist annexations. They could be stopped by politicians and indeed they were stopped many times. Lord Derby scorned the ambitions of the Australians, who wanted to have virtually the whole of the Pacific: ''I asked them whether they did not want another planet all to themselves and they seemed to think it would be a desirable arrangement if only feasible. The magnitude of their ideas is appalling to the English mind.''[24] These subimperialists did not get what they wanted. On the other hand, governments could do very little when there were no local initiatives or when there was opposition in parliament.

This means that we should be careful with such concepts as ''scramble'' and ''partition.'' They are not things that existed in reality, but constructions of the mind, historical concepts, interpretations. That is perfectly all right. Historians cannot do without a certain ''realism'' in the philosophical sense of the word. But one should realize that because these are constructions of the mind and not processes in nature, there are no laws of causation that link one event to another. Therefore the search for a *prima causa* of the partition is useless.

What, however, we could probably agree upon is a certain chronological scheme, a framework. We can then distinguish a first or initial phase from 1879 to 1885; a second stage—the heyday of partition—from 1885 to 1895; and an epilogue from 1895 to 1912. In this sense 1885 was the point of no return. But such a scheme, of course, is only an analytical tool, an instrument to aid understanding of a complex reality.

Such a scheme cannot explain why the scramble happened when it did, but it can help us in analyzing the conditions that had to be fulfilled in order to make it possible, although not inevitable. Thus, the medical requirements for survival in Africa had to be created and there had to be the military and technical superiority of Europe to make the price to be paid for the partition an acceptable one. These conditions were not fulfilled in the early nineteenth century. But there was another condition, too, a political one. The two characteristics of the partition period—as compared with earlier and later years—were (1) that there was something for everybody; and (2) that everybody wanted something from Africa. Thus, we can determine the time limits of the partition. The first characteristic disappeared about 1914—when Africa was partitioned. The second one only came into being after 1870. Before that the political conditions for such a situation were not fulfilled: Germany and Italy had not yet been unified and France had no motive for getting seriously involved in these matters. There was nobody to challenge Britain's informal empire and thus there was no partition. But all this does not mean that after that the partition *had* to happen. Politics is the realm of freedom, as Hegel said.

The other question is not of chronology but of typology. The partition was one form of imperialism among others. The question is: why did imperialism in Africa take this form rather than another? Let us then first see what is typical about imperialism in Africa. The most interesting thing about the partition was not that it began but that it was never stopped. Once the partitioning had started, one partitioned and partitioned until there was nothing left to partition. Why did this happen? The best way to answer this question is perhaps by asking another one: what could have stopped it? There are two possible answers to this: (1) a massive resistance by Africans; or (2) a major international crisis. Both would have raised the price of the partition to an unacceptable level. None of these occurred. Why not? Why was Africa partitioned while China was not? Why did the First World War break out because of a problem in the Balkans and not in Africa?

History is about what happened, not about what did not happen. That is why there are hundreds of books on the partition of Africa and thousands of studies on the causes of the First World War. But there are practically no studies on the question of why China was not partitioned nor on the question of why the scramble for Africa did not lead to war between the European powers. These questions are in a way unanswerable. Still, these comparisons can help us to understand what did happen. The partition of China was very much in the minds of men at the end of the nineteenth century. It was supposed to be imminent. Men spoke of the "Africanization of China." But it did not take place. To some extent, of course, the reason for this was domestic. China was a highly centralized polity, an empire. In Africa there was nothing like that.[25] But there is another side to it as well: the international situation was different. Russia was on the march in East Asia and approached China over land. Japan became an imperial power as early as the 1890s. The United States took an interest in China and preached the gospel of the open door. Nothing of this happened in Africa. Here the Europeans were, as it were, on their own, amongst themselves. Here they could reenact their European policies in a new and different context.

The partition of Africa was in the "best" tradition of European politics: it was about territorialization, about borders and boundaries. We often speak of the "artificial boundaries of Africa," but were they any more artificial than the European ones? In a way the partition was nothing but the entire history of Europe since the Middle Ages all over again, but in a condensed form: 400 years of history repeated within 30 years! But there was one great difference: in European history, annexations and wars were followed by peace treaties, boundaries, and maps. In Africa, they started with maps and treaties and war came later, if at all. And if war came, it was not among Europeans but between Europeans and Africans. This explains one of the most curious phenomena of the partition, its peacefulness. Most of the partition took place between 1885 and 1895. When one looks at the map of 1895 in Keltie's *Partition of Africa*, one sees that by then the partition was nearly complete.[26] On the other hand, we know that the decade 1885–1895 was the most peaceful in modern history. In the great statistical study on war by Singer and Small we see, for example, that in that period there was only one great war (between China and Japan) and one smaller war (between the Congo State and the Arabic slave traders).[27] This is to say that during the partition itself there were practically no European or colonial wars.

There are two possible explanations for this strange phenomenon. In the first place, there is the danger of a conceptual fallacy: maybe the application of violence as used in Africa did not fit with the criteria of traditional war, was therefore not classified as such and thus not counted. But there is another explanation as well, namely, that during the heyday of partition very little actually happened in Africa. What these maps illustrate is not reality but fiction. They illustrate the agreements on boundaries as reached in European chanceries and offices, not the occupation itself. This came later and cannot be dated so easily.

This order of things was very different from European history. It was not so much European history repeated as European history upside down. In European history there is first annexation, war, and so on, and finally there are maps that represent the result of all this. In Africa the maps came first, maps that in the beginning represented nothing but themselves. Normally, a map is a representation of reality in a realistic or coded form. Not so "The Map of Africa by Treaty." Here there was no reality to be represented. Here, to use a well-known expression from the 1960s, "the medium was the message."

This explains much of the peacefulness of the 1885–1895 decade. Not much happened except on paper. It also explains why the Europeans could so easily avoid getting involved in major conflicts. Territorial questions were settled in advance. Moreover, these were arrangements about regions that those involved did not know and certainly did not care much about. All this lightheartedness is perfectly illustrated in a speech by Lord Salisbury in the Lords in 1890, where he said: "I will not dwell upon the respective advantages of places which are utterly unknown not only to your Lordships, but to the rest of the white human race.''[28] Africa was ''very light soil'' indeed! The rivalry between Russia and Britain on the Northwest Frontier was known as the Great Game. But compared to Africa, this was not a game, but business. In Africa—apart from the Mediterranean—European rivalry never became more than a game.

Chapter 8

The Netherlands and the Partition of Africa

The Netherlands was almost the only country in Western Europe which took no share of Africa in the course of the partition. This is at first sight surprising. For centuries the Dutch had had a presence on the Gold Coast, while at the Cape they had created the most important white colony in sub-Saharan Africa. True, the Netherlands had given up both possessions before the partition, but by that time the Dutch were the chief traders on the Congo estuary which, after all, was a major flash-point giving rise to the partition. Curiously enough, no one has sought to examine this seeming paradox. It is therefore the aim of this chapter to consider the relationship between Dutch commercial expansion and the origins of partition, and to place this question in the context of the Netherlands' principal imperial interests, in Southeast Asia.

THE NETHERLANDS AND THE CONGO, 1857–1884

In July 1857, the Rotterdam firm of Kerdijk and Pincoffs acquired the African interests of a Manchester merchant, Leopold Samson. This was the start of Dutch commercial activities along the mouth of the Congo River—activities which were soon to reach considerable proportions. Within that same year, Lodewijk Kerdijk, the 26-year-old brother of one partner, departed for the Congo in order to explore the business potential of this region. In 1858 he established the first factory in the Congo, in the village of Ponte da Lenha, followed by a second factory two years later, in Banana.[1] This latter factory, called "Holland," was to become the most important in an enormous network of such settlements. The next year (1861) Lodewijk died, barely 30 years old. His company's trading activities, however, continued to grow. In 1863 the factory "Holland" was considerably enlarged through the acquisition of the properties of the French concern Régis of Marseilles. This company had specialized in the export of so-called "free laborers" to the French colonies in the West Indies. When it became clear that this trade was destined to disappear, Régis decided to sell their settlement in Banana. These properties, situated close to the harbor at the tip of the peninsula, were sold to the firm of Kerdijk and Pincoffs, which gave them the name "Rotterdam." In fact, "Holland" and "Rotterdam" together formed one awe-inspiring entity.[2] In 1879 the "Dutch house" was visited by H. M. Stanley, who was much impressed: "The Dutch know how to make their young men comfortable. The *table d'hôte*, with its varied abundance, may be cited as one proof; the neat frame houses, lofty and cool, another. They have a medico at hand who possesses a well-stocked dispensary; they have a billiard table; they have a number of riding asses. . . . The Dutch are, as usual, far ahead in the style, arrangement, and solidity of their structures."[3] Yet at this very time the enterprises of Kerdijk and Pincoffs were in the course of complete disintegration: the two gentlemen were respectively in jail and on the run. What had happened?

To answer this question, the activities of Kerdijk and Pincoffs must be considered in their totality. The two men were cousins as well as brothers-in-law. Henry Kerdijk was born Henry Polak but he later called himself Henry Polak Kerdijk and in 1866 he assumed the name Kerdijk. He married Adriana Pincoffs, a sister of his partner Lodewijk Pincoffs. Together, they traded in dyes such as madder and indigo. In addition, they were actively involved in shipping, both as shipowners and as traders. When the trade in dyes began to decline in the 1850s, as a result of the emerging chemical industry in Germany, they began to concentrate on shipping and in time they turned their attention to Africa. That was in 1857.[4] As we have seen, business went well at first. Trade expanded gradually and the number of ships as well as factories grew.[5] Banana remained the center of their activities, which in the course of the 1860s eventually covered the entire estuary as well as the coastal regions. In 1871 the company owned 33 factories in the zone between 3° and 9° South latitude; in 1877 there were as many as 44 of these settlements.[6] As a result the Rotterdam concern was by far the most important trading company in this area.[7]

In the single year 1870, they imported to the Netherlands, via the port of Rotterdam, 1,550,000 guilders' worth of merchandise; this was approximately equal to the imports of all English trading companies together.[8] Their import products consisted mainly of palm oil (which was in high demand due to the development of the candleworks in Gouda and Amsterdam), and also included palm kernels, ground nuts, and coffee. The exports to the Congo were considerably more picturesque: one writer gives a list of some 50 articles running from textiles, rifles, and rum to table knives, playing cards, and empty bottles.[9] The method of trading was exceedingly primitive and led to considerable cheating on both sides, as described by one of the agents of the Rotterdam firm, Onno Zwier van Sandick.[10]

Trading was not only complicated, it was also risky, as was to become apparent.[11] At that time, however, business continued to prosper, and as it expanded the legal form of the company also changed. In 1862 the African interests of the Kerdijk and Pincoffs Company were transferred to a limited partnership which in 1868 became a limited company under the name of Afrikaansche Handelsvereeniging (African Trading Association). Prince Henry, the brother of King William III, played an important role in the latter. In addition, the original partnership of Kerdijk and Pincoffs continued to exist.

The interest of such distinguished persons as Prince Henry is proof of the respect that these two Jewish merchants had won for themselves, and not without reason. Pincoffs in particular was the driving force behind many a commercial enterprise. It is impossible to give a detailed account of his many activities here.[12] Let it therefore suffice to mention his role in the expansion of the port, the construction of the New Waterway, and the establishment of the Bank of Rotterdam. Of the two partners, it was Pincoffs who had new ideas, developed plans, encouraged enthusiasm in others, lobbied in the Municipal Council, brought bankers together, and attracted fresh, mainly foreign, capital. He did all this not only for Kerdijk and Pincoffs and the African Trading Association but also for other firms in which he had an interest: the Rotterdam Trading Association, the Netherlands Indies Gas Company, and the Bank Association Limited. He was also active in politics. At the age of 30, he already occupied the Jewish seat in the Rotterdam Municipal Council, and in 1873 he became a member of the Upper Chamber of Parliament, the first Jew admitted to this body.[13] In 1879 he was even offered the post of Minister of Finance, but he refused. This is understandable, since by that time he was already up to his neck in the malversations which were to be revealed several months later in an enormous scandal which was to shock Rotterdam to its very core. In 1877 none other than Prince Henry, the king's brother, had accepted the post of Honorary Chairman of the African Trading Association, an enterprise which had "his special sympathy."[14] The minutes of the meeting convened for the prince's installation cite his exact words: "In the strange times in which we live it is a pleasure for His Royal Highness to support an enterprise which represents Dutch business in far-off places in such an independent and dignified manner."[15]

Prince Henry was not the only one with royal blood who paid attention to the two African traders. The King of Belgium also exhibited considerable interest—which, of course, stemmed from his ambitious plans for Africa. The Netherlands had not been represented at the first Geographical Conference held in Brussels in September 1876. It was, however, present at the Second Conference in Brussels in June 1877. Meanwhile, on 27 April 1877, a National Committee of the Association Internationale Africaine had also been established in the Netherlands. Among the members of this committee, with Prince Henry as chairman once again,[16] one finds the names of H. Kerdijk and L. Pincoffs.[17] This mutual interest was certainly understandable. The Association was, after all, to focus on the region around the Congo River and could in this respect make good use of the services of the two merchants from Rotterdam. On the other hand, Pincoffs, who had already started to doctor the books of the African Trading Association in 1875, continued to get deeper into debt, and here he saw his last chance to unload his disastrous African adventure by turning the business over to the Association. Thus, the Dutch Committee of the Association was important mainly as a forum where contacts between the Rotterdamers and the Belgian king could be established; in the five years of its existence there were few signs of active involvement on the part of the Committee and in 1882 it was dissolved.[18] Part of the remaining funds were turned over to the Dutch Geographical Society. The active chairman of this society, Professor Veth of Leiden University, had regularly criticized the lax attitude in the Netherlands toward the exploration of Africa, urging that expeditions be organized. With part of this money, therefore, the Society equipped the first and only Dutch-sponsored African expedition which left for Angola under the leadership of Daniël Veth, the chairman's son. This expedition was, however, doomed. It was a total disaster and most of the group, including Daniël Veth himself, died.[19]

In the meantime, however, as a result of the activities of the Committee, contacts were established between the merchants from Rotterdam and the Belgian king. Leopold was highly impressed by the scope of the trading activities of the Dutch firm. He sent his confidant, Jules Greindl, Secretary-General of the Association, to Rotterdam and Pincoffs was received at the palace in Brussels where he was seated next to the queen at the table! The support which Pincoffs promised the Association was indeed very generous. He pledged free transport to and within the Congo, free hospitality at his factories, and the support of his agents.[20] Moreover, the African Trading Association was second only to Leopold as a source of capital for the Comité d'Etudes du Haut-Congo, Leopold's new creation. Pincoffs was therefore an exceedingly powerful member of this Comité, as is apparent from the fact that he was able to change their plans: under Pincoffs' influence the Comité decided to begin with exploration rather than commercial activities. Only after that would the Comité turn to business operations. Two separate enterprises were to be set up for railroad construction and trade exploitation, respectively.[21] Pincoffs, whose last hope was to transfer his firm to this last one, the trading company, even managed to have a non-competitive clause included in the articles of the Comité.[22] Stanley was rather suspicious of these proceedings, and even Leopold was not particularly happy about the power of the man from Rotterdam; but for the time being he had to protect the international nature and the humanitarian-scientific cloak of his organization.[23]

For Leopold, therefore, the press report that appeared on 15 May 1879 was not inopportune.[24] It stated that the African Trading Association had suspended all payments, that one of its directors, Kerdijk, had been arrested in Antwerp after an unsuccessful suicide attempt, and that the other director, Pincoffs, was a fugitive from justice. The very words of the official police bulletin describing the fugitive evoke the fall of the man who only a short time before had been named the "Providence of Rotterdam."[25] The bulletin read: "1.7 metres long, round fat face, pale colouring, dark hair turning grey, dark eyebrows, gray beard, shifty eyes, high forehead, hooked nose, thin lips, round chin, slow wheedling voice; special characteristics: somewhat waddling gait due to obesity which is also evident at neck, throat and hands; clothing: usually dark.''[26]

The cause of this dramatic fall was related to the complicated nature of trade in Africa. Pincoffs' African business venture had increased in volume and reputation but not in equal measure in stability and profit. As a matter of fact, according to some, his enterprise had never been very healthy: even the first factory was said to have cost too much money.[27] In any event, several setbacks were to follow, such as the premature death in Banana of young Kerdijk and the fire in the factory shortly afterwards. The main problem, however, was the hazardous and complicated nature of the trade itself. The assortment of goods exported to the Congo was, as we have seen, highly varied. As Muller explained in a statement, ''The negroes prefer first this article, then that; it was therefore necessary to maintain a large selection of goods and to continue exporting.''[28] This is fine as long as the return is sufficient—but that was just the problem because the goods meant for Europe might fail to appear, due to a single crop failure or a natural calamity. Such setbacks occurred several times in the 1870s.[29] In such cases Pincoffs needed credit to carry him through this period, and credit means trust. To establish and hold this trust, Kerdijk and Pincoffs not only dealt in royal contacts and distinguished board members; they also declared high dividends of 9 and 10 percent for many years.[30] In order to make this possible, they falsified the books, drew up accommodation papers and transferred large sums of money from one firm to the other and back again. Pincoffs' enterprises represented a capital of 24 million guilders in all—at that time an unheard-of amount which Pincoffs switched around without interference. No one ever heard of, or suspected a thing about this swindle. The directors had been lulled to sleep by the soft, soothing music of Pincoffs' dance of the millions.

Thus, the African Trading Association perished in the tremendous scandal of 1879, only to recover quickly out of the ashes as the ''Nieuwe Afrikaansche Handels-Vennootschap'' (New African Trading Association). The man who played the leading role in this Operation Phoenix was the other Dutchman with important African interests at that time, Hendrik Muller. Muller's African activities as shipowner and trader had been concentrated along the Gold Coast, but after the Dutch territories there were turned over to the British in 1872 he transferred his business to Liberia. Muller therefore did not know the Congo intimately, but he was the only person in Rotterdam—or anywhere in the Netherlands—who knew anything about the process of trade in Africa, and his reputation was sound. For this reason, he was called upon to save whatever he could out of Pincoffs' bankrupt estate. And Muller was successful. He liquidated the African Trading Association, arranged a settlement with the creditors and even managed to restore trust in the future of this firm. On 20 August 1880, the reconstruction was complete. Out of the residue of the African Trading Association, the New African Trading Association was created with Muller and his co-liquidator W.C. Schalkwijk as managing directors, together with the former superintendent of the African Trading Association in Africa, A.A.P. Jung, who was indispensable because of his expert knowledge of the situation in the Congo.[31] Thus, the damage arising from this bankruptcy that caused such a sensation in Rotterdam was kept to a minimum in Africa. In fact, by tacit consent the company continued to function, maintaining and expanding its interests and activities in the Congo during the 1880s—when this region became the subject of ever-increasing interest in international diplomatic circles.

The important commercial role of the Dutch was well-known in these circles. Between 1880 and 1884 diplomatic reports indicated that without a doubt the Dutch had a very large, some said the largest, commercial interest in the Congo. At least this is what the Dutch ambassador to London, Count Van Bylandt, wrote in a note for his Minister of Foreign Affairs on 2 December 1882.[32] Minister Rochussen, however, reprimanded him; he felt that this passage was inaccurate because "as the British statesmen must know their interests are greater than ours."[33] As a result of this ministerial intervention, the memorandum refers only to "intérêts fort considérables."[34] Later, Van Bylandt was to defend his text by saying that in 1877 officials of the British Foreign Office had told him that the Dutch factories were "much more important than those of any power."[35]

This discussion typifies the confusion which surrounded the controversial question: who had the greater interest in the Congo, the Netherlands or Britain? In part, this is a question of criteria. Some may have used the quantity of goods as a measure, others the value of these goods or the number of factories or the number of employees. There is, of course, also an essential difference between the goods imported into the Congo and those exported from the Congo. The most important source of confusion, however, was the difference between the volume of trade and the economic significance of that trade. Without a doubt the Dutch merchants had the largest sales volume in the Congo but the British still had the greatest economic interests.[36] To begin with, there were many British trading companies active in this region; furthermore, British merchants had a large share in the Dutch firm which, as we have seen, was financed mainly through foreign capital. However—and this is the most important factor—the Rotterdam trading company exported predominantly British goods, mainly cotton, rifles, and gunpowder. Anstey estimated that British products accounted for more than 60 percent of the goods exported to the Congo by the New African Trading Association.[37] These goods were first imported into Holland and therefore were included not in the statistics for the Britain-Africa trade but in those for the Netherlands-Africa trade. What this amounts to—and this is essential for a proper understanding of Dutch diplomacy concerning the Congo—is that, as far as the Congo was concerned, the economic interests of the Netherlands were in fact solely the commercial interests of the New African Trading Association and that Dutch products were barely involved, with the exception of some textiles, Dutch gin, and gunpowder.

DUTCH DIPLOMACY AND THE CONGO QUESTION, 1877–1884

Dutch diplomatic interference in the affairs of the Congo already existed in 1877, as indicated by the contacts between Van Bylandt and the Foreign Office. At that time the Netherlands and Britain together successfully resisted Portugal's claims to part of the African coast at the mouth of the Congo River. Both countries were sufficiently involved to want to protect their merchants by challenging the pretension of the Portuguese government, notorious not only for its protectionism but also for its corruption.[38] In 1882 an identical situation appeared to develop when, as a result of the Brazza-Makoko treaties, France and, in reaction, Portugal as well, began to activate their claims to these regions. It is not surprising that the Dutch minister again turned to his British colleague.[39] This time, however, he had no success, because as a result of French activities in the Congo in the interim period, the British government had revised its position regarding Portugal's claims and was now supporting them. This was to result in the Anglo-Portuguese treaty of 26 February 1884, a treaty much disputed within Britain as well as beyond its borders.

In the Netherlands, too, this treaty led to protests. The Dutch government received several petitions from various chambers of commerce, including, of course, Rotterdam but also Tilburg and the textile centers in Twente.[40] The Minister of Foreign Affairs, Van der Does de Willebois, had to answer interpellations in both chambers of Parliament—addressed in the Lower Chamber by the M.P. for Rotterdam, J. van Gennep,[41] and in the Upper Chamber by Hendrik Muller. The second debate is particularly interesting because it clearly showed that the minister was fully aware of the fact that a new situation had developed in Africa—a situation, moreover, which offered the Netherlands more disadvantages than advantages.[42] As the Dutch ambassador to Brussels put it: "Without a doubt, it would have been more pleasant and better for the Rotterdam firm if the situation had simply remained as it was."[43] The minister knew only too well, however, that an irreversible process had commenced: the politicization of Africa. This was a situation that the Netherlands had to handle with the greatest of care. The major danger was that it would be squeezed between its two powerful neighbors, Germany in Europe and Britain in Asia. In Van der Does's instructions to the ambassador to Berlin concerning the coming conference, this view is expressed very clearly: "After all we must constantly bear in mind that, whatever the outcome of the conference may be, on the continent we remain the weak neighbours of Germany and in the Netherlands Indies we remain in continuous contact with Great Britain and thus, we are always open to difficulties."[44]

For this reason, Van der Does's reaction to the Anglo-Portuguese treaty was exceedingly cautious and he awaited further developments. These were not unfavorable, because Britain encountered national as well as international resistance to ratification and an international conference was required to solve this problem. On 8 October 1884, the minister received an invitation to the conference.[45] Two days later Van der Does informed the Cabinet which authorized him without further discussion to request the king's permission to accept the invitation.[46] This was granted, and on 15 October 1884 the Dutch government announced through its envoys to Berlin and Paris that it accepted the invitation and would be represented at the conference by the envoy to Berlin, F.P. Van der Hoeven.[47]

The conference was not to begin until 15 November. During the intervening period the situation in the Congo had to be studied and tentative positions determined regarding the points on the agenda to be included in the invitation. For the former, of course, the expertise of the New African Trading Association was exceedingly important. When asked, this company was happy to provide all the necessary data together with a map and a list of all its factories in this region.[48] Moreover, the head agent for this company in Banana, A. de Bloeme, was included as a consultant in the Dutch delegation.[49] As for the agenda of the conference, the invitation listed three items: (1) freedom of trade in the region of the Congo River; (2) freedom of navigation on the Congo and Niger Rivers; (3) the establishment of regulations concerning the further occupation of territory along the African coasts by European powers.[50]

The first two points caused no problems: the Dutch government was fully in accordance with these proposals.[51] The third, however, was an entirely different matter. It meant in effect that any claim by a European power to territory along the African coasts would only be acknowledged if that power had also established effective authority there. This worried the Dutch minister. He did not object to the establishment of such regulations for the African coast, but he strongly opposed their introduction anywhere else. Here is a glimpse of the fear that the agreements reached in Berlin would eventually affect the situation in other parts of the world, and therefore also in the Netherlands Indies. It was in fact because of a situation in the Netherlands Indies earlier in 1884—the so-called *Nisero* incident—that the concept "effective occupation" had such unpleasant connotations. At that time the Dutch government made shamefully inadequate attempts to liberate the British crew of the ship *Nisero* from the hands of the Sultan of Aceh, who was supposedly under Dutch authority. This authority therefore proved to be ineffective and in Britain there was talk of direct intervention, of approaching the sultan himself, which would have been a violation of Dutch sovereignty. Consequently, Dutch-British relations were strained that year, and it is easy to understand Dutch alarm at the phrase "effective occupation."[52] Thus, one of the most important objectives of Dutch diplomacy in Berlin was to limit all discussions to West Africa alone. As the Dutch minister wrote: "The Netherlands is directly involved due to Dutch possessions in the Netherlands Indies, since later on occupation could be attempted under the pretext that Dutch authority and occupation were not effective and that—by analogy or according to the text—the decisions of the Conference of Berlin should also be applicable there."[53] To be on the safe side, he added: "You will not introduce my references to our possessions in the Dutch East Indies into the discussion: this might be *a priori* imprudent.''[54] This missive appears to be typical of the diplomatic approach of the Netherlands throughout the Berlin Conference: one talked about Africa but thought about the Indies.

THE BERLIN CONFERENCE, 1884–1885

When the Conference was opened on 15 November 1884, it soon became apparent that the delegates would not adhere strictly to the agenda. To start with, Britain made it quite clear that it did not wish the territories along the Niger River to be considered in the same manner as those along the Congo River. It considered the region of the Niger to fall exclusively within the British sphere of influence. In the second place, the British delegate, Sir Edward Malet, emphasized the humanitarian task of the Conference. The European powers had to protect and civilize the native population and therefore the import of goods detrimental to such aims, such as alcohol, rifles, and gunpowder, should be forbidden.[55] Third, there was the problem of the size of the free trade zone in the Congo.

As far as the first point was concerned, the Netherlands, which did not have any interest in the region of the Niger River, supported the British claims. Since Germany also agreed, the question was quickly settled. The other two proposals were not so straightforward. Malet's humanitarian ideals were excellent, but the products exported by the Dutch consisted predominantly of the very goods of which Malet disapproved,[56] while his proposal was strenuously resisted by German distillers from Bremen and Hamburg.[57] For the Dutch minister, however, political concerns were much more important than commercial interests, and once again this can be attributed to the Netherlands Indies. The Netherlands, he wrote, had just had problems in Aceh with the interloper trade in alcoholic beverages carried out by the inhabitants of the Straits Settlements. Now that the British government had been so friendly as to combat this trade, the Netherlands could not afford to distance itself from the British passion for morality just to protect the interests of a small group.[58] In fact, the eventual solution to the problem was quite favorable to the Netherlands. A proposal to combat or forbid this trade would imply the need for border patrols and customs agents which in turn would be a contradiction of the major principle of the conference, namely, free trade. Most of the participants were unwilling to go along with this. Therefore, they chose a solution without obligations: the Conference expressed the wish that this type of trade be reduced.[59]

The third point, the size of the free trade zone in the Congo, was also to cause Dutch diplomats some problems, and again the difficulty was not the proposal itself but the likely consequences for the Netherlands Indies. The general aim of the conference was to make the free trade zone as large as possible. The Netherlands was, of course, in full accordance with this view. Indeed, it supported every proposal to enhance free trade and even took the initiative by introducing an amendment to facilitate free access to the Congo.[60] Nonetheless, there remained grounds for objecting to the general principle of free trade, as distinct from free trade in the Congo region. Van der Does pointed out to the envoy in Berlin the danger that when a free trade zone within Africa was defined, mention might be made of the Indian Ocean. This ocean, after all, included "our own Archipelago. . . . It is in fact this Archipelago that we must consider—without talking about it—whenever an extension of the agenda of the Berlin Conference is under discussion."[61]

Other suggestions which were discussed included a proposal from the United States concerning the neutrality of the Congo and a British plan for a "slave declaration" in which they urged that a general embargo be declared on slave traffic. The American plan, which the Netherlands was quite willing to support, was not successful because of French and Portuguese opposition. Ultimately, they agreed to accept a so-called "facultative neutrality," a meaningless formula since, of course, any country that so wishes may declare itself neutral.[62] As far as the British slave declaration was concerned, the Netherlands again objected that a general declaration implied a broadening of the scope of the conference. Since this objection was shared by other countries, the declaration was finally limited to the Congo.[63]

In the course of the conference the discussions in Berlin took place not only in the official chamber but also and especially in the lobbies. One of the most important aspects of the Conference was that simultaneous bilateral negotiations were being carried out in Berlin between the various countries and the Association Internationale du Congo—Leopold's last creation—concerning recognition of her sovereignty and the definition of her territory. The Rotterdam trading house strongly urged recognition of the Association because it promised free trade.[64] The Dutch minister who, as always, was more cautious, felt that a small country should not be too bold in this respect. Recognition, therefore, did not take place until 27 December 1884, in the form of a treaty between the Netherlands and the Association. In this treaty, the Association granted all Dutch citizens total exemption from import and transit duties in exchange for recognition.[65]

The Conference ended on 26 February 1885 and the next day the minister sent the General Act to the king. In an accompanying statement he declared that he was highly satisfied with the course of the conference: only Africa was discussed, Dutch neutrality had not been damaged and free Dutch trade had been guaranteed.[66] The same satisfaction is also evident in his speech to the Lower Chamber the day before: "I am exceedingly pleased, and so, I am sure, are all of you who are listening, that I can add that the Netherlands succeeded in achieving everything it had aimed for in the interests of trade."[67] The men from Rotterdam were also pleased. In the annual report of the New African Trading Association for 1884, we find the following: "The results of the Congress in Berlin, that our chief agent Mr A. de Bloeme attended as a delegate for the Netherlands, were favourable. The basin of the Congo River and its tributaries were declared open for free trade to all nations.''[68] A similar enthusiasm is apparent in the annual report of the Rotterdam Chamber of Commerce. It referred to King Leopold as ''that excellent monarch,'' praised his plans for a free state with a system of free trade and, in mentioning the conference, stated that this ''as is known . . . led to very satisfactory results.''[69]

There were also more skeptical reactions. The unfortunate explorer Daniël Veth wrote on 15 April 1885:

> All the decisions of the Congo Conference give rise to a multitude of questions which I would like to have answered in full. How in the long run is the Association Internationale going to cover her costs if import duties may not be levied? It would seem to me to be highly unlikely that one will be able to find in Europe a number of fools who will provide sufficient money to support a large crowd of loafers in Africa.[70]

Skepticism is also apparent in a newspaper article by Tobias Asser, who himself had attended part of the conference as legal adviser to the Dutch delegation. In the *Algemeen Handelsblad*, Asser said that the decisions were ''paper regulations'' which ''when passions are roused'' would be ignored by all concerned.[71] The same newspaper had already observed, on 23 January 1885, that the future would show who had been more astute regarding the Congo—the Netherlands or Belgium. These were prophetic words, as later events were to demonstrate. If one considers the many conflicts which rapidly developed between the New African Trading Association and the agents of Leopold's Association, it is difficult to believe in the general enthusiasm in the Netherlands following the Berlin Conference.[72] But it is clear that the Dutch honestly believed in the sincerity of Leopold's intentions and promises. In the light of later developments, this seems surprising, but in Berlin belief in free trade was so widespread that the results of the Conference induced a premature euphoria.

In any case, few people in the Netherlands took an interest in the Berlin Conference. Those interested were mostly to be found at the Foreign Office, where the minister gave his personal attention to Dutch policy regarding West Africa. The other ministers did not interfere and the question never arose in cabinet meetings. In Parliament the Congo question was discussed four times: on three occasions in 1884 and once in 1885.[73] Otherwise it was not a subject of interest in the 1880s. Parliament's concern was not revived until 1889 when the problem of the Congo Free State became prominent. This lack of activity on the part of Parliament only reflects the level of public opinion: no one really cared very much about Africa. The press considered the Conference only in terms of international relations and as such applauded it as an important step forward in the relations of the civilized nations.[74] There was hardly any attempt to influence governmental policy; nor was the government urged on to greater activity. There was one group which called for more active Dutch participation in the colonization of Africa: the Dutch Geographical Society; but it was not very successful. The only real pressure group was, as we have seen, the New

African Trading Association. Their interests were certainly taken seriously, but they were obviously considered secondary to national interests, as seen by the minister. Because this company truly monopolized trade with the Congo, it was strong from the commercial point of view; but politically it was weak. This was due to the fact that a large proportion of the exports to the Congo consisted of foreign goods. So the interests of an important Dutch industry were not at stake. The combination of Dutch gin and gunpowder, however explosive, was not strong enough to sway the priorities of Dutch diplomacy.

CONCLUSION

The general conclusion which can be drawn from this case study is obvious. The Dutch did not want to play a political role in Africa and watched unhappily from the sidelines as this part of the world became involved in political conflicts. They would have much preferred Africa to remain an object of commercial endeavor rather than political strife. When they realized that Africa had become a political question, they accepted that reluctantly, since this situation created more dangers for the Netherlands than possibilities. On the one hand, the possibilities of an ''informal empire'' were reduced; on the other, the contradictions inherent in the position of the Netherlands as a colonial giant and a political dwarf became increasingly evident. Abstention and neutrality: that was the motto.[75] The main purpose of Dutch foreign policy was to maintain the integrity of the realm in Europe and overseas, and this required cordial relations with Germany and Britain. In comparison with this, African interests were infinitesimal. Besides, the future of Africa was viewed with some skepticism. Economically, it was thought to be almost insignificant; emigration was, of course, never even considered; natural resources were presumed to be meagre. ''These are not Californias,'' wrote a journalist of the Rotterdam newspaper *De Maasbode*.[76] Nor was there the slightest question of what Leroy-Beaulieu called ''*colonisation moderne*,'' that is, a capitalistic exploitation and *mise en valeur* of Africa.[77] Plans for investment in railroads, harbors, and so forth did not exist. The Dutch approach to Africa was purely commercial.

At the time of the Berlin Conference, the Netherlands was still the second largest colonial power in the world and its commercial interests in the Congo were quite considerable. The fact that despite this it did not play a political role in the Congo or anywhere else in Africa, but remained the only uninvolved western European power, was not a question of chance or impotence: the small countries had enough opportunities—as was proved by Belgium and Portugal. It was the result of unwillingness. In the Netherlands—at least in this decade—the political will to operate as an imperialist power was non-existent. Whenever it was necessary to act in such a manner, the Dutch did so hesitantly, with reluctance and often with dread. Dutch behavior was that of a ''saturated'' power, so far as the colonies were concerned, a power which was forced protestingly along the path of imperialism.[78]

Part III

Decolonization and After

Chapter 9

Toward a History of Decolonization

FORGOTTEN PROBLEM

Decolonization has finished.[1] It definitely belongs to the past, but somehow it has refused to become history. A great deal has already been written on this subject, and yet it seems that there is little to say about it. After the Second World War, the colonized countries wanted to become independent; they struggled with their oppressors and threw off the yoke of colonial rule. Within a few years they all achieved their aim. That is the song that has now already been sung for about 30 years, in various keys, it is true, but with a remarkable consistency of tune and melody. The entire colonial history seems to have been no more than a prologue to an inevitable and triumphant independence. A new Whig interpretation of history has come into being.[2]

Consequently, there has been no real historical debate on decolonization. Just how surprising this is becomes clear when one looks at the other end of the same story, that of modern imperialism. In this case, already during the imperialist period itself, we find a theory and a discussion developing. Hobson, who opened the debate on imperialism, asked the question as to why the sudden expansion from Europe into Africa took place. He himself also gave an answer: this phenomenon was the result of economic problems in Europe. Because of the development of capitalism, new markets were being sought for the capital that could no longer be profitably invested at home. This was the beginning of the great debate on modern imperialism. A comparable debate on the origins and course of decolonization, on the question of guilt, on good and evil, and so forth, has not yet taken place, although it now seems to be beginning. Collective and comparative volumes like *Decolonization and After. The British and French Experience*; *The Transfer of Power in Africa*; *Les Chemins de la décolonisation de l'empire colonial français, 1936–1956*; *India and Indonesia from the 1920s to the 1950s*[3]—all published between 1980 and 1986—are useful contributions to this, while also authors like J. Gallagher, D.A. Low, R.F. Holland, T. Smith, J.A.A. van Doorn, J. Bank, P.C. Emmer, M. Kuitenbrouwer, to mention just a few, have offered new interpretations, often of a comparative nature.[4] That this should happen was to be expected, as becomes evident if we compare this subject with other major historical questions. Then we see that discussions almost always arise after a certain period of time, usually as a result of one of the two following causes: either new documents become available to the public or the political situation changes. For instance, the great debate about the First World War arose when the German government published a huge amount of source material on German diplomacy which was intended to counter the German *Kriegsschuld* argument. There are now also major series of publications of source material on decolonization available which facilitate research on the subject.[5]

The other source of revisionism is the changing political situation. That was the case, for instance, in the discussion about the cold war, in which, especially under the influence of the Vietnam War, the Americans took over the role of scapegoat for a number of years, a role which had initially been played very successfully by Stalin *cum suis*. In this respect, things have certainly changed since decolonization. The emerging countries have long ago lost their innocence. Starting with the atrocities carried out during the partition of India, the massacres of 1965 in Indonesia, the Cultural Revolution in China, the Khmer Rouge in Indochina, the appearance of such individuals as General Amin, Marshall Mobutu, and Emperor Bokassa, the picture of "the good colored" has been seriously undermined. The contrast between the dark night of colonialism and the rosy dawn of independence has lost some of its sharpness. While there is no question of a revaluation of the colonial system, it can be established that discussions about the merits of colonial government have now at least become possible. In this respect, we see a kind of demythologizing taking place. There is now a better insight into the importance of the colonies for the motherland, and also a more objective appreciation of the developmental aspects of colonialism has become possible.

Another aspect of decolonization—and one that has been discussed for some time—is that of the importance of decolonization as a turning point. Did decolonization mean the end of the colonial era, or was it rather the continuation of it, albeit in a different form, that of neocolonialism? A great number of very different answers have been given to this question, which are closely connected with the interpretation of the colonial period itself. I shall return to this point in the conclusion, but will first look into the process itself and ask two major questions: (1) why decolonization occurred when it did, and (2) why it developed the way it did. In other words, what we must consider is the chronology and the typology. After that we can venture into an evaluation.

DECOLONIZATION: AN EXPLANATION

To the question as to why decolonization occurred when it did occur, the short answer runs as follows. In the long run decolonization was inevitable. In the course of the twentieth century, the demand for independence became increasingly insistent. After the Second World War, the demand became irresistible. With this answer, we have unconsciously, as it were, introduced the Braudelian scheme that is nowadays so familiar to the historian. Braudel has demonstrated that it can be useful to study historical events in three different time perspectives: the short-, medium-, and long-term perspectives. In the case of decolonization, this scheme of interpretation indeed seems to be especially useful, because it brings out various aspects of it and clarifies its historical position.[6]

Let us begin with the long-term perspective. Decolonization is usually taken to mean the events that took place between 1945 and 1975. By 1975, decolonization was indeed practically complete. Within this period, two important episodes can be distinguished: the decolonization of Asia, which largely occurred between 1946 and 1949 (1946 the Philippines, 1947 India and Pakistan, 1948 Burma and Sri Lanka, 1949 Indonesia) with Indochina as the major exception; and the second episode, the decolonization of Africa, which began in 1960 ("the year of Africa"), culminated in 1962 (Algeria) and was virtually completed in 1964, but for an aftermath that lasted until 1974.[7]

But, of course, this is not the full story. If colonialism is placed in a wider historical context, it can be seen that decolonization had already begun much earlier. The first major decolonization occurred during the transition from the eighteenth to the nineteenth century, in the form of the American Revolution and the dissolution of the Spanish and Portuguese empires in South and Central America. This new order was sealed at the Congress of Verona and confirmed by the Monroe Doctrine. In the Western Hemisphere, only the Caribbean (and the Falkland Islands, as would be realized much later) remained outside this decolonization process. What the Americas had in common was that they were real colonies in the old, the classical sense of the word. That is, settlements, new nations overseas such as New Holland, New England, New France, New Spain; in short, the New World. The decolonization of the middle of the twentieth century affected completely different areas. Although in some cases it concerned what could be called settlers' colonies (for example, Algeria, Kenya, and Rhodesia), the European colonists were always very much in the minority. Even in the most spectacular case, Algeria, the European section of the community totalled less than 10 percent. In the Dutch possessions, the number of Europeans, seen from the Dutch point of view, was considerable. In Indonesian eyes it concerned a negligible minority. Whatever these colonies were, they were not new worlds.

A second feature that these areas had in common is that they had been brought under European authority only a comparatively short time earlier. For almost the whole of Africa and Indochina, colonialism was a matter of less than a century, sometimes even significantly less (Belgian colonial history scarcely takes up more than 50 years, the history of the French protectorate over Morocco not even that). At first sight this obviously does not apply to India and Indonesia, but even here it would be wrong to think in terms of a history of centuries. Of course, a Dutch and somewhat later an English presence had already been felt very early in these areas, but this had little to do with colonialism in the real sense of the term. It had been a question of trade and commercial companies. The true colonial history of Java begins about 1830 and that of the rest of Indonesia half a century or more later. The British colonial period in India only really began after the Mutiny and the winding up of the Company in 1857. The centuries-old Portuguese presence in Angola may go back to the sixteenth century, but we must bear in mind that until 1900 it remained essentially confined to the coast and the immediate hinterland. In other words, the colonial period existed for only approximately a century, sometimes slightly more, often considerably less.

Beside the two above-mentioned spectacular, violent decolonizations, there was a third, practically invisible decolonization. That was the silent history of the British dominions. It is a history which is scarcely spectacular, but is no less important for that. The development of Canada, Australia, and New Zealand from colonies to dominions and then to independent states is in one sense the true success story of the British Empire. The history of South Africa from the Pyrrhic victory in the Boer War to the break with England in 1961 is the one black page in this otherwise glorious book.

What all this means is that there were in fact three decolonizations, the first in the Americas and the last in Asia and Africa, violent and often accompanied by wars; the one in between Britain's white dominions peaceful, supple, and gradual. It also means that decolonization has a lengthy history, a history that takes up almost two centuries. This is as much a relativization of the question "why then?" as the beginning of an answer to it. Thus, we have returned to the short answer we began with and to the division into three time levels.

As seen from the long-term perspective decolonization was inevitable. It was the logical outcome of the colonization process itself. This is not only wisdom after the event. The colonizers were also aware of it. This consciousness is certainly highly developed in British colonial thinking, but it is not entirely absent from French ideology, either. The difference is that in the English version, the colonies were to become independent states by the end of colonialism, whereas in French thinking the colored peoples would become colored Frenchmen as the result of this process. The idea of overseas compatriots was only viable to the British with respect to the white dominions where the British race could not be distinguished from the inhabitants of England itself. The fact that the French had very few such possessions perhaps explains this difference to some extent. The ideology behind the French Revolution might explain something, too. More important than this difference was the question as to when the end of the colonial period should take place. When would the colored peoples be ''ready'' for it? Many statements of French and Dutch colonial figures from the 1930s demonstrate that, in the general opinion of the period, that time was still very far off; it was a matter of centuries.[8] In general, the English are credited with having a more flexible attitude and a better insight into the developments. But this should not be greatly overestimated. As late as 1954, prominent Englishmen declared that Cyprus would ''never'' become a sovereign state, and as late as 1960, it was considered inconceivable that a date in the foreseeable future could be set for when Kenya would become independent.[9]

This is to say that medium-term developments are more important to understanding the timing of decolonization. From the beginning of the twentieth century, there has been a structural change in the balance of power in the world. The demographic factor has played an important role in this. The European population growth stagnated, while in Asia there was a population explosion. As a matter of fact, this was, to a considerable extent, the result of improved hygiene and a raised standard of living, and therefore indirectly a result of colonialism. Furthermore, after the First World War, the leadership of the world economy shifted from Europe to America. Europe had finally lost its world hegemony.

One other new development from the 1920s and subsequent years was the increase of nationalist movements, and that was also to some extent the result of colonialism. Colonialism had formed a small elite of Westernized people who believed in the equally Western nationalist ideology. The nationalist movement consisted mostly of the children of the above-mentioned elite, which had originally collaborated with the colonial rulers. The new elite came to the conclusion that they had more to gain by resistance than by collaboration and they managed to instill these sentiments into a large section of the population. Here we are confronted with a crucial problem in the history of colonization.

Colonial history cannot be reduced to a simple dichotomy of colonialism—decolonization, submission, or freedom. It is—and always has been—a history of collaboration and resistance. There was resistance during the establishment of the colonial system (the colonial wars), under colonialism (taxation and famine riots, peasant revolts, etc.), and at the end of it (wars of decolonization, military actions, and pacification), but in all these phases there was clearly also cooperation at the same time. The important matter is the balance between the two, and the terms under which cooperation occurred. The growth of nationalism after the First World War, and above all in the 1930s, was an indication that the ''terms of collaboration''—to use the phrase coined by Ronald Robinson—had to be reconsidered. In this case, it would become the end of one specific form of cooperation, the colonial system.[10]

Ultimately, we are left with the problem of exact timing, that is, the short-term history. The answer to this question is as simple as it is conventional. The balance of power had fundamentally changed after 1940–1945, which placed the anti-colonial movement in a far stronger position. We saw the world hegemony shared by the United States with its clear anti-colonial program, and the anti-imperialist Soviet Union. By this period the European countries were in a generally weakened position. England's problems were largely financial and economic, while in the case of France and the Netherlands they were political and moral. The occupation of such colonies as Indonesia and Indochina by Japan made a restoration of colonial power necessary—something quite different from the mere continuation of it.

All of these elements combined to create a situation in which the anti-colonial movement very quickly came to the boil, as if it were in a pressure cooker. Additionally, political changes were taking place in Europe where left-wing governments, or governments with strong leanings to the left—and therefore traditionally anti-colonial—had come into power. This political change within Europe itself made a firm colonial restoration policy even more difficult. The colonial consensus in the mother countries had received a shock. It was clear that the colonial period was over.

DECOLONIZATION: A MODEL

Let us now look at our second topic, the various forms of decolonization. Why did decolonization proceed the way it did? This question can best be answered by an analysis of the three forces that determined the outcome of the process: the colony, the mother country, and the international factor. In this respect, it can, of course, be said that of these three, the colonial factor was the primary force, and that therefore the nationalist movement was the *prima causa* of decolonization.[11] This remark is not untrue, but neither is it very helpful. Even though the beginning and the end were the same, there were major differences in the manner in which decolonizations took place, and for the people concerned these were of primary importance. Decolonization shows a whole range of differing procedures that run from a peaceful transfer of power, as in India, to bloody and long-lasting wars (*sales guerres*), as in Indochina, with all kinds of variation in between. Sometimes in economic and cultural areas the bond between the mother country and the ex-colony remained more or less as it was (that is what happened in a large number of African colonies). Sometimes, the break was complete (as was the case for the Netherlands and Indonesia). Mostly, the conflict was played out between the government of the mother country and the nationalist leaders, but sometimes the white colonists themselves took matters into their own hands (as in Rhodesia and Algeria) and in this way an extra factor came into play.

This pluriformity—and here mention has only been made of the extremes in between which the process took place, and not of the many variations in between—makes it well-nigh impossible to arrive at generalizations about good and bad, successful and unsuccessful decolonizations. Nevertheless, vague general notions on this subject exist. In general, for example, the English have been praised for their flexibility. But the problems they left behind were certainly not insignificant: the partitioning of Palestine, British India, and Cyprus, for example; the revolt in Rhodesia; and, of course, the South African—not to mention the Irish—question; these are just some of the inheritances of British colonialism. Although the English were not involved in major decolonization wars, they lost many human lives and large sums of money in the winding-up of their Empire. They frequently withdrew voluntarily, but nevertheless, they did play a leading role in the Suez venture of 1956. The French usually have a poor reputation for decolonization because of Vietnam and Algeria. This is not entirely unjustified, but the rather more quiet developments in Morocco and Tunisia, and the harmonious transfer of power within Black Africa must also be credited to their account. The Netherlands has been accused of having wanted to hold on to Indonesia for too long, and Belgium has been accused of having abandoned the Congo too abruptly. Of course, it is easy to be wise after the event.

More important than such generalizations—or moralizations—is an analysis of the effect of the various forces. The politics of the mother country are seen to have been an important factor. In this the one can be credited with more wisdom, statesmanship, and determination than the other. Additionally, of course, the political and constitutional situation in the one country was different from that in the other. In the Netherlands and France, there were coalition governments and constitutional problems that caused complications. In England, such constitutional problems did not exist and, furthermore, there was—and still is—a two-party system with a clear-cut majority government. As far as the mother country is concerned, it was, moreover, important whether it was a major or a minor power. Naturally, England and France had more resources at their disposal than Holland, Belgium, and Portugal. However, this was not such an important factor, as becomes evident from a comparison between the Netherlands and Portugal, both small countries, but with very different methods of hanging on to their colonies. The influence of the Second World War is also of importance. During the war, the Netherlands and France were both occupied, a confusing and traumatic experience. Following the blow of 1940, France felt the need to recover its dented prestige and the Netherlands thought that its future was dependent upon Indonesia. On the other hand, for England, the Second World War had been a proud and triumphant experience. The ideology of a colonial power is also of importance, and after the American Revolution, England recognized the need for a clear tradition of gradual progress and responsible government on the one hand, and indirect rule on the other. Up to a point, decolonization was always considered to be a possibility for the future.

Actually, the second factor, the situation in the colonies themselves, seems to have been more important. In this case, the fundamental difference is the one between administrative and settlers' colonies. Wherever a considerable white population had settled and taken over a large portion of the land, the decolonization process created painful conflicts. That can be seen in the Netherlands Indies, in Algeria, in Kenya, in Rhodesia, and in Angola. But this factor does not explain everything, because there have also been areas like Indochina, New Guinea, Malaysia, the Falklands, and so on, where this factor was absent and where there were major conflicts all the same. Other elements must have played a role in those cases.

Other important factors were the power of the nationalist movements and their potential association with communism. In general, it can be said that the nationalist movement had deeper roots in Asia than in Africa, that a larger elite had come into being there, and that its sense of nationality was more anchored in precolonial times. The Asian self-consciousness stems from the beginning of this century (the Russo-Japanese War of 1904–1905 is often mentioned in this connection). Education, even tertiary education, was available on a relatively large scale. There was an awareness of history in countries like India, Indonesia, and Vietnam, which gave room for a sense of nationalism, and which offered a picture of a past of national greatness. All this was absent or present to much a lesser extent in Africa, where the nation-state was a colonial invention.

The importance of communism in all this becomes clear if Indonesia and Indochina are compared. This also brings us to the third and last force, the international factor, in particular the attitude of the United States and the conjuncture of the cold war. In general, the United States was against colonialism, which is evident from its attitude to England and the Netherlands, but especially after 1947, it was also strongly against communism. For this reason it supported the French in their struggle against the communist leader of Vietnamese nationalism, Ho Chi Minh, and later even took over the role of France in Indochina. In the case of Indonesia, however, it played Sukarno's game, because it hoped to use him in its containment strategy.[12] The politics of Portugal with respect to its African colonies also received American support, because Portugal was an important ally, and had important strategic locations to offer. Politics with respect to South Africa were and are also influenced by similar strategic considerations.

It can be proposed as a general conclusion that the colonial powers all found themselves in more or less the same situation. Clearly, after 1945, their positions had been weakened. They all had to contend with strengthened nationalism in the colonies, a weakened consensus in their own countries, and an unfavorable international situation. The actual process of decolonization was, however, very different, depending on the effect of the three forces mentioned above. England, France, and the Netherlands were all three confronted with a new, powerful nationalism in their colonies after 1945. England conceded to the Indian wish for independence. France and the Netherlands, in Indochina and in Indonesia, respectively, followed another course, that of resistance. The difference between these and England was that in both cases the mother country and the colony had been occupied during the Second World War. Both countries were looking for a new solution and a new relationship but did not want to work with the nationalist leaders: Ho Chi Minh, a communist, and Sukarno, a collaborator with the Japanese. After this, their ways parted too, this time under the influence of the international factor. The Netherlands gave in to pressure from the United States (and world opinion) and resigned itself to the independence of Indonesia, while France, supported by America, was able to hold on for a long time. The interaction of these three forces determined the speed and course of the transfer of power. The result, however, was always the same: independence.

THE SIGNIFICANCE OF DECOLONIZATION

What was the meaning of all this? What changes did decolonization bring about? Was it a turning point? Opinions on this have developed over time. Originally, to propose it in the most general terms, decolonization was regarded as an important caesura. It had brought an end to the colonial period and several centuries of Western dominance. This theory was accompanied by great optimism about the future, as much in the new countries as in the West where there was a strong belief in developmental politics and social engineering. In the United States, it was hoped that the new countries would be converted to the blessings of democracy and the market economy, and would therefore join the Western camp. America's vision of the past was strongly dominated by the contrast between colonialism and independence.

In fact, this situation did not last for very long. In the West and in the United States in particular, there was fairly rapid disappointment at the lack of inclination of its pupils toward economic liberalism, at the criticism directed at the multinationals, the imperfection of democracy and, above all, at the inclination toward the neutralist politics of the Third World. There was no less disenchantment in the new nations where there was great disappointment at the actual consequences of decolonization. General welfare scarcely improved, development stagnated, indebtedness grew, and exploitation remained, even though it took on another form. The multinationals turned out to be even harder rulers than the colonial regents and governors had been. Dependence remained, and was, so it is said, "structural." In this perception the United States, far from being the leader of the anti-colonial movement, became the commander of international imperialism. In this way "liberal optimism" was replaced by "radical pessimism," to use A.G. Hopkins's happy formulation.[13] This all found utterance in theories about *dependencia*, structural imperialism, center-periphery relations, and the development of underdevelopment.[14] The image of the West was no longer dominated by the break with colonialism, but by the continuation of Western domination, in one form or the other.

This tendency was further strengthened by another discussion in the field of colonial history, that about imperialism. In the 1950s and the following years, the British historians Gallagher and Robinson developed the concept of "informal empire," that is to say, of economic domination without political expression.[15] These ideas—very fruitful for an analysis of the English experience of the nineteenth century—also relativized the contrast colonialism-independence, albeit this time from the other end, the establishment of the colonial systems.

Of course, neither of these historiographical developments was entirely separate from the other. In fact, in their analysis of British imperialism of the nineteenth century, Gallagher and Robinson were inspired by the example of post-1945 American imperialism, which was just as informal. As a result, the interpretation of imperialism was considerably refined. The uniqueness of the colonial period was put into a wider perspective. It was seen as an episode in a much longer process of Western expansion that had taken on various forms, of which colonialism was only one expression and which still exists today.

Does this imply that the significance of decolonization can now be dismissed altogether? The answer to this is no. In many ways, decolonization was certainly an important caesura, even though its significance needs to be relativized and refined with respect to time and place. In some cases, decolonization was a great shock, a cruel break. This, for instance, was the case with the Netherlands and Indonesia. The relations between the two, be they political, economic, or cultural, virtually came to a complete end. For the mother country this meant a total political and economic reorientation. The Dutch answer was industrialization, European unification, and Atlantic orientation.[16] In the case of India, political decolonization did not occur simultaneously with the loosening of the economic ties. This happened gradually in the subsequent years. The result of this was that, by about 1960, the economic influence of England in India had all but completely disappeared.[17] In the case of Indochina we see that, after the long decolonization conflict with France had ended, the conflict was continued in the form of an even more long and drawn-out war with the United States. Actual independence in Indochina, therefore, came much later than at the severing of the link between the mother country and the colony. But when it came, the break with the former colonial power and even with the whole Western world was radical and complete. All of these occurrences were completely different, but in none of them can it be maintained that decolonization made no difference.

In Africa we see, inasmuch as it concerns sub-Saharan Africa, that, in general, there has been a certain continuity in the period following decolonization. The ties with the former mother countries have not been completely broken. Links have remained in the areas of education and economic affairs, while at the same time a certain degree of political association has often remained. In the case of France, this influence is indeed far-reaching: it is still very clearly present in many of its former African colonies, in economic and monetary forms, via developmental cooperation and education, via political activities, and sometimes even by means of open military interventions. This is much less true in the former Belgian and Portuguese colonies. The North African countries, finally, practice a much more independent political line and are strongly orientated toward the Arab world.

In all these cases, it can be established that decolonization did not mean the end of the problems for the areas concerned. In some respects, it can even be argued that there was a worsening of the economic situation and an increased dependence on the world economy. Optimism about a new beginning and a better life has increasingly given way to doubt, skepticism, and resignation. The problems are gigantic. Africa in particular provides us with a picture of ecological and economic misery that knows no equal. Also, in the political area there is but little optimism. Most of the Third World countries have experienced racial and religious riots, massacres, dictatorships, political assassinations, and continuing systematic corruption. It can scarcely be maintained that the world overseas has become a more peaceful (or more prosperous) place since decolonization. But that is not what decolonization was about.

Colonialism was a certain form of power politics, a form in which the political identity of a particular social group had ceased to exist. The colonial countries, no matter how divided and hostile they might otherwise have been, cooperated in keeping that order going, and in legitimizing it. Since decolonization, a completely new world order has appeared. There are still weak and poor countries alongside rich and powerful countries, and we still find many of the rich and powerful countries in the North and many of the weak and poor countries in the South. But the relationships between these have changed drastically. There is no longer a communal strategy of the powerful toward the weak states. On the contrary, there is great division between them. This has led to a struggle for clients between East and West and the result of this was that the negotiating position of the former colonies has been considerably strengthened. If the present world order is compared with that of a hundred years ago, it can be seen that not only Europe has an essentially different position, but so do the countries of Asia and Africa. This is the true meaning of decolonization.

Chapter 10

Post-Imperial Holland

The ten years between 1940 and 1950 were undoubtedly the most dramatic decade in Dutch history since the establishment of the Kingdom of the Netherlands in 1813 or, indeed, the creation of the Dutch nation in the sixteenth century. In 1940 the Netherlands became involved for the first time in almost 150 years in a large-scale armed conflict in Europe, and was forced to relinquish the neutrality so long cherished. Five dramatic days of war were followed by five dark years of enemy occupation, during which a totally unprepared population was confronted with the colossal questions of collaboration and resistance. Dutch losses as a direct result of the war are estimated at about 250,000.[1] Barely liberated, the country plunged once more into war—the greatest ever fought by the Dutch army. In 1947, 170,000 men saw military service in Indonesia, including over 100,000 who had been conscripted following a revision of the constitution. In the conflict more than 2,500 of these men were lost, but only 10 percent of fatalities occurred during the two short and militarily successful "police operations." The rest were killed in the guerrilla wars before and after the conventional actions.[2] These political and military activities were accompanied by stormy public agitation and discussion in the Netherlands. In 1949, Indonesia was granted independence. Since the seventeenth century it had been the most important, and since the nineteenth century almost the only overseas Dutch colony.

War, occupation, war again, and finally the loss of an empire were together more dramatic events within ten years than Dutch history had provided in the course of several centuries. Contemporaries assumed that the impact on the people would be enormous. In the Netherlands the years following 1945 were characterized by hope and fear: the hope of a new society which would arise out of destruction, the fear of total ruin if the colonies were lost. None of this was going to happen.

GREAT EXPECTATIONS

During the war many visions of a new postwar society marked a major difference from the Napoleonic occupation. Then the ideal for the future could be summed up in the words of the Proclamation of Liberation: "The old days will come again." Now the aim was not recovery, but renewal, the construction of a new society, the disappearance of the old factions and "*verzuiling*" (the religious segmentation of Dutch society). Surely, all this would be possible now that a common kinship had been found in a time of need.

In contrast to the dream of a new society was the nightmare of the loss of empire. While in the Netherlands total regeneration was the order of the day, as to the Dutch East Indies there was only one thought: restoration. Restoration of the ties between the mother country and the colonies, and restoration of the triangle of commerce, Netherlands-Indonesia-America, which, according to the experts, was essential for the revival of the Dutch economy. The possibility of a future for the Netherlands without the Indies was therefore not even taken into consideration, except as a state of disaster which had to be prevented. This view is strikingly expressed by a slogan common at that time, which had been the title of a forgotten pamphlet written in 1914, *Indië verloren, rampspoed geboren* ("The Indies gone, prosperity done").[3] Just as some nineteenth-century English and French authors had given warnings that without colonies their countries would sink to the rank of the Netherlands, so now in the Netherlands people spoke of being reduced to the position of Denmark. What, one wonders, would the Danes have felt about the loss of their own colonies?

The idea of total dependence upon its colonies is unique to Holland, where it has been traditional for almost two centuries.[4] Numerous authors had exhausted themselves in creating metaphors to explain the economic significance of the Dutch East Indies to their readers. Indonesia was called a horse pulling the cart of Dutch economy, a milk cow (a comparison made by Paul Leroy-Beaulieu),[5] the goose that laid the golden eggs, and so on. But even the entire animal kingdom was not enough to illustrate the significance of the Indies: they were also called the column upon which the Netherlands rested, the sheet anchor of its national existence, the plank upon which it floated.[6] Little wonder that the decolonization of Indonesia was never discussed in the Netherlands; it would have been like discussing the pros and cons of divorce during the wedding.

The nationalistic movement which developed in Indonesia in the 1930s was therefore not taken seriously. The most powerful politician in the Netherlands at that time, Dr. Hendrik Colijn, himself a former colonial army officer and director of Royal Dutch Shell, holder of innumerable high offices between the wars, called it the work of a "superficial layer of the population, as thin as the silver skin of a grain of rice''—an image every colonial would understand.[7] Another former director of Royal-Dutch, B.C. de Jonge, Governor-General from 1931 to 1936, was even more explicit: ''We have worked here in the Indies for three hundred years and we will need another three hundred years before the Indies might possibly be ready for some form of self-government.''[8] In her famous speech of 7 December 1942, Queen Wilhelmina presented as a policy for decolonization a poorly defined and unrealistic proposal for a Commonwealth. But this is better characterized as an improvised concession to the language of the times rather than a map of the road to independence.[9] Fear of a mutilated, withered Holland without colonies continued to dominate the visions of the future.

In reality, however, there was no room for either dreams or nightmares. The expectations of renewal never materialized. The underground press experienced only a short-term flowering once it came above ground. *Verzuiling* of press, radio, trade unions, and education became stronger than ever. Political renewal met the same fate. The Communist Party enjoyed a brief popularity due to its activities in the Resistance (after 1941), but after 1948 quickly fell to a membership of a few percent. The most important new party was the Labour Party (PvdA), which took the place of the prewar Socialist Party (SDAP). Stripped of such socialist idiosyncrasies as pacifism and republicanism, it was to become a broad left-wing popular movement, a house of many mansions. However, its time of flowering was also short. In 1946, it was the largest party in the country; at the elections of 1948 the Catholic Party regained the leading position. The followers of the PvdA remained at or below the prewar levels of the SDAP. Politically, the country was dominated by the confessional parties (Catholic and Protestant), exactly as it had been in the interwar years. In fact, the restoration was more complete than in 1813, when at least a united kingdom took the place of the former republican confederation.

Nor were the sombre prophecies about a future without colonies fulfilled. There was no question of an economic collapse. On the contrary, the Dutch economy showed spectacular growth. The increase in the national income per capita averaged about 3.5 percent per year between 1950 and 1970: seven times as much as in the first 40 years of the century. This means that real income just about doubled. Unemployment, too, remained fairly constant at a very low level (in 1957: 1.2 percent), in spite of a spectacular population explosion from 10 million to 13 million between 1950 and 1970 and the loss of the colonial sector.[10] Satisfactory as they were, these developments were in no way extraordinary and the Netherlands fared neither better nor worse than neighboring states, whether they lost their colonies or not. The heady brew of recovery and rehabilitation was followed by the tipsiness of the consumer society and the welfare state. No imperial hangover ever really declared itself. At first glance, therefore, it appears that decolonization had little influence on Dutch history. However, closer study reveals that it left its mark on various fields of politics and society.

AN IMPERIAL HANGOVER

That some kind of imperial hangover did in fact exist first became apparent in the development of relationships with Indonesia. The conflict with the Republic was accompanied by considerable public agitation, which, after the transfer of sovereignty, abruptly gave way to a thunderous silence. The Indonesian question was considered closed. But relations with the young nation were to reveal how poorly the past had been absorbed. At the time of the transfer of sovereignty the recently formed Dutch-Indonesian Union, which was to be the framework of the new cooperation, was described in grandiloquent terms, yet this structure was to collapse even more rapidly than the French *Communauté* or the British Commonwealth. The nucleus of the conflict was the future of New Guinea. In the absence of agreement, it was decided that this territory would remain Dutch for the time being. The Dutch government adhered to the standpoint that this large island was not part of Indonesia, and believed that the region could be used as a resettlement area for those who would not feel at home in the new republic, especially the Eurasians and Europeans. In anticipation of further negotiations, the Netherlands therefore tentatively retained this last jewel out of the once glittering "Girdle of Emeralds."

The relationship between the two countries, however, deteriorated rapidly. In 1956, Indonesia withdrew from the Dutch-Indonesian Union; in 1957, Dutch firms were nationalized; 1960 saw the start of a military confrontation over New Guinea. It seemed as if the entire drama would be played out again. Again Dutch troops were sent to these far-off places, again war threatened and again the attitude of the United States was decisive. When it became obvious that America would not give any support, the Dutch government retreated rapidly. In 1962 the Accord of Washington was signed and, after a short interim period, New Guinea became part of Indonesia.

The attitude of the Netherlands toward New Guinea is curious. Why did the Dutch government clasp this country and its 700,000 Papuans so warmly to its bosom? There is no rational explanation. Of course, numerous ethnological, historical, judicial, and moral arguments were presented: Indonesia had no right to New Guinea; the Dutch had a duty to the Papuans. In addition, there was a political argument: the Netherlands must defend the freedom of the Far East, which seemed likely to fall prey to communism. Undoubtedly, this was a very important consideration. Because of the cold war, America had drastically revised its starry-eyed view of liberation movements in Southeast Asia. The Dutch government was perfectly aware of the "domino theory"; it hoped—and expected—that America would support its democratic and most loyal European ally in a conflict with what was seen as a semicommunist, demagogic, Asiatic dictatorship. However, these aspects did not genuinely explain Dutch policy concerning New Guinea. The true motives were injured pride, an obstinate search for national grandeur, and a deep antipathy toward the traitorous former subjects. The Dutch attitude did not develop from rational considerations but from what Lijphart has called ''the trauma of decolonization.''[11] The policy of the Netherlands at that time can only be explained as atavistic, a more or less instinctive return to the colonial habits of ''chastisement,'' ''pacification,'' and ''police operations''—three concepts which made up the Dutch vocabulary as far as colonial wars were concerned. That New Guinea became the object of this policy was not based on its great economic significance: that was negligible. The reason was that New Guinea was seen as the exact contrary of the Netherlands. Even in the elementary school, every child learned that the Netherlands was Nature's stepchild when it came to the distribution of raw materials; all could see that the country was cold, wet, and heavily populated. In contrast, New Guinea appeared to offer everything that Holland missed: space, warmth, and raw materials. As far as the latter is concerned, it is interesting to note that the New Guinea crisis coincided with the sensational discovery of natural gas in Groningen. These findings were (and are) not only of enormous economic and monetary significance, but they also changed the age-old image of the Netherlands as a country poor in natural resources and thus contributed to the formation of a new national image and a new national awareness.

THE NETHERLANDS IN A NEW WORLD

The Dutch strategy in the New Guinea question was based in particular on expectations of American support. This orientation toward America is another example of the influence of the Second World War and decolonization on Dutch political thinking and actions. Foreign policy after 1945 represented a break with traditions which had survived for many decades, even centuries. The change arose from a fundamental reevaluation of the position of the Netherlands in the world. The long-established aim had been to maintain the international system of law, neutrality, free trade, and imperial relationships. During and after the war the initial reaction was to return to these ideals; hence the great efforts to retain Indonesia, and the enthusiasm for the United Nations. However, decolonization and the cold war meant that, although the main objectives—safety and free trade—remained the same, the means of securing them had changed. Instead of neutrality and collective safety, Dutch diplomats looked for safety to the Atlantic Alliance. Enthusiastic and dedicated to these new international links, their loyalty to American leaders was total. And this in turn explains why a deep bitterness developed during the New Guinea crisis about the American betrayal (as many saw it) of the United States' most faithful and loyal NATO partner.

Trans-Atlantic enthusiasm was accompanied by the counterpoint of an equally fervent passion for Europe; partly because increased trade with Europe, it was felt, must close the gap left by the loss of Indonesia. Dutch diplomats eagerly supported every initiative toward European cooperation and, more especially, unification. Their concept of unification was influenced by two ideals: a supernational Europe and a Europe enlarged by including Britain. That these two ideals were to a certain extent contradictory was, of course, well-known but seldom expressed. The major goal was the inclusion in an expanded Common Market of the United Kingdom, the country with whom the Netherlands had the closest historical and psychological ties. Supranationalism, on the other hand, was not based on a reasoned analysis of the advantages and disadvantages, but on a historic distaste for the power politics of the major powers. It lent a romantic haze to the European movement, and offered victory over the power of protectionist, warlike states. In the Netherlands there was widespread consensus in favor of this new foreign policy that was simultaneously supranationalistic and pro-British, both European and Atlantic. The fact that these aims were logically irreconcilable was publicly spelled out in particular by French politicians. The Dutch reaction to this Cartesianism was one of indignation, distaste, and ridicule of "French vanity."

A third major element in Dutch foreign policy was a lively interest in development aid. It was in this field above all that compensation was to be found for the smarting loss of global influence, for the dwindling of the Netherlands after a centuries-long presence in Africa and, even more importantly, in Asia. However, this desire to help underdeveloped countries should not be dismissed as neocolonialism. Subjectively, this policy is based on the same idealistic elements which informed colonial policy during the so-called ethical period. A remarkable instance of this continuity appears in a book of recollections by a number of overseas administrators.[12] The most striking aspect is that the authors consider themselves not so much as colonial civil servants, but, rather, as development experts *avant la lettre*. A more material argument for granting development aid was also put forward: that enlargement of the Third World's purchasing power would lead to the creation of the export markets for the products of the industrialized nations. But idealism and trade interest cannot alone explain this collective enthusiasm. It appears to be an instinctive Dutch reaction, the reaction of a people used to living in many parts of the world, willing and successful emigrants, extremely interested in travel and foreign countries, yet still Calvinistic enough to enjoy such sinful pleasures only when they are justified by a good cause. Development aid is the most apolitical element in Dutch politics. Since the 1970s the enthusiasm for Europe has waned, the Common Market's capitalistic nature has been criticized, NATO has come under attack, the United States is no longer an idol. But development aid is as popular as ever. In contrast to the European and Atlantic policies, which signified a break with age-old traditions, it satisfies the deepest beliefs and traditions of the Dutch nation.

ECONOMIC RECOVERY AND REORIENTATION

The new enthusiasm for Europe was based not only on political ideals but also on economic necessity. When in 1949 it appeared that the economic triangle, Netherlands-Indonesia-America, could never be revived, a reorientation of the Dutch economy was obviously necessary. It is no coincidence that, in the same year, there appeared the first memorandum on industrialization, giving the preliminary outline of the new Dutch economic structure.

Although the economic significance of Indonesia was considerable, it certainly was not as important, or even necessary, to the Netherlands as many claimed. According to Derksen and Tinbergen, the contribution of the Dutch East Indies toward the Dutch national income was 13.7 percent in 1938. Of the entire national capital 7.5 percent was invested in Indonesia; this accounted for 40 percent of Dutch investments in foreign countries. Profits, too, were highly exaggerated: such frequently quoted figures as 15–20 percent were pure fantasy. In 1936, a "depression year," the average return on investments in the Indies was only 2 percent, rising to 3.9 percent in 1938, a "normal year" according to Derksen and Tinbergen. This rate barely differed from that derived from other investments.[13]

From the standpoint of employment, however, Indonesia was much more important: according to the 1930 census, 72,000 Dutchmen were working there. The percentage of civil servants among them was striking: 26.8 percent worked directly for the government; added together with those working in other branches of government service, such as education, postal services, and the national railway, more than 43 percent were employed by the government. In this connection, however, it should be noted that at least 50 percent of the Dutchmen in the Indies were "stayers" (i.e., born and raised in Indonesia), so that only a few thousand jobs were open each year to newcomers from the Netherlands, whereas 45,000 new jobs per year were needed. However, Derksen, when making these calculations in 1938, pointed out that to formulate the problem in this manner was to oversimplify. In fact, Indonesia was exceedingly important for senior civil servants or men with academic training. Almost as many high-ranking civil servants worked in Indonesia as in the Netherlands. Numerically, indirect employment was even more important. According to a very rough estimate the jobs which resulted from the interaction of the Indonesian sector with the Dutch economy amounted to some 100,000.[14]

Nevertheless, decolonization did not end in economic disaster. Obviously, the commercial enterprises formerly active in the Indies had a fairly difficult time; the agricultural concerns and many trading companies in particular found it hard, sometimes impossible, to adapt themselves to the new situation. In other sectors, the change was made smoothly—the banks, for example, adjusted quickly [15]—and on the whole the Dutch economy successfully withstood the shock. The two main problems were exports and unemployment, to which the Dutch answer was industrialization. New industry had to produce exportable goods and provide jobs for a rapidly expanding population; at the same time, an active emigration policy helped to keep unemployment down. During the 1950s, 145,000 Dutch emigrated, mainly to America, Australia, Canada, and New Zealand.[16] In 1960, with the economic boom, emigration fell off sharply. The increasing importance of industry to the economy is illustrated by the fact that in 1938 it provided approximately 30 percent of the Dutch national income; by 1957 this had increased to 42 percent. Industrialization was especially important in the field of the Netherlands' exports, whose nominal value between 1938 and 1961 rose from 1 to 16 billion guilders. In 1938 10 percent of the Dutch exports went to Indonesia. In 1961 this had dropped to zero; but the gap was quickly filled by new markets in Asia (4 percent), North America (2 percent), and Africa (1 percent), and by a 3 percent expansion within Europe (73 percent in 1938, 76 percent in 1961).[17] Only since the 1960s has there been a marked growth in Dutch export to Common Market countries, from 38 percent in 1950 to 56 percent in 1969.[18] At the present, of course, the possibilities of new markets in the Far East are considered to be of great interest.

VICTIMS OF DECOLONIZATION?

Upon the whole, the economic impact of decolonization was mild and the shock was absorbed smoothly. This was also generally applicable to the social sphere; for a truer picture, however, it is necessary to consider in more detail the fate of the various groups which have returned to the Netherlands from Indonesia.

One of the largest groups for resettlement consisted of the 100,000 conscripts who had served in the Indies. Little is known about their adaptation at home. No doubt their experiences had affected these men, generally very young, who had borne guerrilla warfare, contact with an alien society, isolation, and enforced idleness. Occasionally, stories of incidents and excesses came to light, but there was never any question of a public discussion of—let alone inquiry into—the conduct of the soldiers in the Indies. Nor was any general concern shown as to their reception and readaptation at home. Perhaps the most marked result of service in the East Indies is the popularization of Indonesian dishes in the Netherlands. There had, of course, always been returned expatriates, but they were too few and too localized to influence Dutch eating habits. Now there developed a passion for Indonesian food and Indonesian restaurants. Nasi, bami, and egg-rolls have become an integral part of Dutch culture. Once or twice a week many housewives prepare an Indonesian meal (or what they believe to be such a meal) and there are no less than 2,180 Chinese-Indonesian restaurants in the country.

A second, even larger, body of repatriates were the Indonesian Dutch. They came in waves, the first of which occurred between 1945 and 1948. Members of the first group, in many cases, came to the Netherlands for rest and rehabilitation, but did not intend to remain there. The second wave, which developed between 1949 and 1951 as a result of the transfer of sovereignty, consisted mainly of civil servants and military personnel. Neither they nor the group arriving between 1952 and 1955 proposed to return to the East. The latter, somewhat lower in social status than the earlier repatriates, were often Eurasians or Europeans who had never been in the Netherlands; these people had waited to see which way the wind would blow. A fourth and last wave came during 1957–1958 as the result of nationalization. Included in this group were the *spijtop-*

tanten, those who had at first chosen Indonesian nationality, but subsequently felt that they were not treated as full citizens, and so came to Holland.

The total number repatriated is not known and is exceedingly difficult to determine at this late date because the definition of repatriation is not clear and the records were kept carelessly. A reasonable estimate, however, would be about 250,000 people.[19] In the same way, little is known about how they fared. Economically, hardships were few: jobs were easy to find at a time of increasing prosperity. Socially, however, the repatriates encountered many problems, such as the loss of status and adaptation to a different and often simpler way of life. The greatest difficulties were probably experienced by the "stayers"—Dutchmen born and raised in the Indies—to whom the Netherlands were an unknown foreign country. They included many Eurasians who had had difficulty in finding acceptance even in the colonial society. In contrast, the higher-ranking, academically trained colonial civil servants had few problems. These mostly took up satisfactory second careers in the civil service, administration, the judiciary, and the universities. Their numbers, however, were very limited.

The most important and enduring social problem developed after the arrival of a group of 12,000 South Moluccans. The origin of what today is called the Moluccan question stems from the Dutch conflict with the nationalistic government of the Republic of Indonesia. By the Accord of Linggadjati on 15 November 1946, the Netherlands recognized the Republic of Indonesia as the government which exercised de facto power over Java and Sumatra. But Indonesia consisted of many other regions and in various parts of the Archipelago Dutch power had already been reestablished at an early stage. Wishing to maintain its influence in Indonesia as far as possible, the Netherlands government found it necessary to restrict the power of the Republic by means of the "federal policy." Indonesia would become a federation, in which the Republic of Indonesia (consisting of Java and Sumatra) would be no more than one state among others. Numerous states were to be created (eventually there were sixteen) and the whole federation would form the United States of Indonesia, linked to the Netherlands by the Dutch Indonesian Union. At the time of independence, sovereignty was handed over to these "United States of Indonesia."

Predictably, the nationalist movement of the Republic saw in this policy only a strategy of "divide and rule." They were therefore not particularly inclined to respect the federation and, immediately after the transfer of sovereignty, a strong drive toward unification developed, which found a general echo among the people. But the Moluccans who lived in the federal state of East Indonesia showed a decided resistance to the loss of their independent rule to the government of the Republic. When it became obvious that the federal state of East Indonesia was to be eliminated, the Moluccans set up the Republic of the South Moluccas (25 April 1950) on the island of Ambon. After fierce battles, this area was occupied during 1950–1951 by the central Indonesian government.

The resistance of the Moluccans arose from their historical ties with the Dutch government. They had long provided many of the soldiers for the Netherlands

Indies Army. At the time of the Moluccan uprising this army had practically been disbanded, but there were still 4,000 Moluccan soldiers awaiting discharge. They understandably did not want to submit to the Indonesian government, fearing that they would be considered as traitors, and a Dutch judge ruled that they could not legally be forced into this position. The Moluccans wished to move to New Guinea (at that time still Dutch) or Ceram, which was continuing to fight the central government; however, neither alternative was acceptable to the Indonesian government, nor therefore to the Dutch government. The only remaining choice was to depart for the Netherlands, a decision taken in February 1950.

It was presumed that the Moluccans would only remain in the Netherlands temporarily, as is obvious from the fact that the 4,000 families, 12,500 people in all, were housed in camps. This group, therefore, stayed together in the camps, was cared for by the government, was not permitted to work and remained completely isolated from Dutch society, awaiting a return to Indonesia and dreaming of an independent republic. In the 1950s this situation began to change. Increasing prosperity made it possible for the Moluccans to take part in the work process, a return to the East Indies became less realistic as the relationship with Indonesia deteriorated. Instead of the camps, residential areas in various Dutch towns were made available for housing. This group of Moluccans, about 90 percent of whom belong to the Evangelical Moluccan Church, now numbered 32,000.[20] They enjoyed the benefits of a flourishing economy and an emerging welfare state. Nevertheless, the nucleus of the problem remained. The Dutch government considered the Moluccan question to be a social problem, a matter for the Minister of Social Welfare. The Moluccans considered it as a political problem, the responsibility of the Minister of Foreign Affairs. In 1975, impatient with the attention of social workers, they turned to up-to-date methods of terrorism. On three occasions, in 1975, 1977, and 1978, they occupied a school, a train, an embassy, a consulate and a county house, killing several people in the process. The Dutch government developed unexpectedly successful tactics—persuasion, exhaustion, and military power—to end these actions. Dumbfounded, the people watched the television screens, as jets dived over one of their trains and tanks attacked one of their schools. The indiscriminate killing of Dutch citizens did indeed draw attention to the Moluccan question but hardly gained public sympathy. The result of these activities is that the Moluccan question is considered more seriously, though not that their political aims have been accepted by the government.

The first Moluccan terrorist action occurred in 1975, the same year in which immigration from Surinam reached its zenith, in anticipation of the colony's independence, which was to be granted in November 1975. Thereafter, the Surinam people could indeed enjoy the vast sums in development aid which the Netherlands was to pay as alimony in this divorce, but they could no longer expect the extremely favorable social benefits available to Dutch citizens. The lure of these fabulous payments was great. In 1973, 11,000 Surinamese came to the Netherlands, in 1974 almost 18,000, and in 1975, when independence was breathing down their necks, nearly 40,000 took one-way tickets to Amsterdam Airport. At least, the Dutch felt, there could never be more than 385,000 immigrants since that was the total population of Surinam. By 1975, a total of 115,000 Surinamese had settled in the Netherlands. Not only was this a very large group for such a densely populated country—it just about compensated for the total emigration surplus of the 1950s—but it also involved a group of easily recognizable colored people. The Dutch realized in 1975 that they had in their midst not only a dissatisfied Moluccan population—32,000 strong—but also over 100,000 potentially dissatisfied and poorly adapted Surinamese. The 250,000 repatriated Indonesian-Dutch were smoothly assimilated into Dutch society. But now it suddenly became clear that the inheritance of the colonial past also included 150,000 colored inhabitants. This belated discovery that the Netherlands had become a multiracial society caused the country its first true imperial hangover.

COLLECTIVE PSYCHOLOGY

It is apparent that decolonization had several unfavorable effects in the Netherlands: various sectors of commerce recovered only partially or not at all from the shock; the trauma of the loss of empire had a negative influence on Dutch politics; failure to settle the Moluccan question has saddled the country with a dangerous inheritance. On the whole, however, the shock was absorbed without too much trouble. The feared economic disintegration never occurred; on the contrary, prosperity increased as never before. Adaptation to the new state of international affairs proceeded fairly smoothly. The assimilation of 250,000 Indonesian Dutch was barely noticed. When, in 1969, H. Baudet published an article about "The Netherlands after the loss of Empire," he could justifiably argue that, for the Dutch, colonization appeared to be a turned page, the past a closed book.[21]

Ten years later, however, the picture looked somewhat different. In the course of the 1970s there have been several crude reminders of the imperial past, not only the activities of the Moluccans and the arrival of the Surinamese but, even earlier, heated discussions on the behavior of Dutch troops in Indonesia. Moreover, similar *crises de conscience* developed in the same period following revelations about the behavior of Dutchmen in the Second World War. The years 1940–1949, which were thought to be dead and buried, were suddenly revived. How can this strange situation, this sudden passion for the "truth about the past" be explained? The paths of collective memory are inexplicable and there is no clear answer to this puzzling question. However, this much is certain: to find an explanation, the correlations between the events of the years 1940–1945 and those of 1945–1949 must be considered. Both periods were dominated by war, although in different forms. In the first war, Holland was the unsuspecting and innocent victim; in the second war Holland was itself the aggressor. The first case involved a clearly defined situation affecting the entire Dutch population; the second was a war in a far-away country, whose aims were vague and controversial and which ended badly. It is understandable that after 1949 public interest concentrated mainly on the years of the occupation, a period when it was not difficult to distinguish between heroes and villains. Moreover, the distribution of good and evil left the Dutch with a very satisfying self-image: against the wicked Germans stood the courageous Dutch, initially caught unawares by events but soon united to engage en masse in resistance against the oppressor. Of course, there were evil Dutchmen, but they were exceptions; the worst were quickly punished and the others were soon set free. It was not suitable in a period of reconstruction and cooperation to overemphasize such problems and so alienate parts of the population.

There thus developed a generally accepted view of the history of the war, which was expressed in numerous commemorative volumes and memoirs and was crystallized in 1960–1964 in a long television series on the occupation—the first major television success in the Netherlands. The director of the State Institute for War Documentation, L. de Jong, who directed this series, became a national hero, the unassailable guardian of the tree of knowledge, whose institute was a shrine for the sacred relics of this past. The history of the Dutch war in the Indies, on the other hand, received virtually no attention: no institute, no television series, no scholarly articles, official or unofficial. In contrast to the stream of literature about the Second World War, there exist only a few unread novels and some forgotten memoirs. Colonial history was out of favor: at the universities it attracted very few students.[22] In short, there existed no historical view of colonization and decolonization; no one needed it; it was the past, but it was not history. It was simply pushed aside, obliterated, wiped out. Of course, many war veterans knew that unspeakable things had happened, but only a few had actually fouled their hands with these acts. The rest knew what had happened, but they kept quiet and accepted no strictures from outsiders. There was in fact almost no criticism. The Dutch soldier by definition never took part in excesses; that was something Germans did. Thus, one past fell victim to legend, the other to oblivion.

Around 1970 the whole situation suddenly began to change. Public opinion was shocked by two affairs which bore a certain resemblance: the Hueting question and the Weinreb case. The first attacked the myth of the good Dutch soldier, the second the myth of the resistance. The Hueting affair developed from a television program on 17 January 1969, in which a veteran of the colonial war, the psychologist Hueting, revealed details of excesses by Dutch troops in Indonesia. This was a bombshell, and reactions ranged from angry denials by former soldiers to demands that the guilty should even now stand trial. The government did what it had to do: it ordered an investigation. The report, which appeared very quickly, was vague and said little, restricting itself to recording a few incidents. In some of the controversies surrounding the matter, Dutch soldiers were compared with the SS. This is an interesting illustration of the connection between the two periods. The words "war crimes" could only be used within the framework of reference of the Second World War and were indelibly associated with the concept of the SS. The suggestion that Dutch soldiers could have committed war crimes therefore relegated them to the same level as the Germans. But this in turn was inconceivable because the entire historical picture of the war was based on the contrast between the Dutch and the Germans.

Like the Dreyfus affair, the Hueting scandal concerned the honor of the army. But this was only half the story: the other part, the fight for rehabilitation of an unjustly convicted man, was provided a short time later by the Weinreb question, the only difference being that Weinreb was not innocent. It began when Weinreb, a Dutch Jew who was found guilty of treason after the war, published his memoirs in 1969, in which he contended that, instead of being a traitor, he had in fact played a very dangerous and subtle game with the Germans.[23] The details of this highly complicated question are not relevant here. After a long and thorough inquiry it was concluded that Weinreb had been guilty. What is important here is that many were moved by Weinreb's image of himself as the lonely fighter amidst a suffering, passively collaborationist population. Furthermore, his resistance was not based on nationalism but on humanity and his only weapon was his intellect. These were aspects which particularly appealed to the younger intelligentsia: they implied criticism of the establishment and appeared to offer an alternative form of defense to take the place of NATO and its nuclear weapons.

These two affairs illustrate the *crises de conscience* which appeared so frequently in the Netherlands in the 1970s—but not only in the Netherlands. The entire Western world was to learn this need for adaptation, purification, and catharsis, with Vietnam and Watergate as the symbols of moral issues in foreign and domestic politics. The difference between America and the Netherlands in this respect is, however, that the Dutch found issues not only in current political problems but also in the recent past. The acid test in Dutch politics is still the individual's attitude during the Second World War. This is now, apparently, even more important than ever before—which is an indication of how poorly the past has been assimilated. The years 1945–1949 have been erased, while the years 1940–1945 have become legend so that the discovery of every new transgressor produces a dramatic shock.

This preoccupation with moral problems, which at first glance appears to be something new, is in fact a traditional element in Dutch politics, characterized for centuries by a tendency toward moralism and puritanism, and in foreign politics a preference for neutrality. In this sense the 1950s and 1960s, displaying less attention to the moral elements in politics together with enthusiasm for European and Atlantic ties, were an anomalous period in Dutch history. The 1970s, on the other hand, despite all the criticism of the establishment and the rise to power of a new generation, appear to be much more traditional. Moralism was again linked with neutralism: organizations such as the Common Market and NATO were sharply criticized. As ever, this neutralism was based on a certain conviction of moral superiority: the true calling of the Dutch is not to be an ally but an example. Formerly, it used to be said that the Kingdom of the Netherlands was a ''light in a world of darkness,'' in more recent days it was mentioned as the ''guide'' showing the way to zero growth and environmental protection. This feeling of moral superiority, combined with commercial realism, is probably the most lasting element in Dutch political culture, a frame of mind apparently unaffected even by such major events as war and decolonization.

Chapter 11

Overseas History, 1945–1995

This chapter is on overseas history, an interesting but by no means easy subject. For what *is* overseas history? Strictly speaking, there is no proper definition of it or, rather, what it is depends on where one stands. From the British perspective, for example, practically all history is overseas history, including part of the history of the United Kingdom itself. To paraphrase a well-known French expression: everybody's history is overseas history for somebody else. This is obviously not what we have in mind when we use the term here, so then what is it? A practical solution of this problem can be found by examining the contents of publications which carry this term in their titles. The French *Revue française d'histoire d'outre-mer*, published by the society of the same name, is essentially a journal devoted to the history of European, and particularly French, expansion overseas and of former French possessions. This is not surprising, as its original name was *Revue d'histoire des colonies*. In the same vein the French as well as the Belgian *Académies des sciences d'outre-mer* used to be known as *Académies des sciences coloniales*. The German-language series of *Beiträge zur Kolonial- und Überseegeschichte* combines the two terms. The British are lucky enough to have their Commonwealth, which is why there is a *Journal of Imperial and Commonwealth History*, a much more elegant combination than "Imperial and Overseas History." In the Netherlands the Royal Colonial Institute changed its name to Royal Tropical Institute, but somehow the term "tropical history" was never accepted.

It is not difficult to understand what was going on here. After 1945 the term "colonial" became increasingly unattractive and institutes that wanted to continue their existence had to find different (preferably more neutral) names. However, it was not simply a matter of changing names. There was also a change of approach and interest. Overseas history developed into a much broader field of study than colonial history used to be. It deals not only with colonial systems and the encounter between Europeans and non-Europeans in general, but also with the economic, social, political, and cultural history of the non-European peoples. It is precisely here that problems arise, because not only theoretically but also in actual practice, overseas history has developed into such a vast subject as to become unidentifiable. Of course, there are some elements that give a certain cohesion to the field. In the first place, the overseas historian normally deals with two types of sources, on the one hand European, mostly archival, sources and on the other, non-European, written, or, as is often the case in African history, non-written sources. Because of the lack of traditional sources the assistance of other disciplines is necessary, hence the role of disciplines like archaeology, linguistics, and anthropology in overseas history. Overseas history therefore tends to be more interdisciplinary than other fields.

Apart from this, the overseas historian must also familiarize himself with civilizations other than his own. This generally supposes a broader—and somewhat different—education than is normally the case, as well as a greater demand for linguistic skills. This is the reason why overseas historians are often found in orientalist or Africanist departments, at least in Europe (the situation in the United States is different). And even when they are appointed in history departments overseas, historians feel the need to collaborate with other specialists on the same area, such as linguists, anthropologists, or art historians. This is not the case with historians of Europe. A specialist in French history will not normally work in a department of French studies nor will he feel the urge to go to conferences on French studies. As it is typical for overseas historians to learn about civilizations other than their own, they have to collaborate with other disciplines to reach a better understanding of that particular civilization or society. But they also have to keep in touch with other historians in order to understand what is going on in their own discipline. The tension between the area approach and the disciplinary approach is a well-known phenomenon.

There is another reason why, historically speaking, there is a certain unity in the field of overseas history. Most of the overseas world formerly belonged to the colonial world and is now supposed to form part of the Third World. This is why in some circles the expression "Third World history" is in use.[1] But the very idea of a "Third World" is now disintegrating, as it no longer reflects reality. In retrospect, it even seems strange that countries like India and Indonesia were supposed to form one world with Sudan and Mali for the sole reason that they were all former colonies and are still relatively poor. To equate overseas history with Third World history therefore does not seem to be a good idea, all the more so as the history of the United States clearly belongs to overseas and indeed to colonial history but not to Third World history.

The question can be raised whether overseas history, if it is supposed to include the history of the whole world apart from Europe (or "the West"), is a subject of study at all. This problem is the result of the success of overseas history after the Second World War, when the rise of overseas history was to some extent due to a reaction to former colonial history. A great backlog had to be made up, and a great leap forward was made. The new nations vindicated their own national past. The "people without history" finally found one and the results of this movement were impressive. Overseas history has become so vast and so varied that it can no longer be considered as one specific field of history. In order to survive, overseas history will need some form of reconceptualization. Before discussing this, we should sketch a brief outline of the history of the subject.

THE HISTORY OF OVERSEAS HISTORY: A SURVEY

In one form or another, history has been practiced in most civilizations. In Indonesia the chronicles or *babads* go back very far. The Hindus in India took little interest in history, but the Muslims had a greater interest and a stronger sense of chronology, though they too only drew up chronicles of events. In Japan and China a historiography was developed comparable to traditional European history which, in its modern scientific form, was only developed in the West in the nineteenth century. It is characterized by what is called "the historical method" (chronology, philology, textual criticism, hermeneutics) as well as a particular type of historical thinking. Awareness of the uniqueness of events, the notion of development and succession over time but also the notion that each period has a specific character with its own values and standards, are characteristic of this. The German historical school played a major role in this development, which is why some of the most famous historical notions are still best known in their German form: *Historismus, Verstehen, Zeitgeist.*

The historical interpretation which resulted from this was extremely Eurocentric. *Weltgeschichte* in fact came down to European history, for in the framework of general history non-European peoples played no role. They were considered as people without history (Hegel) or people of eternal standstill (Ranke). Apart from the traditional ancient civilizations, they came into the picture only at the moment they submitted to and were conquered by the Europeans. This does not mean that there was no interest at all in civilizations other than Western ones, for this existed in the form of what was known as oriental studies. The impetus for these studies was, on one hand, the Bible and linguistics, and on the other, colonialism. After the Renaissance many European universities not only created chairs of Greek and Latin but also of Hebrew and Arabic. Later on, departments of Middle Eastern and/or Arabic studies emanated from these subjects. Comparative and historical linguistics, a popular subject in the nineteenth century, stimulated the study of Sanskrit, which in turn gave rise to chairs and institutes for the study of Indian civilization.

An even more important stimulus came from colonialism. The training of colonial civil servants became a part of European university education in the nineteenth century. Courses on languages and colonial administration could be found alongside courses on imperial or colonial history. While they focused primarily on the European point of view, these courses also paid some attention to overseas peoples. It is interesting to see that as early as 1897 a search committee for a chair in the history of the Netherlands Indies gave preference to a candidate because he could also pay attention "to the indigenous point of view."[2] Apart from the colonial subjects themselves, other overseas peoples became objects of study. In the Netherlands, for example, the Chinese were studied because of the important Chinese community in the East Indies, the Japanese because of the "yellow peril," and Islam because of the danger of "Muslim fanaticism." The result of this was that two groups of historians came into being: a small group in departments of oriental studies who studied other civilizations in their own right, and a much larger one who taught history proper, that is, the history of Europe and its colonies. Even though they were based in the same university, the two groups would rarely collaborate.

The situation changed drastically after 1945, partly for external and partly for internal reasons. The external reasons are obvious: decolonization, the decline of Europe, the emergence of the new superpowers. These events led to a rethinking of the role of Europe in world history and a questioning of the Eurocentric approach. The decline of Europe became as important a subject of study as its previous rise to power. The Dutch historian Jan Romein proclaimed the end of the *European Era* and the beginning of the *Asian Century*, to quote the titles of two of his books.[3]

But apart from political and ideological reasons there were also internal developments, changes in the way history was studied. The postwar period witnessed the rise of social and economic history. Historians became less interested in political and military history and more interested in subjects such as material civilization, *mentalités*, everyday life, the common man, and so on. In this respect, at least until the eighteenth century, European history was not so different from non-European history. Under the impact of the *Annales* school history became less teleological, less "whiggish." Structure replaced evolution as the central preoccupation. Continuity became as important as change and therefore the opposition between Europe (change) and Asia (continuity) became less relevant. In this approach the nation state was no longer the central unit of historical analysis; therefore, the opposition of motherland and colony was less important. The new approach was more in terms of villages, towns, regions, social groups. This made the antagonism between the colonialist and the nationalist approach less sharp, and there were also practical changes. A growing influence came from American historians, for their departments of history had always been less parochial than European ones, and they played an increasing role in Asian and African history. Moreover, the former colonies themselves developed their own history departments. To be sure, for a long time Western historians still dominated the field, as they were better educated and had easy access to important holdings in European archives. The indigenous elites were more interested in fields other than history. The task of developing the economy and building the nation was more urgent—and more rewarding—than that of writing history.

A curious situation resulted from this. On one hand, the impact of Europe on the concept of history itself became even stronger than before. Historians from Asia and Africa often came to Europe to study history or at least to finish their education. They worked in Western archives and they turned to Western models to learn how history was to be studied and written. Thus, like the Japanese after the Meiji revolution, they learned history from the West.[4] In their own civilization they found no references. On the other hand, their interpretation was, of course, very different and sometimes strongly anti-Western. The young nations needed "a usable past" and "usable" meant nationalistic and anti-colonial.[5] Thus, the question was not only one of colonialist versus nationalist historiography. It concerned the place of the West in world history in general. European historians themselves also questioned the Eurocentric approach to overseas history. A new impulse for this debate came from the discussion about the origins of underdevelopment stemming from the disappointment of postcolonial change. The original optimism about a bright new future now that colonialism had ended faded away when it became clear that the economic and social problems of the former colonies were permanent (or structural) rather than temporary.[6] This time the opposition was not that of colonialism versus nationalism but of Left versus Right. The neo-Marxist critique of colonialism became very influential in the Western world itself.

Thus, the development of overseas history after 1945 was a dialectical process. First there was an emancipation movement in non-Western historiography, which resulted in an impressive explosion of historical research and production in Asia and Africa. The non-European countries discovered their own pasts and offered their own interpretations of it, but it was precisely then that the problem of overseas history manifested itself in a new form. Today everybody accepts that Africans and Asians have their own histories, and that they are as rich and interesting as that of Europe. The question, however, is whether we can stop here and simply consider world history as the sum of a great number of autonomous regional histories. Most historians would agree that we should try to do more and study how, in one way or another, these various civilizations have become interconnected, how today's world situation has come into being. The real challenge of overseas history is to offer a modern form of world history. This is an ambitious goal but, as Fernand Braudel has said, we need ambitious historians.[7] A possible outline of this can perhaps be found in the new history of European expansion that has developed in the last three decades or so. But before examining this we shall look first at the spectacular development of Asian and African history in the same period.[8]

ASIAN AND AFRICAN HISTORY

Both in India and Indonesia, history in its modern scientific form was introduced by the colonial power. In India the foundation of the Asiatic Society of

Bengal in 1784 can be considered as the starting point. The official British historiography of India was highly Anglocentric. As Nehru once remarked about the British: "Real history for them begins with the advent of the Englishman to India; all that went before it is in some mystic kind of way a preparation for this divine consummation."[9] However, an interest in historical studies soon began to develop among the new Indian intelligentsia. In the middle of the nineteenth century, as a reaction to the rather condescending approach of the colonial historians, Indian historians developed their own historiography, and in the late nineteenth century the rise of the nationalist movement gave a strong impetus to this, so that by the 1920s and 1930s there existed a considerable group of professional historians. The names of well-known scholars such as R.K. Mookerji and R.C. Majumdar bear witness to this, and therefore, when independence came in 1947, Indian professional historiography was already in a strong position.

The transfer of power itself also stimulated the writing of history, and there was a demand for popular texts and schoolbooks. The government stimulated the study of the recent past and particularly of the nationalist movement. In 1952 the Ministry of Education ordered the compilation of a history of the Indian freedom movement, and R.C. Majumdar was appointed director of the project. Majumdar's conclusions were very different from what the government had expected, but he published his interpretation all the same. This debunking of the nationalist myth was a clear indication of the high standard of professionalism that had been reached by the Indian historians.[10] Although British historians are still playing a leading, if not *the* leading, role in Indian history, Indian historians themselves have become increasingly important. The *Cambridge Economic History of India* as well as the *New Cambridge History of India* are convincing demonstrations of this.

In Indonesia the development was somewhat different. Compared to India, there were fewer university-trained persons in general and practically no professional historians at all during the colonial period. The nationalist movement was also weaker than it was in India, and nationalist intellectuals expressed their feelings in literary rather than scholarly works. Thus, there were practically no professional Indonesian historians before independence. The government of the Republic stimulated the study of the past but from a clear political perspective (ideological pressures were strong). In 1957 the first national congress of historians was held. There it became clear how little research had yet been done, but from then on history as a scholarly discipline was developed. The main figure in this was Sartono Kartodirdjo, who introduced a new social-science-inspired form of history which pays special attention to rural history.[11]

In the meantime, it was Indonesian history that led to an interesting debate about a new Asiacentric approach to Asian history. John Bastin, in his inaugural lecture at Kuala Lumpur in 1959 about *The Study of Modern Southeast Asian History*, greatly stimulated this discussion,[12] but the question itself had already been raised much earlier. It was introduced by J.C. van Leur in his dissertation about early Asian trade, which was published in 1934.[13] Van Leur, who died very young (at the age of 34) in the Battle of the Java Sea, was to have a lasting influence on Indonesian history and indeed on Asian history in general. The originality of his work lies in two things: the abandonment of the Eurocentric viewpoint and the application of sociological categories.[14]

However, Van Leur's criticism is at the same time more general and more fundamental. He questions the periodization of history and the place in it allotted to Asia. For instance, in a well-known article he examines why period labels such as "the eighteenth century" were applied to Indonesian history. He concludes that there was no point in this since none of the great changes which typify European history of this period can be traced in the Indonesian past. Up to 1800 it simply remains part of Asia.[15]

The question of the role of Europe in Asian history was of vital importance for the postindependence historiography. In this respect one can distinguish two schools, the minimalist and the sentimentalist. The minimalist school minimalizes the role of the Western factor in Asian history, claiming that this was virtually non-existent, while the sentimentalist school maximizes the crimes and misdeeds of the West. Although, logically speaking, the two views seem to be contradictory, they can sometimes both be found in the work of one scholar (for example, the Dutch sociologist W.F. Wertheim or the Indian historian K.M. Panikkar).[16] Thus, the debate was not altogether clear and the concepts themselves are ambiguous. But the two questions: "Was Western influence good or bad? Was its impact great or small?" are still intensely debated today, and understandably so. They are vital for our interpretation of the past as well as our understanding of the present, as we shall see later.

In the nineteenth century the European approach to Asian history became increasingly dominated by feelings of European superiority and a conviction of Asian backwardness. This, however, was only a fairly recent phenomenon since European historians had traditionally shown a great respect for the ancient civilizations of Asia. This was very different from the European attitude toward Africa, which had always been regarded as an ahistorical continent and the African people as a people without civilization and thus without history. The most famous formulation of this opinion is to be found in the Jena Lectures given by Hegel in 1830–1831 and published as the *Philosophy of History*. Here he wrote: "At this point we leave Africa, not to mention it again. For it is no historical part of the World; it has no movement or development to exhibit. . . . What we properly understand by Africa is the Unhistorical Undeveloped Spirit, still involved in the conditions of mere nature, which had to be presented here only as being on the threshold of the World's history."[17]

Hegel had a great influence on Karl Marx, and classical Marxist writings reflect the same line of thought. A late echo of this can be found in the work of the Hungarian Marxist historian of Africa, Endre Sik, who wrote in 1966:

> Prior to their encounter with Europeans the majority of African peoples still lived a primitive, barbaric life, many of them even on the lowest level of barbarism. Some of

them lived in complete, or almost complete, isolation: the contacts, if any, of others were but scattered skirmishes with neighbouring peoples. The *State*, taken in the real sense of the word, was a notion unknown to most African peoples, as classes did not exist either. Or rather—both existed already, but only in embryo. Therefore it is unrealistic to speak of their "history"—in the scientific sense of the word—before the appearance of the European invaders.[18]

There is no doubt that such opinions were by no means a monopoly of Marxist historians. Just one year before Sik's book appeared, the Regius Professor of Modern History at Oxford, H.R. Trevor-Roper, compared the histories of Britain and Africa, describing the latter as being little more than "the unrewarding gyrations of barbarous tribes in picturesque but irrelevant quarters of the globe."[19]

How things have changed in 30 years! Nobody in his right mind would argue any more that African history does not exist, not even in Oxford. The development of African history has been spectacular. Perhaps it has been the most vivid, dynamic, and innovative field of history since the emergence of the new social and economic history in the 1920s and 1930s. One could argue that the *Journal of African History* has been the most innovative journal since the founding of the *Annales*. Indeed, the two developments are to a certain extent comparable. Social historians, such as those of the *Annales* and others, began to ask questions that had not been asked before and of which no mention was made in traditional sources. New sources had to be discovered and new techniques developed to reexamine old sources in a new light. The same situation exists with African history. Sources are scarce, at least traditional ones. For cultural reasons the Africans have produced less written material on African history than the Europeans, and for climatic reasons, little of this has been handed down to us. This means that most of the sources are exogenous. They come from foreigners, be they Greek, Roman, or Arabic; travellers, geographers, European merchants, or administrators. Technically speaking, much of African history is pre- or protohistory (or ethno-history, as it has sometimes been called).[20]

The very scarcity of sources has given an enormous stimulus to the development of new techniques and methods. The past had to be investigated with other means. Again, the comparison with the *Annales* and its *nouvelle histoire* is relevant. In both cases archaeology, cartography, linguistics, onomastics have been applied. Anthropology has also played a major role in African history. Indeed, the distinction between the anthropologist and the historian is by no means very sharp.

The most famous of the techniques developed in order to provide new sources for African history was the study of oral tradition. Here the publication of Jan Vansina's *De la tradition orale. Essai de méthode historique* in 1961 was epoch-making. Quickly translated into English (*Oral tradition*, 1965), the book had a tremendous impact on African history.[21] Halfway between the naive and the skeptic, Vansina developed a method for using oral tradition in a critical way and thus for employing it in serious history writing. Vansina divided the oral tradition into five categories (formulae, poetry, lists, tales, commentaries) each with its various subdivisions. He argued that oral tradition should not be accepted at face value and that it should only be used after critical examination, paying attention to the impact of social significance, cultural values, and the personality of the writers. It should also, as far as possible, be checked with other sources, for example, archaeological findings or written documents. Some historians (and anthropologists) were more skeptical about oral tradition and believed, with due respect for Vansina, that he overestimated its possibilities, but it is undeniable that his work and ideas have greatly influenced African history.[22]

Whatever possibilities oral tradition and other unorthodox sources offer, the fact remains that as far as written documents are concerned Africa is rather deprived. It is true that this also goes for certain periods of European history for which documents are also very scarce, as well as for pre-Columbian America, pre-Cookian Australia, and so on, and that therefore African history is exceptional but not unique. All the same, a historiography of Africa comparable to that of Europe seems impossible. Long-term developments can be studied but a strictly factual or *événementiel* history is often impossible. At the moment the structural or long-term approach is in vogue in European history as well, but this is a matter of choice. In Africa, structural history is not a choice but the only possibility. One is not seduced by it, but condemned to it.[23]

In the last decades a number of African historians have appeared in the international forum, and their role is becoming increasingly prominent. All the same, one should acknowledge that the great leap forward in African history was mostly due to European and American historians, especially British ones. The *Journal of African History*—the first issue of which appeared in 1960—was, as Terence Ranger has said, "the combined manifesto, charter, programme and shop-window for the field."[24] Roland Oliver's seminar at the London School of Oriental and African Studies has been called "the premier setting in the world for the presentation of new work on Africa's past."[25] Oliver's and Fage's *Short History of Africa* sold over a million copies and is probably the single most influential book on African history.

French historians have also played an important role, albeit a more modest one. In 1961, Henri Brunschwig, a former student of Marc Bloch and Lucien Febvre at Strasbourg, was invited by Fernand Braudel to introduce African history at the Ecole des Hautes Etudes. His seminar became a meeting place for French and African scholars. Yves Person, the author of a monumental and innovative history of Samori, and Catherine Coquery-Vidrovitch not only wrote important books themselves but also brought the subject to the University of Paris.[26] Other universities (Aix, Bordeaux) also offered courses and seminars in African history, and a great number of African students presented doctoral dissertations at French universities.

The contribution of American universities was significant, particularly that of the three main schools of Yale, UCLA and, above all, Madison (Wisconsin). Those American historians who played a leading role in the second and third generations of African historians were mostly former students of Curtin and Vansina at Madison. At the moment important historical schools also exist at various universities in Africa itself (Nigeria, Kenya, Zaïre). The period of European dominance is clearly over.

In retrospect, much of the debate about the possibilities and impossibilities of African and Asian history looks rather futile, not only because of the decrease in the feeling of European superiority but also due to the changes in the study of history itself. The antagonism of colonialist versus nationalist makes sense within the framework of political history, but in other fields of history we find a different approach. Social history is studied at the level of the village, the region, the ethnic group. Cultural history is analyzed on a much bigger scale than that of the nation state. Concepts like Hindu or Javanese civilization or "the world of Islam" are relevant here. Economic history works with large unities like the Indian Ocean, or Southeast Asia or even the world economy. In this type of approach the opposition—colonial versus anti-colonial—does not make much sense.

Does this mean that the impact of colonialism on overseas history is over and that Western and non-Western attitudes have found a complete equilibrium? Not necessarily, for in two respects there still exists a degree of Western dominance. In the first place, as a result of colonial expansion a great quantity of books, documents, and other materials about the overseas world were brought over to Europe and are now available in European archives and libraries. This means that in order to study their own past non-European historians will have to continue to come to Europe. In the second place, and also to a large extent as a consequence of colonialism, in the Western world a great tradition has been founded in the field of non-Western studies, in which it still plays a major role. On the other hand, there are practically no African or Asian historians who study European history and society. As long as the West has its Orientalists but the East has no "Occidentalists" there can be no real equilibrium.

On balance one can say that the development of African and Asian history was a natural and a necessary phenomenon, but it also leaves us with a problem. While it is true that African and Asian history is to a large extent autonomous, it is also true that since about 1500 the history of Africa and Asia has become connected to that of Europe. Asian history is much more than an extension of the history of Europe, but it cannot be completely isolated from European history, either. The central development of modern history is the increasing interconnection and interweaving of various formerly isolated civilizations and economies. This has resulted in the "modern world system" (Wallerstein) and the "civilization of modernity" (Eisenstadt) that we have today. One cannot understand this process by considering only isolated parts of history, for that would be missing the central theme of modern world history. World history cannot be considered as identical to European or Western history; neither can it be conceived of as a series of isolated developments. To tackle this problem is the central concern of the history of European expansion as it has developed in the postdecolonization period.

EXPANSION AND REACTION

The study of European expansion was also influenced by external as well as internal factors. The rapid fall of the colonial empires, for example, led to a questioning of their previous apparent stability. The rise of the American empire, an empire without colonies, stimulated a rethinking of both informal and formal techniques of imperialism. The emergence of China led to a reappraisal of the country's scientific and naval possibilities and thus to new questions about the differences between Chinese and early European expansion.

On the other hand, internal factors changed the nature of expansion studies as well, and the general trend in favor of social and economic history also manifested itself in this field. Questions about monetarization, shipping, gold and silver, the profits of empire, and so on, were asked in a new way and these could often be answered with the aid of a computer.[27] Social history became a fashionable subject and this stimulated the study of migration, the slave trade, race relations, urbanization, and *mentalités*. Political science influenced political history by suggesting the study of such topics as decision-making, public opinion, the role of special interest groups, and so on.

Although at the theoretical level the traditional distinction between a first and a second phase of expansion was questioned, in actual practice the division of labor between modernists and students of contemporary history is still very visible. Traditionally, in early modern expansion the emphasis is on the great discoveries, ships and navigation, companies and trade, migration, plantation systems, and slave societies. Charles Boxer and J.H. Parry wrote successful books aiming at an overview of the seaborne empires.[28] The Minnesota series on the history of *Europe and the World in the Age of Expansion* also offered a series of textbooks on these topics. In many of these fields new approaches were offered, new questions were asked, and new techniques applied. Glamann, Steensgaard, and Chaudhuri published pathfinding studies of the Indian Companies, Curtin did pioneer work on the slave trade, Chaunu on the Atlantic world, Bailyn on migration, and many more could and should be mentioned.[29] Many of the questions discussed here are closely related to major topics of debate in European history such as theories about the origins of capitalism, "Phase I and II," the general depression of the seventeenth century, the price revolution, and so on. It should, however, be acknowledged that no general theory of European expansion was offered. While in the history of nineteenth- and twentieth-century expansion the debate was dominated by the concept of imperialism, there was no such thing in early expansion studies, at least not until Immanuel Wallerstein launched his theory about the modern world system.

Immanuel Wallerstein, a social scientist from Columbia University, first studied African decolonization and development problems. His way of thinking about these topics was influenced by *dependencia* and underdevelopment theories. However, Wallerstein turned to history because he believes that these problems of development can only be fully understood in their global context and in a historical perspective. The historical work he feels most familiar with is that of the *Annales* group and particularly that of Fernand Braudel. There is indeed a strong similarity between Wallerstein's ideas and the conceptual framework of the third volume of Braudel's work on *Material Civilization, Economy and Capitalism.*[30] Wallerstein's main publication so far is a (planned) four-volume study of what he calls *The Modern World System.* The first volume, which came out in 1974, offered the analytic framework of the project.[31] It was a source of inspiration for many other scholars and led to an interesting debate on the origins of European expansion and capitalism.

Wallerstein argues that the world economy of today goes back to the end of the fifteenth century. Here we find the beginnings of a world system that developed fully in the sixteenth and seventeenth centuries and was already mature before the Industrial Revolution. The "systemic turning point" can be located in the resolution of the crisis of feudalism which occurred approximately between 1450 and 1550. By the period 1550–1650, all the basic mechanisms of the capitalist world system were in place. In view of this the Industrial Revolution of about 1760 to 1830 can no longer be considered as a major turning point in the history of the capitalist world economy.

The world system, according to Wallerstein, is characterized by an international economic order and an international division of labor. It consists of a core, a semiperiphery and a periphery, the location of which changes over time (regions can ascend to the core or descend to the periphery). Modern history is in fact the history of the continuing integration into this world system of ever more parts of the world. The world system works in such a way as to make the center receive the profits, thus exploiting the periphery. This is brought about by international trade, which is considered as a zero-sum game: the profits of one party equal the losses of the other. The profits of international trade made the Industrial Revolution possible, which in turn only confirmed existing unequal relations and reinforced the development of underdevelopment.

Wallerstein's work was well received by social scientists but rather more critically by historians who in particular criticized the great weight given to international trade in the model. Some argued that preindustrial economies were not able to produce such a significant surplus as to make an important international trade possible. Before the coming of steamships, transport facilities were very limited. Around 1600 the combined merchant fleets of the European states only had the tonnage of one or two (around 1800 of seven or eight) of today's supertankers.[32] Even in trading nations par excellence, such as Britain and the Dutch Republic, trading for export represented a very small percentage of the GNP (and export to the periphery only a small percentage of the total overseas trade).[33] The capital accumulated in Britain as a consequence of overseas trade cannot have represented more than 15 percent of the gross expenditure undertaken during the Industrial Revolution.[34] Generally speaking, the effects of European expansion on overseas regions were not very important. In Asia the impact of overseas trade was only regional. Both in India (textile) and Indonesia (cash crops) only limited regions were affected by European demand. As far as Africa is concerned, the trade in products was very limited. Much more important was the Atlantic slave trade. Recent research, however, tends to minimize the long-term demographic consequences of this. In the Americas and the Caribbean the impact of European expansion was the most dramatic, not so much because of trade but because of the demographic decline of the original population.

An interesting point of Wallerstein's theory is his questioning of the very concept of an Industrial Revolution and thus of the distinction between preindustrial and industrial colonialism. This distinction was a central argument in the classical theory of imperialism, a theory that has dominated the historiography of late-nineteenth- and twentieth-century European expansion.

IMPERIALISM

Although the word imperialism had been in existence since the 1860s, imperialism as a historical concept only began with the publication of J.A. Hobson's *Imperialism: A Study* in 1902.[35] In order to explain imperialism Hobson argued that, as a consequence of the capitalist system, the British economy suffered from underconsumption. This meant that surplus capital could not be profitably invested in England itself. Therefore, in his famous words, the capitalists were "seeking foreign markets and foreign investments to take the goods and capital they cannot sell or use at home."[36] Thus, the theory of capitalist imperialism was born.

Hobson's theory was soon taken over, adapted, and made more sophisticated by Marxist thinkers, especial Germans such as Karl Hilferding and Rosa Luxemburg. In doing so, these authors also changed Hobson's argument. Whereas to Hobson the flight of capital was a typical but not a necessary consequence of capitalism, for the Marxists imperialism became an inevitability. The most famous formula is to be found with Lenin, who in 1916 called imperialism "the highest stage of capitalism." Although the differences between Hobson and Lenin are evident, it soon became commonplace to refer to the "Hobson-Lenin thesis." In fact, this became a standard explanation of European imperialism during the 1920s and 1930s.

Only in the 1960s was the general discussion on imperialism reopened. Clearly, decolonization as well as the rise of the American economic empire had much to do with this. In 1961 the British historians J. Gallagher and R. Robinson published the book that was to be the single most influential reexamination of British imperialism: *Africa and the Victorians*.[37] The year before, Henri Brunschwig had published *Mythes et réalités de l'impérialisme colonial français, 1871–1914*, an essay which set the tone for all later studies on French imperialism.[38] New interpretations of Belgian, German, Italian, Portuguese, and, eventually, Dutch imperialism followed. Thus, we might speak of a historiographical revolution.[39]

The books mentioned above removed the traditional, simple explanation of imperialism in terms of economic needs, though they did not give an analysis of the economic aspects of imperialism. In order to tackle this immense question it was not only necessary to solve a great number of theoretical and methodological problems, but also to collect and analyze an enormous amount of data. Again the computer made this possible. Two American historians, L. Davis and R. Huttenback, very appropriately connected with the California Institute of Technology, did precisely this for the subject of British imperialism. They collected a huge amount of data and analyzed this with very sophisticated methods. Their book *Mammon and the Pursuit of Empire*[40] seems to offer the definite answer to the old and famous question: Did the Empire pay? The answer, somewhat disappointingly, is: No! After 1880 the initially high rates of profits on colonial investments fell below comparable returns from other overseas destinations or even Britain itself. Thus, Hobson and Lenin were wrong about the relation between surplus capital and the urge of overseas expansion. The dependent colonies were not major recipients of City capital. There can be no doubt that this is not the whole answer, because Davis and Huttenback also argue that for some capitalists these investments were far from marginal.[41]

In France, under the influence of Brunschwig's arguments, even Marxist authors have accepted his vision that the economic aspects of French imperialism were negligible. In an attempt to rescue the Marxist interpretation they have argued that French imperialism was to be found elsewhere, in Russia, the Ottoman empire, and so on. This dialectical exercise resulted in the conclusion that French colonialism was not imperialist and French imperialism not colonial.[42] In order to find a more empirical answer to the question of economy and empire, Catherine Coquery-Vidrovitch took the initiative of setting up a data bank of French colonial trade (1880–1960). Her Parisian colleague, Jacques Marseille, was the first to make extensive use of this rich documentation for his dissertation *Empire colonial et capitalisme français: histoire d'un divorce*.[43] Marseille's conclusion is that there was a break in the relation between capitalism and colonialism. In the initial period, 1880–1930, French industry needed the outlet of the protected colonial market, and the marriage of colonialism and capitalism was a happy one. In the second period, 1930–1960, protectionism became an obstacle to sorely needed industrial modernization. Divorce became inevitable. But decolonization was already under way. The end of Empire in 1960 was a blessing for capitalism.

So much for Europe, but what was the impact of imperialism on the overseas world? This is a complicated subject on which a passionate debate has been going on ever since the question was raised. There are few things on which the debaters agree but one fact is undeniable: the real impact of the West on the overseas territories only took place after the Industrial Revolution. What were the effects of this? Of course, colonialism was organized in such a manner as to promote the interests of the colonial power. This implied burdens of various kinds for the colonized peoples. However, beyond the domain of basic truths such as these there is a vast zone of problems that cannot be answered simply. There is the well-established phenomenon of deindustrialization (notably in the case of the Indian textile industry). There is also the problem of specialization in cash crops. On the other hand, there are long-term developments resulting from investment in infrastructure (mining, roads, ports), the improvement of administration, education, health. To draw an economic balance sheet of colonialism is extraordinarily difficult, not only because of the lack of data but also because of theoretical problems.

If, as modern research has convincingly demonstrated, the simple explanation that imperialism was the result of capitalism is unacceptable, the question remains: What *was* the reason? Why was there "an age of imperialism" at all? As far as Britain is concerned the answer to this question was also given by Gallagher and Robinson. They argued that there was none. The very concept of an age of imperialism (1880–1914) is a fallacy. To consider this period as the zenith of British imperialism is to misunderstand its real nature. The increasing number of red areas on the world map during the 1880s and 1890s might seem to suggest that Britain's power was increasing. In reality, however, this was not an indication of strength but of weakness. Britain was more powerful in the early nineteenth century when it ruled by informal means than in the later years of formal political rule.[44]

The concept of informal empire is very attractive and very inspiring because it explains a great number of important phenomena. It also gives a much broader meaning to the term "imperialism." In this type of analysis imperialism exists in different periods and in different forms. The task of the historian is to explain the transition from one form to another. In Gallagher and Robinson's argument the reasons for this are not to be found with the politicians in Europe—who preferred informal empire anyway—but in changing situations overseas. Imperialism is considered as a system of collaboration between Europe and non-European forces. The changing forms of imperialism result from changes in terms of collaboration.[45] It is obvious that in such an analysis decolonization also loses much of its importance as a turning point. If there exists an informal imperialism before Empire, logically there can also be an informal imperialism after Empire.[46] Here the debate on imperialism is connected to those on decolonization and underdevelopment.

DECOLONIZATION AND AFTER

Decolonization has only recently become a subject of historical analysis and debate and is finally emerging as a subject for historical analysis rather than an act of God or the result of the laws of nature.[47] Decolonization is no longer exclusively described as the history of the acts of political leaders in a short time span (1947–1962). Its long-term, structural and conjunctural aspects are also given attention. The analysis of the various forms of decolonization centers around the three forces that were at work, the colonial power, the situation in the colony, and the international factor. The interaction of these forces decided the forms but not the outcome of the process because, whatever the differences, the outcome was always the same: independence. But here a question arises. What did independence really mean? Was the end of Empire also the end of imperialism or was it the continuation of it by different means? Here the subject of decolonization is connected to another topic, the theory of dependency.

The *dependencia* theory was first put forward by the Argentinian economist Raúl Prebish in 1947 and then further developed in the 1960s by Latin American scholars and by North Americans interested in Latin America. The theory was born from the observation of the permanency of Latin America's problems: poverty, inequality, slums, external debts, the dominance of foreign capital: in a word, dependency. The theory of dependency argues that this situation is not the result of a lack of development but of underdevelopment. Originating in Latin American studies, the theory was further worked out and refined to become a universal one applicable not only to Latin America but to the entire Third World. The Third World is seen as the periphery of a world economic system in which the center, that is to say, the West, is accumulating the profits and keeping the periphery in a situation of permanent dependency. Thus, underdevelopment is not a situation but a process. The Third World is not undeveloped, but it is being underdeveloped by the West. André Gunder Frank formulated its most catching formulation: "the development of underdevelopment."[48]

The theory of dependency was soon applied to various parts of the Third World, particularly to Africa. Samir Amin wrote extensively on the subject and Walter Rodney published his successful book about it with the arresting title *How Europe Underdeveloped Africa*.[49] The problem with the theory is that in order to explain the particular (under)development of Africa it has to make the continent dependent upon foreign influences during most of its history. This line of thought was somewhat contradictory of the main trend which developed in African history in the same period, which underlined the autonomy of African history. Africans were no longer seen as mere victims of European expansion but to a large extent as masters of their own destiny. While neo-Marxists embraced the theory of dependency, classical Marxist historians and anthropologists underlined the autonomy of African history and even tried to discover an "African mode of production."[50]

Both the theory of dependency and the concept of informal empire were of great heuristic value because they questioned some of the fundamental assumptions of overseas history and thus changed our interpretation. The very concept of an age of imperialism with a clear-cut beginning and end can be disputed, at least as far as Britain is concerned. The zenith of the British Empire is now sometimes placed in the eighteenth century, its decline already beginning in the nineteenth. Not surprisingly, the question has been asked: "Why did the British Empire last so long?"[51] The danger with concepts and theories like these is that their meaning is overestimated and they become the new orthodoxy. It is a useful corrective to existing interpretations to relativize the importance of turning points such as the beginning of imperialism or the transfer of power, but we should not also underestimate their historical significance. The loss and eventual recovery of political independence are important enough historical caesurae, and it is no use letting their concrete historical significance fade away in some rather abstract concept of dependency.[52] Perhaps it is more useful to stay somewhat closer to the concrete historical process and to give full attention to the specific and unique aspects of European expansion. This brings us back to the question we started with: "What is overseas history?" or rather: "What will it be in the future?"

CONCLUSION

In 1979, when P.C. Emmer and I published a volume of essays entitled *Reappraisals in Overseas History*, we also had to ask ourselves the question: "What is overseas history?" We then argued that it is a much broader concept than the history of European expansion, for it "deals not only with the encounters between Europeans and non-Europeans, but also with the economic, social, political and cultural systems of the non-Europeans themselves."[53] This is true. As we have seen here, there are in fact two different and clearly distinct forms of overseas history: the autonomous history of Asia and Africa and the history of European expansion. But as we have also seen, this situation is not satisfactory. If there are autonomous histories of Africa, Asia, America, Australia, and so on, there is no point in throwing all these histories into one basket, for the sole reason that they are not European, and calling this "overseas history." The reason why this was done was that after 1945 overseas history had to find a new focus, and colonial historians and their students turned to Asian and African history itself. It was some time before these fields proved their rights of existence. In the meantime, the term "overseas history" served as a neutral and therefore convenient cover for their activities. This form of overseas history can thus be considered as an emancipation movement. It can be compared with the emergence of women's history or black history or, in an earlier period, the history of the working classes, the peasants, and so on. As soon as the emancipation is completed the subject changes its character. From the professional historian's point of view it will continue to exist as a specialization, a special field of interest, but for the public it becomes part of "general" history.

This is clearly also the case with both African and Asian history. They have proved their rights of existence, just like European or American history. So this particular branch of overseas history is bound to disintegrate into African or Asian history, and so on. But there is another side to it as well. Just as some but not all of European history can be understood as autonomous history, the same goes for the overseas world. Over the last five centuries or so the histories of various parts of the world have become interconnected and various civilizations have influenced one another. This is the other topic of overseas history and the importance of this aspect of modern history is increasingly understood. In this form overseas history has gained a distinct place in the field of modern history, not as a special discipline or subdiscipline but as a particular form of world history.

At the moment it seems that there are two approaches, two ways of dealing with the problem of world history. One of them can perhaps be labelled historical macrosociology. This type of history is characterized by a social-science approach. It singles out a specific social phenomenon or topic, like state formation or revolution or dictatorship, and analyzes this in various historical contexts. Thus, one can distinguish similarities and dissimilarities between, for example, events in sixteenth-century Europe and twentieth-century China. The aim of the game is to learn more about social processes in general.[54] The other approach is more traditional insofar as it tries to distinguish a certain pattern in the development of modern history and considers the writing of history as the description of concrete historical processes and events. History is also studied in a comparative way but within the framework of chronological developments. There is more interest in the differences between various developments and the uniqueness of certain events than in their similarities. The conceptual framework is that of the unification of the world as a consequence of the expansion of Europe and the rise of the West.[55] Both approaches are characterized by a strong desire to transcend traditional boundaries, parochial views, and nationalist bias. In the end they have the same goal: to make the specific Western discipline of history applicable to world history. This is necessary because "our civilization is the first to have for its past the past of the world, our history is the first to be world history." These words were written by the Dutch historian Johan Huizinga more than half a century ago.[56] The challenge of drawing the consequences from them is one we are still facing today.

Chapter 12

Overseas History in the Netherlands after the Second World War

Is history science or art? This is a problem which has been on people's minds for more than a century and certainly it is an interesting question. But within the framework of this contribution it is not really important, for, whether one practices art history or history of science, one faces the same problem. On the one hand, such a history is first and foremost a history of the work and achievements of individuals. A history of science which does not deal with the work of Copernicus, Newton, and Einstein is as useless as a history of art in which Rembrandt, Rubens, and Michelangelo do not figure. Art and history are and will remain foremost the work of individuals of genius. On the other hand, it is also true that a history of art or science which confines itself exclusively to a series of sketches of individuals and their work is not satisfactory either. Artists and scientists do not work within a vacuum. As one discerns tendencies and trends in art, likewise within the field of science one finds schools and paradigms. In order to understand works of art and science we have to look closely at influences and examples, at the time-spirit, the spiritual climate, and so on.

The same applies to the practice of history. This, too, is the work of individuals. Of course, there are rules and methods, but each work of history in the end bears the mark of the individual author. Here also some individuals stand out and masterworks are sometimes the result. The history of historiography is right to pay a good deal of attention to the work of historians like Ranke and Burckhardt, Pirenne, and Huizinga. But historiography on its own is not enough; one should also pay attention to the time and place in which historians were writing. In order to understand the work of a historian, one should realize that he belongs to a national culture as well as to the international scientific community. In contrast to the natural sciences, in historiography, national factors and traditions play a part. Moreover, it should be pointed out that in order to study history, not only the work of a few talented persons, but the historical production in its totality is important. Historical knowledge and insight are the results of an extensive collective activity of many, often unknown, sometimes even anonymous scholars and researchers. In modern historiographical studies attention is duly given to these general aspects, and to such a degree that in this field of history also quantitative, "cliometric" approximations have found their places.[1]

In this chapter, therefore, we cannot confine ourselves to the discussion of a few important works and a few influential historians, and not even to a survey and analysis of historical production as a whole, but we should place them in their proper contexts and perspectives. This implies that to begin with we have to enter into the factors which have given rise to the overseas studies in the Netherlands and determined their development. These could be named the exogenous factors, the influences from outside. We all know how important these factors are, especially in history which, according to the title of one of Jan Romein's works, operates *In opdracht van de tijd* (Per order of time).[2] Modern German historiography, to give only one example, has been influenced profoundly by recent German history. The rise of African history, to take another, is linked with decolonization, just as an interest in Eastern European history is connected with the cold war. Likewise, the development of overseas historiography in the Netherlands has been determined to a high degree by similar external factors.

Apart from this we have to pay attention to the developments within the discipline of history itself, the endogenous factors, so to speak. These occur beyond boundaries of countries and are autonomous to a certain extent. As we all know, the writing of history has changed character radically since the Second World War. In this connection it suffices to mention the word *Annales* in order to denote some of the major changes. Like every other branch, overseas history has been influenced by these developments.

The examples named so far (decolonization, *Annales*) have been taken from the recent past. In order to understand the present-day situation, and to place it into perspective, we have to go further back than the postwar period and take a look at developments over a long and medium-long period, for these continue to make themselves felt. Therefore, we should not only discern three levels of analysis (the individual, the national community, and the international scientific world), but three time perspectives as well: long, medium, and short term.

For this reason we will take a look at the development of overseas studies in the Netherlands first, then discuss the historiographical developments which influenced overseas history. After that, the influence of these two factors on the practice of overseas history in the Netherlands after 1945 will be dealt with. Finally, an attempt will be made to examine and analyze that historiography itself.

OVERSEAS STUDIES IN THE NETHERLANDS: HISTORICAL BACKGROUNDS

The initial impetus to the pursuit of overseas studies in the Netherlands was given by those studying the Bible at the theological faculties. Naturally, this study focused especially on the world of the ancient Near East. Bible study stimulated philology, the study of Hebrew and other Semitic languages, Arabic, and the Arab world. Similar studies developed at practically all Dutch universities and often led to considerable scientific efforts in related fields, such as archaeology and the ancient history of the Holy Land and the ancient Near East. These are the origins of an orientalistic tradition, still in existence, which centers around philology and textual criticism. For our investigation, however, the effects of the overseas expansion itself were far more important.

Two phases of the Dutch overseas expansion may be distinguished: the *ancien régime* (seventeenth-eighteenth centuries) and modern time (nineteenth-twentieth centuries). These two periods were very different in character. The Dutch colonial realm of the *ancien régime* was a "seaborne empire," a realm of maritime expansion, supported by the great companies, the "VOC" (United East India Company), and the "WIC" (West India Company). This expansion was worldwide, but superficial. It was a realm of lines and dots, without great territorial claims and without much profundity. The presence of the Dutch extended, for a shorter or longer period of time, over the Americas (New Amsterdam, the Antilles, the Guyanas, Brazil), the coasts of West and South Africa, great parts of South and Southeast Asia and the Far East (India, Ceylon, Burma, Indochina, Thailand, Indonesia, Japan, Taiwan). Apart from this, very intensive commercial ties often existed, even in regions where no settlements, fortresses, or footholds had been founded by the Dutch (e.g., North Africa and the Mediterranean world).

This resulted in a very great wealth of sources and documents on the older history of the overseas world. Sometimes they concern only a short period of Dutch occupation, as was the case in Taiwan (1624–1662), at other times a very long-standing presence, as in Deshima in Japan, where the Dutch were the only Westerners present, from 1639 to 1854. Often Dutch record offices, especially the National Archives in The Hague, contain data on the history of regions which have never been part of the Dutch colonies, and which are not normally related to Dutch history. A striking example hereof is Morocco. The series *Sources inédites de l'histoire du Maroc*, conceived by the French Comité du Maroc at the beginning of this century, comprises six tomes of Dutch sources for the years 1578–1660 alone.[3] Continuation of this series for the rest of the seventeenth and eighteenth centuries would mean the publication of at least another ten volumes. This great wealth of files explains why researchers from many parts of the world regularly visit the National Archives in The Hague.

The second phase in Dutch colonial history, which started with the Congress of Vienna—and here we have come to the medium term—was a period of contraction, but also of intensification. The Dutch colonial realm was confined from that period onward, apart from some possessions in "the West," and until 1872 on the Gold Coast, to the Dutch East Indies. For a long period Java was almost exclusively what it was all about. These regions came under colonial influence to a much more intensive degree than before, in the economical sense (*mise en valeur*) as well as administratively. The economic and administrative problems arising at this led to the development of colonial studies and an academic education for colonial civil servants. The study of the Islam (as practiced by Snouck Hurgronje) and the adat law (as by Van Vollenhoven), were of great practical importance. Owing to this, the study of the Far East was promoted, too. In 1855, J.J. Hoffmann was appointed as professor of Chinese and Japanese languages in Leiden. The presence in Indonesia of a large Chinese population group advanced the study of sinology. In 1874 a special chair for Chinese was established. The Japanese language was less in demand for a time.[4] An increasing interest in indigenous cultures stimulated the practice of the archaeology and ancient history of Indonesia. Apart from that, colonial history and cultural anthropology were included in the university curriculum, whereas linguistic research (e.g., of the Javanese) expanded considerably. These studies were and are practiced especially in Leiden where, since 1903, the Colonial civil servants were educated (from 1925 until 1950 another Colonial School existed in Utrecht, the so-called "Oil Faculty"). Thus, the studies of Indonesia and the Far East were added to the tradition of the study of the Near East.

Another nineteenth-century development was that of language theory and historical linguistics. Historical linguistics, inspired by the research of the Indonesian languages mentioned above, led to an increasing interest in the development of the Indo-European languages and Sanskrit. The study of Sanskrit obtained an important place in the Faculty of Letters and in its turn to a large extent stimulated an interest in the Indian languages and culture. Centers for the study of Indian culture were developed in Leiden (The Kern Institute) and later on in Utrecht.[5]

Developments after 1945 were of a completely different character compared to those of the previous period. The Second World War caused a clear break. World politics after 1945 were dominated by two major processes: decolonization and the cold war. Both influenced the study of overseas history. The Japanese occupation of the Dutch East Indies in 1942 meant an abrupt end to a long period of the Dutch political presence in Asia. After the war the Dutch government made an attempt to recover its former position but, as we know, without success. In 1949, Indonesia became independent. Only New Guinea (Irian Barat) remained for some time under Dutch authority. This was a heavy burden on the relations with the Republic of Indonesia. Dutch-Indonesian relations remained very tense and finally led to an almost complete rift. In 1962 the Netherlands gave up New Guinea, but the relations with Indonesia were only normalized in a later phase. Decolonization led to reduced funding for, and interest in non-Western studies. The interest in colonial studies disappeared with the loss of job opportunities and professional training. On the other hand, the fast industrialization with the accompanying need for export possibilities led to a new interest in regions like Africa and Latin America. The tremendous increase in influence of the United States stimulated the historical study of this new superpower, as would also be the case *mutatis mutandis* later on with the Arabic world and Japan.

Apart from these political events new developments also took place in the field of the social sciences. The years after 1945 showed an exceptional increase in popularity of the social sciences, including non-Western sociology as well as cultural anthropology. Next to these and in relation to them there was a great interest in the problems of the developing countries, which led to the rise of development studies. This form of social science in general was strongly influenced by American sociology, and was, generally speaking, ahistorical in character.

CHANGES IN HISTORY

The developments in overseas history were thus influenced to a high degree by external, political, social, and economic factors. However, the changes in the discipline of history were no less important. Long- , medium- , and short-term developments can be distinguished here also.

History as a science is a Western invention. To be true, we do find certain forms of interest in the past in all cultures, but modern historical science, with its special methods and techniques (philology, text-criticism), its philosophic foundation in historicism, its specific chronological notions of diachrony and synchrony, is typically Western. That's why it can be said that history has been a Western monopoly for a long time. Non-Western history was not practiced at all, or hardly at all, by the concerned nations themselves, and even if it was practiced, this was done in a manner totally different from that in the West. This situation continued until very recently. Historiography has been exported from the West. Even in countries like Japan and China historiography is only a recent phenomenon.

Western historiography in its turn was dominated strongly by national and European chauvinism. As a consequence it was restricted almost exclusively to the West. The overseas civilizations were looked upon as dead civilizations, the overseas nations as nations of perpetual standstill. They knew no development, and as a consequence no history. This idea gained general acceptance in the nineteenth century, and this leads us to the medium-term developments. In this century of nationalism, history was dominated to a very high degree by what was called "fatherlandic" history. That which was practiced in addition to this, under the name of "general history," was in fact nothing but the history of the development of Western civilization. This situation basically remained unchanged until the Second World War, even though exceptions existed; for example, Huizinga in the Netherlands.

Thus, a certain division of labor came into being. Those non-Western nations who had once known a high degree of civilization, became the subjects of a special field of study, Orientalism. Those nations who, in the opinion of those days, were either not civilized, or were less civilized, also got a discipline of their own, namely, that of ethnology. The "regular" historians restricted themselves to the history of Europe, and sometimes of North America. This division continues until today. The majority of history departments in the Netherlands devote little or no attention to non-Western history and most universities have no other facilities available for it, either. Apart from a single exception, non-Western history is only taught at Leiden. These non-Western historians—and this is very different from the situation in the United States—are not to be found within the section of history, however, but in the orientalistic departments, that is to say within the sections for the Languages and Civilizations of China, Japan, India, Indonesia, and the Middle East. Generally speaking, those historians were schooled there, too. Thus, the regular and the non-Western historians, although working within the same faculty, are divided from each other functionally as well as organizationally.

The ethnologists, called anthropologists today, even find themselves within another faculty, namely, that of the social sciences. This is a recent development, which has its drawbacks. In order to bridge this gap, Leiden University has brought the scholars of non-Western societies within the faculty of social science and their colleagues from the faculty of letters have been brought together in the Centre for Non-Western Studies (CNWS), just as the Western and non-Western historians before them already had started to cooperate in the Institute for the History of European Expansion and the Reactions to it (IGEER).

As we have seen, non-Western history was practiced mainly in the orientalistic departments. That goes without saying. And yet there was another, less obvious department, where this also took place, namely, that of "fatherlandic" history. The explanation of this lies in the strong preoccupation which nineteenth-century historians had with the nation-state. The national point of view dominated historiography. The overseas regions, which were under the political authority of a European country, were seen as parts of that country, and their history was dealt with as part of the history of that country. Dutch national history therefore did not deal with the Netherlands only, but also with its colonies. This tradition continues until today and, next to obvious, practical reasons, like the availability of the source material, tradition is one of the factors which led to the fact that in the Netherlands there remains a strong tendency to deal especially with the history of Indonesia. The same applies to other countries. In Britain, India is a special subject of study, in France, Indochina, and so on. The term "colonial" has disappeared, perspective and method have changed, but this division of labor has remained.

Since the Second World War, especially from the 1960s onward—and herewith we have arrived at the short-term developments—great changes in the study of history in Europe have come about. To put it very simply, these changes may be called the *Annales* revolution. In the very first place, this consisted of a considerable broadening of history, not only but also in a geographical sense. The European outside world received more attention. In a thematic sense, interest also broadened. The history of economics, society, and *mentalité* tended to become more important and political history less so. This led to a weakening of the meaning of national points of view, which tend to be of less importance outside political history. International and comparative studies appeared. This new approach obviously had its consequences for overseas history, too.

By shifting the emphasis from political to social and economic history, the nation lost its position of being the most important historical framework. In European history, social history is often practiced in the form of regional studies. Also in overseas history, the traditional political frameworks (Dutch East Indies, British India, etc.) are usually nowadays broken down into districts, which are studied as independent units. Hereby the agricultural sector receives a great deal of attention. History is studied on the level of a geographical unit or an ethnical group which, by the way, sometimes converges with that of the precolonial nation. At the same time it is transcended too; in cultural history, for example, by means of concepts like the Malay Archipelago; in economic history, in the study of the development of transnational economic systems: the Indian Ocean, the Atlantic World, the Chinese Sea, or even comprising all in *The Modern World-System*.[6] As a result the colonial aspect of history became less relevant. For a colony is a political notion and this notion has less significance for economy and culture. At the same time the attention for the structural elements in European history, the "longue durée" or the "histoire presqu'immobile," made the distinction between nations with and without change less convincing. This is the reason why Western history became less "different" from non-Western history. Moreover, Western history proved to have its own primitive aspects, for which a great deal of interest arose. Anthropologists began to include European nations in their fields of interest, in addition to the exotic nations.

DEVELOPMENTS AFTER 1945: GENERAL TENDENCIES

Up until now we have discussed the social-political developments and some general trends in historiography after 1945; we now have to consider how these developments influenced the study of overseas history in the Netherlands after the Second World War.

Because the relations with Indonesia were broken off almost completely, the intellectual and scientific contacts were also lost. Therefore, the Dutch historians did not play a role in the education of the Indonesian historians. In this the Dutch differed from the British and the French. Nor did Indonesian historians visit the Netherlands. Naturally, the language factor did play an important role here.[7] On the other hand, Dutch historians and students turned away almost en masse from overseas and Indonesian history. Colonial history was out of favor and the term disappeared from the vocabulary and was replaced by neutral terms like overseas studies or studies of the tropics or of the East-West relations. Another development also took place, namely, an increasing interest in general instead of national history arose. Moreover, within the field of general history a broadening of the traditional interest could be discerned: from Western Europe to Europe in general, to North America, and later on, but to a lesser degree, also to Latin America.

In consequence of these contrasting movements, namely, contraction and broadening of traditional interest, a certain conceptual confusion arose among the historians. The unifying point of view of colonial history, whereby the overseas nations had been included in the historical picture only after they had come into contact with the West, had been lost. *The Pilgrimage of Humanity*—to quote the title of a well-known Dutch history book—apparently included more pilgrims than those from Europe alone.[8] History had to become world history, but the question remained from what perspective such a world history should be written. New stimuli arose from different sides. In Amsterdam the historian Romein and the sociologist Wertheim, both inspired by Marxism, demanded attention for the increasing importance of Asia.[9] They did not look upon the history of Asia from a colonial perspective, but from the point of view of development and emancipation. Colonialism was strongly rejected and decolonization was joyfully hailed as the beginning of a new era. This new approach was not without importance. Wertheim's work was interesting because it dealt with the problems of modern Indonesia within a broad Asiatic context and from a vast historical perspective. Moreover, he stimulated many students, so that in this respect one could almost speak of an Amsterdam School. Romein himself did not write a great deal on Asiatic history, apart from a general work called *De eeuw van Azië* (The Asian Century). He confined himself mainly to discussing the differences in development between Europe and Asia. In addition to a tendency to criticize colonialism, there was also a movement which drastically reduced the importance of the colonial period and the relevance of the European presence in Asia. The few centuries of European colonialism, so the argument ran, had left hardly any influence on the age-old history of Asia. They figured merely as "scratches on a rock." A vigorous expression of this view is found in the work of the historian Resink, naturalized as an Indonesian; for example, in his *Indonesian History between the Myths*.[10]

This development was connected with the new historical *Annales* insights which emphasized the importance of long-term development and introduced concepts like "structure" and "longue durée" into the historical jargon. Furthermore, there was the increasing interest in social and economic history and the accompanying need for interdisciplinary studies. The importance of the social sciences for history was emphasized, especially of cultural anthropology in the case of overseas history. The techniques and aids of social history (diagrams, statistics, etc.) were given more room. Conversely, sociologists would become more interested in the historical dimensions of their study after an initial "development fever" and a strong belief in "social engineering." Thus, history and the social sciences began to converge again. Now that the distinction between nations with and without history had been abandoned, the difference between history and social science became less relevant. The recent, but rather abrupt division of history into three sections: history, oriental studies, and social sciences, was hereby put into perspective.

All these developments resulted, theoretically, in a discussion about the Asian- or Indonesia-centric approach of history, which should be preferred[11] to the traditional Europe- or Hollando-centric approach, and on a more practical level in a number of important studies in which an attempt was made to reconstruct the Asian economy and society of former centuries on the basis of the VOC records. The major work by M.A.P. Meilink-Roelofsz on *Asian Trade and European Influence in the Indonesian Archipelago between 1500 and about 1630* illustrates the latter point.[12] Both trends had been inspired by a work of earlier date, by J.C. van Leur, which for various reasons deserves our particular attention here.

Van Leur was born in 1908 and met an untimely death in the battle of the Java Sea in 1942. Like many other important specialists in the field of Indonesian studies, he had studied Indology in Leiden. He got his Ph.D. at the age of 26 with a thesis called *Eenige beschouwingen betreffende den ouden Aziatischen handel* (Some Observations Concerning Early Asian Trade).[13] This was to become a classic. He became a civil servant in the Dutch East Indies and was soon promoted, but he also remained active as a scholar. This is evident from the fact that the bibliography of this part-time scholar, who was barely 34 years old when he died, comprises almost 50 titles. Many of these relate to contemporary problems such as the world crisis and thus bear evidence of his broad interest and social engagement.[14]

The originality of Van Leur's work lies in the fact that he anticipated the two developments which were about to characterize postwar historiography: the defeat of the Eurocentric approach and the application of sociological concepts. His criticism of the Eurocentric point of view was embodied in his famous words that most historians "see the Asiatic world from the deck of the ship, the ramparts of the fortress, the high gallery of the trading house."[15] Van Leur is right in considering this to be unsatisfactory and anachronistic. He considered as ridiculous the idea that the arrival of three Dutch ships at the roadstead of Bantam in 1596 could have influenced the history of Asia in a decisive way.[16] He felt that the VOC should adapt itself to the Asiatic world and not vice versa.

Van Leur's criticism, however, is more basic and fundamental. He questions the aim of the whole traditional periodization of history. In a long essay he examined the meaning of the concept "the eighteenth century" with a view to Indonesian history, and came to the conclusion that this was a typically European concept, which is meaningless to the Malay Archipelago. Up to 1800 this region simply remained part of Asia.[17]

The second original aspect of Van Leur's work lies in the application of sociological ideas, especially those of Max Weber. By using Weber's concept of the *ideal-types*—such as agrarian cultures, patrimonial-bureaucratic states, and the like—he described Asiatic history in terms of a general, universal history, but with its own idiosyncratic character. In this way justice can be done to the individual character of the different cultures without discussing them in too abstract or general categories or disposing of them simply as being exotic and incomprehensible.

Van Leur's work is not based upon elaborate or original source research. Its essence is the essay form. His work consists of erudite and stimulating exercises in the field of comparative history. His significance lies especially in the discussions he opened, and the new research which was stimulated by it.

THE HISTORICAL PRODUCTION: A SURVEY

The fact that Dutch interest in colonial history and the history of the former colonial world was minimal after decolonization becomes evident in a concise, cliometric research into the subjects of dissertations which were defended at Dutch universities in the 1960s and 1970s.[18] The authors of the pertaining study found out that in these years a total of eight colonial-historical dissertations were published. Out of a total of 282 dissertations this is very little (less than 3 percent). Later on this was improved on, as is evident from the fact that two of these were published in the 1960s and six in the 1970s, which is a threefold increase. In terms of percentage their number also increased (less than 2 to almost 4 percent). The same may be seen when we look at the dissertations, not only on colonial history, but also on the former colonial regions. The number then rises to sixteen. (Out of a total of 282 that is almost 6 percent.) Here, too, we can see that the 1970s with eleven (out of a total of 164 that is almost 7 percent) clearly score better than the 1960s with five dissertations (a little over 4 percent at a total of 118).[19]

Of course, one has to be very careful with such figures—we are talking about very small numbers, the definitions are none too clear, dissertations are not the only criterion for developments in historical research—but one can see herein an indication that P. Blaas's suggestion of 1983 is correct, namely, that one of the three characteristic innovations which took place in Dutch historical research in the 1960s is the rise of an "internationally orientated and thematically arranged European expansion history."[20] The foundation (in 1974 in Leiden) of the Centre (later Institute) for the History of European Expansion and the Reactions to it (IGEER), as well as the name itself, confirm this impression. The list of dissertations defended in Leiden in the field of expansion history between 1974 (the year of the foundation of the Centre), and 1990, illustrates the same. No less than 35 dissertations have been defended in this field in Leiden in those 17 years. At issue here are dissertations on the history of European expansion only. Historical publications of a social-scientific or orientalistic tenor have not been included herein. From the subjects, a very varied field of interests as to time, region, and theme emerges, which is not confined at all to Dutch colonial history.[21]

Our impression is confirmed when we include in our considerations non-Western history in the broadest sense, including those dissertations which were supervised by professors in the departments of oriental studies and of social sciences. For this purpose a simple source is available—be it only for a very limited period of time—namely, the list of dissertations which the Dutch historical journal (*Tijdschrift voor Geschiedenis*) has published annually since 1983. Based upon this we can draft a survey of the production of dissertations from 1982 up to and including 1990. Within these 9 years a total of 82 dissertations have been published on the subject of overseas history, of which 13 could be classified as orientalistic and 20 as social-scientific. The remaining 49 relate to the actual expansion history, of which 15 discuss the ancient period and 34 the nineteenth and twentieth centuries, with a clear emphasis on the latter period and the very recent past. We will leave it at these short cliometric exercises and emphasize once more their very limited significance. One thing however is quite clear—and that should be our point in this connection—namely, that since the 1970s a systematic, extensive and broadly orientated study of non-Western history has taken place, in which the history of European expansion holds a central position.

HISTORIOGRAPHY: PATTERNS AND THEMES

If, after these remarks on the historical production after 1945, we now attempt to offer some general characterizations, a number of remarkable constants stand out.[22] To begin with, there is the very important production of source publications in different fields. Next to the publication of archivalia and other surveys of source material, which form an indispensable tool for the historian, there are the publications of the sources themselves, which can be in various forms. The Linschoten Society, founded in 1908, specializes in the publication of itineraries, especially from the seventeenth century. These are of great importance to our knowledge of European expansion. Since 1909 there have been more than 90 volumes in this series and the work still continues.

For the history of the VOC, the series *Generale Missiven van Gouverneurs-Generaal en Raden aan Heren XVII der Verenigde Oostindische Compagnie* (General Missives of Governors-General and Councillors to the Gentlemen XVII of the Dutch East India Company), begun by Coolhaas in 1960 and continued by Van Goor, is of great interest. These reports of the administration in Batavia contain priceless material on the complete Asiatic operations of the VOC.[23]

Another type of source publication—in fact, more a form of source adaptation—is the great work by Schöffer, Bruijn, and Gaastra, *Dutch-Asiatic Shipping in the 17th and 18th Centuries*. This is a good example of serial or quantitative history. Inspired by similar studies on Sevilla and its trade with America and on the Sont-Tollgates, the editors made a quantitative survey of all ship movements between the Dutch Republic and Asia during these two centuries. This publication, which was worked on between 1968 and 1987, contains a wealth of data on the demographic and monetary histories of Europe and Asia, but also on nautical and maritime historical matters. Apart from the two volumes of statistical data there is an extensive introductory volume which contains a data analysis.[24]

For the VOC, other publications should be noted, such as the *Daily Register of the Zeelandia-Fortress*, which is an important reference to the early history of Taiwan. The first volume of this edition was published in 1986.[25] All these works were published in the series Rijks Geschiedkundige Publicatiën (Governmental Historical Publications). The history of the Dutch presence in Deshima in Japan is of increasing interest. The publication of the chartularies of the daily registers makes this important source material more easily accessible.[26]

For later centuries, as one may expect, interest especially focuses on Indonesia. The Dutch Historical Society took the initiative of publishing a series of sources on aspects of Dutch colonial politics in the twentieth century (educational policy, the nationalistic movement, etc.), edited by Kwantes and Van der Wal.[27] Van der Wal was also behind the extensive publication of sources referring to the Dutch transfer of power to Indonesia, which was effected under political pressure. After his death the work was continued by Drooglever and Schouten.[28]

A very important source of economic history is the series set up and published by Creutzberg under the title *Changing Economy in Indonesia. A Selection of Statistical Source Material from the Early 19th Century up to 1940*. This series contains statistical surveys of numerous economic activities in the Dutch East Indies such as commerce, agriculture, and so on. The work was continued after his death.[29] Needless to say, countless other publications of sources can be mentioned, such as Snouck Hurgronje's advices, Baud's correspondence, the Titsing Papers, the Jansen Diary, and so on,[30] but we must confine ourselves here to the most important long-term series, and now have a look at the historical production in the true sense of the word, that is to say, at historiography itself.

Is it possible to recognize a general pattern or at least to denote a few tendencies in Dutch overseas historiography after 1945? The answer is: yes, they are visible and they do not differ greatly from the developments in historiography in general. To begin with, there is the inevitable specialization. Few historians these days feel called upon to write long historic syntheses. Monographs and articles have become the most important vehicles of science. These monographs, especially if they are extensive, are often dissertations. The articles are increasingly published in specialized rather than in general periodicals. Compilations containing congress or conference contributions are increasingly prominent. Usually, we find in these the summaries which individual authors cannot give or do not dare or wish to give. Major summaries on the history of Indonesia or on Dutch colonialism, as were published before the war, no longer exist. The *Nieuwe algemene geschiedenis der Nederlanden* (New General History of the

Netherlands) offers a number of important survey articles which may be seen as an impetus to summary.[31]

As regards the themes, here too, a strong shift in interest can be observed. The history of government, administration, and politics in general has seen attention shift in favor of economic history. For the time of the companies in particular, one sees that economic and commercial history has received paramount attention. In this field one sees clearly a sustained and systematic study, which is shown in a number of important dissertations. As these were directed and stimulated mainly by the adaptors of *Dutch-Asiatic Shipping*, one could almost speak here of a Leiden VOC-school. In view of its character as a commercial enterprise, this interest in the running of the VOC speaks for itself. What is more, the VOC archival material, as various historians from Asia have shown, also offers excellent possibilities for studies in the economic and social history of the Asiatic societies themselves.[32] The study of the Dutch source material and of the Dutch overseas history is certainly not only of interest to Dutch historians alone. On the contrary, great names like that of Boxer, Glamann, and Steensgaard illustrate the important role of foreign historians in this field.[33] They have meanwhile been joined by a whole group of historians from Asia. The emphasis, however, is on the seventeenth century while the eighteenth century receives considerably less interest.

Quite striking, especially in contrast to these flourishing VOC studies, is the limited attention, also internationally, for the working and records of the West Indian Company (WIC). Attention is almost exclusively given to the spectacular, but economically not very important slave trade and plantation economy. In view of the importance of the WIC and the West in general, this is regrettable. The Dutch presence in North America and in Brasil was of short duration, it is true, but the business activities of the WIC were very important for the Netherlands until 1800. This is different for later centuries. Surprisingly enough, a larger number and more important studies were published about those later centuries. These are often carried out not by historians, but by sociologists like Van Lier and Hoetink. And it is truly remarkable that historiography on the West Indies was influenced by sociological and anthropological approaches so much earlier than those about the East Indies.[34]

The WIC also exercised authority over West Africa for a time. The VOC had authority over South Africa until the English occupation in 1795. After that the Dutch presence in Africa was limited to some fortresses on the Gold Coast, which were transferred to the English in 1872. Important archive collections exist in the Netherlands on both regions, West and South Africa. However, they attract relatively few researchers. In the case of South Africa, political factors played an important part in this.

In general, it can be said that for modern times Dutch research concentrates especially on Indonesia. This is understandable enough. Indonesia, or the Dutch East Indies, was of prime importance to the Netherlands in the nineteenth and twentieth centuries and this was clearly expressed in the colonial historiography.

The large edition of five volumes on the history of the Dutch East Indies by Stapel, published between 1938 and 1940, discusses not only the history of Dutch relations with the whole of Asia, but with South Africa as well.[35] The Dutch East Indies dominated, even retrospectively, our colonial self-image to such a degree that the complete colonial history seemed to be merely the pre-history of the Dutch regime over Indonesia. This concept has now been abandoned. There is even a rather clear dichotomy between the specialists of the Company's period, on the one hand, and those of modern Indonesia, on the other. In the latter field some sort of specialization seems to have become visible. Indonesian historians work especially on their own internal, cultural, and social history, often at a regional level. Dutch historians, on the contrary, are guided more by questions which concern Indonesia in general, economically and politically as well as militarily and administratively, and also by the cultural history of the substantial group of Dutch people who lived in Indonesia. The most striking example of the interest for the latter is the success of the periodical *Indische letteren* (Dutch East Indian Literature), which has been published since 1986. As its name denotes, literature is the main topic, but other cultural-historical subjects also arise and this in the spirit of the man, who was its great source of inspiration, Rob Nieuwenhuys.

Economic history also attracts a lot of attention. One can speak of a great tradition in this field evoked by names like Boeke and Burger. Apart from the traditional interest in Java, the Outer Possessions have also been included in these studies in the last few years. The statistical material, as collected by Creutzberg and his staff members, has been mentioned and praised already. It is this work which has given us a great deal of knowledge about the economic importance of the East Indies for the Netherlands, and about the economic aspects of colonialism. Apart from the work of Creutzberg, that of Baudet and Lindblad deserves to be mentioned here.[36] The only missing equivalents for the Netherlands are comprehensive economic analyses and surveys like *Mammon and the Pursuit of Empire* by Davis and Huttenback, or Jacques Marseille's *Empire colonial et capitalisme français*.[37]

This leads to another striking absence, namely, the study of Dutch imperialism or, rather, the study of the Dutch colonial history in terms of the imperialism debate. An exception should be made for one particular part in this debate, namely, the collaboration thesis. On the Indonesian side interest in this problem is illustrated by Taufik Abdullah's work on brokers and middlemen, the *schakel society*, as he has called it.[38] There is a great deal which could be said about the reasons for this gap (ideological factors, such as an anti- or un-imperial self-consciousness, but conceptual problems as well).[39] More important is that now we dispose of a book which can be seen as a convincing effort to fill this gap. It is M. Kuitenbrouwer's *The Netherlands and the Rise of Modern Imperialism*. It is remarkable that this book caused some reaction, but did not initiate a great debate on Dutch colonialism.[40]

In addition, we should note some critical works on the excesses of Dutch colonialism, such as one by J. Breman, who may be seen in some respects as the successor to the Amsterdam anti-colonial school of Romein and Wertheim.[41] Other excesses—namely, those by the Dutch army at the time of the police actions—became the subject of study of the sociologist J.A.A. van Doorn, who had been involved in these actions as a conscript, and who also wrote on the Dutch colonial establishment.[42]

The delicacy of these matters became evident on the publication of the Dutch historian L. de Jong's great historical work on *The Kingdom of the Netherlands in the Second World War* when the volumes dedicated to the Dutch East Indies were published. Volume 11, which deals with the war in the Dutch East Indies, is over three thousand pages long. As is customary with De Jong, he went far back in his introduction, for Indonesia as far back as Jan Huygen van Linschoten's voyage in 1583, and for Japan as far as around the year zero. In his epilogue De Jong continued as far as decolonization. That was in Volume 12, in which four hundred pages were devoted to this subject. In these works De Jong, who has often been thought of as right-wing, shows himself as the old-fashioned social-democrat he really is. This became evident in his criticism of Dutch colonialism. That he had once been a left-wing opponent in the Labour Party against the postwar East Indies politics was shown by his critical treatment of the decolonization politics and the military action.[43] These two issues in turn caused sharp reactions and comments in public opinion. It is more striking and revealing however, that this first, extensive synthetic treatment of this last phase of Dutch colonialism, as well as, for that matter, De Jong's whole work, has hardly ever caused any arguments in professional circles. Perhaps the work was thought to be too old-fashioned and too colossal, certainly too ideological and moralizing. In any case, this is not due to lack of interest in decolonization problems. The party political sides of decolonization, the internationally political as well as the military sides have received real and serious interest, which also includes the curious question of New Guinea.[44] During the last few years this question has resulted in manifold publications, journalistic contributions, and the memoirs of those involved, as well as dissertations and other scholarly publications.[45]

CONCLUSION

The overseas studies in the Netherlands may boast a long and rich tradition. Overseas history has been practiced here for a long time. Colonial history in a more restricted sense, which flourished in the first part of the twentieth century, has not reappeared on the agenda after 1950. It is true that colonial-historical subjects do still figure extensively, but they form part of an internationally orientated approach directed at comparison and generalization. Even when limited and modest in set-up, these studies are being written from the perspective of European expansion and the reactions to this. This perspective is, in the final analysis, that of general or even world history, and not that of national history. That is the great difference from the prior situation.

Because of the long history of Dutch overseas activities there is a great deal of source material at hand in the Netherlands for the study of this history. That this source material has a central position for reasons of labor division and efficiency is a fact both obvious and acceptable. Often this is the history of the regions visited by the Dutch. This material infrastructure and the rich and lively intellectual tradition in the field of oriental studies together make a reasonable case for the Netherlands to be able to continue to fulfill a role of some importance in the field of overseas history. After the war a temporary recession set in, but that was restructured in the 1970s. The number of young researchers interested in this field is great at the moment.

In a long-term view of this whole development, a return to the old situation can in a certain sense be seen. In the past, oriental and overseas studies used to be concentrated especially in Leiden. Because of the enormous growth of the universities in the 1960s, these studies spread all over the country. In the 1980s, however, a tendency toward concentration in Leiden has become manifest. A certain return to old times can be seen in the disciplinary field, too. As we saw, the study of non-Western history has been subdivided into three disciplines in the course of years: oriental studies, colonial history, and ethnology. This division has been strengthened in a later phase by the subdivision into faculties and departments. At the moment, however, a tendency toward cooperation can be discerned, and attempts are being made to come to an integrated historical approach. And with that, as one could say, the circle has been completed.

Notes

PREFACE

1. R. Koebner and H.D. Schmitt, *Imperialism. The Story and Significance of a Political Word* (Cambridge, England, 1964).

2. J.A. Hobson, *Imperialism: A Study* (London, 1902).

3. *International Encyclopedia of the Social Sciences*, s.v. ''Imperialism.''

4. P. Louis, *Le Colonialisme* (Paris, 1905).

5. *International Encyclopedia of the Social Sciences*, s.v. ''Colonialism.''

6. J. Seeley, *The Expansion of England* (Leipzig, 1884; Tauchnitz, ed.), 17.

7. H.L. Wesseling, ed., *Expansion and Reaction* (Leiden, 1978), 4.

1. COLONIAL WARS: AN INTRODUCTION

1. Cf. J.D. Singer and T.M. Small, *The Wages of War, 1816–1965: A Statistical Handbook* (New York, 1972), 38.

2. Thomas Hardy, *The Dynasts*, Part I, Act II, Scene V (London, 1920), 71.

3. C.E. Callwell, *Small Wars, Their Principles and Practice*, 3rd ed. (London, 1906), 40.

4. Ibid, 39.

5. See J.A. de Moor and H.L. Wesseling, eds., *Imperialism and War. Essays on Colonial Wars in Asia and Africa* (Leiden, 1989), 72 ff. and 167 ff.

6. See D.A. Low, *Lion Rampant: Essays in the Study of British Imperialism* (London, 1974), 20 ff.

7. Callwell, *Small Wars*, 82.

8. H. Lyautey, *Lettres du Tonkin et de Madagascar, 1894–1899*, 2 vols. (Paris, 1920–1921), II, 112–113.

9. Cited in Callwell, *Small Wars*, 128.

10. On this see D. Headrick, *The Tools of Empire: Technology and European Imperialism in the Nineteenth Century* (Oxford and New York, 1981).

11. See e.g., M. Crowder, ''Many questions—some answers: African resistance in West Africa—A general view,'' in S. Förster, W.J. Mommsen, and R. Robinson, eds., *Bismarck, Europe and Africa. The Berlin Africa Conference 1884-1885 and the Onset of Partition* (Oxford, 1988), 401–414.

12. See De Moor and Wesseling, *Imperialism and War*, 65–66.

13. Ibid., 69; and H. Strachan, *European Armies and the Conduct of War* (London, 1983), 76–90.

14. See De Moor and Wesseling, *Imperialism and War*, 222.

15. Ibid., 189 ff.; Crowder, ''Questions,'' passim.

16. Cited in G. Padmore, *The Gold Coast Revolution* (London, 1953), 35.

17. Callwell, *Small Wars*, 57.

18. See De Moor and Wesseling, *Imperialism and War*, 211.

19. See D. Rothermund, ''The legacy of the British-Indian Empire in independent India,'' in W.J. Mommsen and J. Osterhammel, eds., *Imperialism and After: Continuities and Discontinuities* (London, 1986), 139–153. They also used African troops on a large, often a larger, scale. See, for example, De Moor and Wesseling, *Imperialism and War*, 99 ff.; Crowder, ''Questions,'' passim.

20. See De Moor and Wesseling, *Imperialism and War*, 50 ff.

21. L. Davis and R. Huttenback, *Mammon and the Pursuit of Empire: The Political Economy of British Imperialism, 1860–1912* (Cambridge, 1987), 145–165.

22. See De Moor and Wesseling, *Imperialism and War*, 121 ff.

23. Cited in G. Bennett, ed., *The Concept of Empire. Burke to Attlee, 1774–1947* (London, 1953), 319.

24. Cited in H. Martineau, *British Rule in India. A Historical Sketch* (London, 1857), 187.

25. Cf. Low, *Lion Rampant*, 24; H. Brunschwig, ''De la résistance africaine à l'impérialisme européen,'' *Journal of African History* 14 (1974), 47–64.

26. See De Moor and Wesseling, *Imperialism and War*, 24 ff.

27. See Joseph Ki-Zerbo, *Histoire de l'Afrique noire: D'hier à demain* (Paris, 1972), 466.

28. H. Lüthy, *Nach dem Untergang des Abendlandes. Zeitkritische Essays* (Cologne, 1964), 372.

29. See J.-L. Vellut, ''La violence armée dans l'Etat Indépendant du Congo,'' *Cultures et développement* 16 (1984), 3–4, 671–707.

30. Ibid., 672.

31. See J.D. Hargreaves, ''Towards a history of the partition of Africa,'' *Journal of African History* 1 (1960), 108 ff.

32. R. Robinson, ''Non-European foundations of European imperialism: Sketch for a theory of collaboration,'' in R. Owed and B. Sutcliffe, eds., *Studies in the Theory of Imperialism* (London, 1972), 118–140.

2. COLONIAL WARS AND ARMED PEACE, 1871–1914: A RECONNAISSANCE

1. J.D. Singer and T.M. Small, *The Wages of War, 1816–1965. A Statistical Handbook* (New York, 1972). For these criteria, see pp. 35 ff. With the exception of several

refinements, the casualty criterium can be stated as: (a) 1,000 deaths per party per conflict for an interstate war, or (b) 1,000 deaths per year per colonial power for an extra-systemic war.

2. Ibid., 38.

3. Ibid., 395 ff.

4. Donald Featherstone, *Colonial Small Wars, 1837–1901* (Newton Abbot, 1973), 5 ff. The Boer War is, of course, not included in this survey of "small wars."

5. H.L. Zwitser and C.A. Heshusius, *Het Koninklijk Nederlands-Indisch Leger, 1830–1950. Een terugblik* (The Hague, 1977), 13 ff.

6. G. Hanotaux and A. Martineau, eds., *Histoire des colonies françaises et de l'expansion de la France dans le monde*, 6 vols. (Paris, 1930–1931), V, passim.

7. Helge Kjekshus, *Ecology Control and Economic Development in African History. The Case of Tanganyika, 1850–1950* (London, 1977), 149.

8. J.M. Lonsdale, "The politics of conquest: The British in Western Kenya, 1894–1908," *The Historical Journal* 20 (1977), 858–859.

9. A.S. Kanya-Forstner, *The Conquest of the Western Sudan. A Study in French Military Imperialism* (Cambridge, 1969), especially 10 ff.

10. L.A. Davis and R.A. Huttenback, *Mammon and the Pursuit of Empire. The Political Economy of British Imperialism, 1860–1912* (Cambridge, England, 1986), 145–165.

11. Compare, for example, E. Maurel, *L'Armée coloniale. Son recrutement et son haut-commandement* (Paris, 1897); P. Dabry de Thiersant, *L'Armée coloniale de l'Inde néerlandaise* (Paris, 1885).

12. The totals were taken from W. von Bremen, *Die Kolonialtruppen und Kolonialarmeeen der Hauptmchte Europas* (Bielefeld, 1902), and refer to the situation around 1900. The data for the various groups in the *KNIL* come from Dabry de Thiersant, *L'Armée coloniale*, 7 and 8. They refer to the period 1881–1882 but the total differs little from the figures given by W. von Bremen for 1900.

13. See Paul van 't Veer, *De Atjeh-oorlog* (Amsterdam, 1969), 260.

14. Kjekshus, *Ecology Control*, 150–151; J. Iliffe, *A Modern History of Tanganyika* (Cambridge, England, 1979), 200.

15. See Donald R. Morris, *The Washing of the Spears* (London, 1973; Cardinal Edition), 282 and 587.

16. See Van 't Veer, *De Atjeh oorlog*, 211 and 311.

17. See C.E. Callwell, *Small Wars. Their Principles and Practice*, 3rd ed. (London, 1906), 128.

18. See J.C. Witte, *J.B. van Heutsz. Leven en legende* (Bussum, 1976), 63.

19. Callwell, *Small Wars*, 128.

20. Witte, *J.B. van Heutsz*, 43.

21. For Bugeaud, see in particular: Jean Gottman, "Bugeaud, Gallieni, Lyautey: The development of French colonial warfare," in E.M. Earle, ed., *Makers of Modern Strategy* (Princeton, 1944), 234–259; and Ch.-A. Julien, "Bugeaud," in *Les Techniciens de la colonisation (XIXe–XXe siècles)* (Paris, 1946).

22. Callwell, *Small Wars*, 129.

23. Julien, "Bugeaud," 65.

24. Ibid., 66.

25. Gottman, "Bugeaud, Gallieni, Lyautey," 237.

26. See R. Delavignette, "Faidherbe," in *Les Techniciens de la colonisation.*

27. See Witte, *J.B. van Heutsz*, 56 ff.

28. See Van 't Veer, *De Atjeh-oorlog*, 234 ff.

29. For Gallieni, see Gottman, "Bugeaud, Gallieni, Lyautey," 238.

30. Van 't Veer, *De Atjeh-oorlog*, 230.

31. T. Miller Maguire, *Guerrilla or Partisan Warfare* (London, 1904).

32. See W. Laqueur, *Guerrilla. A Historical and Critical Study* (London, 1977), 121.

33. Ibid., 122.

34. The edition used here, the third, was printed in 1906.

35. Callwell, *Small Wars*, 21.

36. Ibid., 25 ff.

37. Ibid., 24.

38. For Wolseley, see in particular Joseph Lehmann, *All Sir Garnet. A Life of Field-marshall Lord Wolseley, 1833–1913* (London, 1964).

39. Callwell, *Small Wars*, 40.

40. Ibid., 40.

41. Ibid., 40.

42. Ibid., 158.

43. Ibid., 151.

44. Ibid., 82. Compare also (Colonel) G.B. Malleson, *The Indian Mutiny of 1857* (London, 1892): "There is only one true method of fighting Asiatics. That mode is to move straight on" (59).

45. See J.S. Gallieni, *La Pacification de Madagascar (1896–1899)* (Paris, 1900).

46. H.L.G. Lyautey, "Du rôle colonial de l'armée," *Revue des Deux Mondes* 157 (1900).

47. P. Lyautey, ed., *Lyautey l'Africain*, 4 vols. (Paris, 1953–1957), III, 146.

48. J.S. Gallieni, *Gallieni pacificateur. Ecrits coloniaux de Gallieni* (Paris, 1949), 226, footnote 1.

49. H. Deschamps, *Les Méthodes et les doctrines coloniales de la France* (Paris, 1953), 159.

50. H.L.G. Lyautey, "Du rôle social de l'officier," *Revue des Deux Mondes* 104 (1891).

51. Lyautey, *Lyautey l'Africain*, I, VII.

52. Gallieni, *Gallieni pacificateur*, 240.

53. Jean Dresch, "Lyautey," in *Les Techniciens de la colonisation*, 138.

54. Ibid., 138.

55. H.L.G. Lyautey, *Lettres du Tonkin et de Madagascar (1894–1899)*, 2 vols. (Paris, 1920–1921), II, 112–113.

56. See, for example, E. Psichari, *Terres de soleil et de sommeil* (Paris, 1908).

57. Lyautey, *Lettres du Tonkin*, II, 292.

58. Compare Paul Louis, *Le Colonialisme* (Paris, 1905), 98.

59. The expression was used by Gaston Doumergue in a Speech to Parliament on 22 November 1894.

60. See P. de Rooy, *Tache d'huile* (M.A. Thesis, Amsterdam, 1971; unpublished), 126.

61. See Laqueur, *Guerrilla*, 420, footnote 61.

62. F. Foch, *Des Principes de la guerre*, 2nd ed. (Paris, 1911), 269.

63. For more details, see H.L. Wesseling, *Soldaat en Krijger. Franse opvattingen over leger en oorlog, 1905–1914* (Assen, 1969), 193 ff.

64. Lyautey, *Lyautey l'Africain*, III, 146.

65. Foch, *Principes*, XI.

66. See note 42.

67. L. de Grandmaison, *Deux conférences* (Paris, 1911), 27.

68. V.G. Kiernan, *The Lords of Human Kind* (Harmondsworth, 1972; Pelican Books), 320.

3. KNOWLEDGE IS POWER: SOME REMARKS ON COLONIALISM AND SCIENCE

1. J.C. van Leur, *Indonesian Trade and Society* (The Hague, 1955), 162.

2. A.D.A. de Kat Angelino, *Het Koninklijk Instituut voor de Tropen en zijn nieuwe taak en doelstelling* (Amsterdam, 1954), 6.

3. A. Sarraut, *Grandeur et servitude coloniales* (Paris, 1931).

4. F.D. Lugard, *The Rise of Our East African Empire* (London, 1893), quoted in R. Faber, *The Vision and the Need. Late Victorian Imperialist Aims* (London, 1966), 121.

5. J.S. Furnivall, *Netherlands India. A Study of Plural Economy* (Cambridge, England, 1944), 392.

6. Quoted in R. Robinson, "European imperialism and indigenous reactions in British West-Africa, 1880–1914," in H.L. Wesseling, ed., *Expansion and Reaction* (The Hague, 1978), 160, note 45.

7. Quoted in the *Times Literary Supplement*, Nr. 4286 (24 May 1985), 571.

8. Cf. also "Colonial wars and armed peace, 1870–1914: A reconnaissance" (Chapter 2, this volume).

9. Cf. "The Netherlands as a colonial model" (Chapter 4, this volume).

10. Cf. L.M.R. Rutten, ed., *Science in the Netherlands East Indies* (Amsterdam, 1929), 295.

11. C.J. Hasselman, *Wording, werking en toekomst; het Koninklijk Koloniaal Instituut te Amsterdam* (Amsterdam, 1924), 36.

12. R.F. Ellen, "The development of anthropology and colonial policy in the Netherlands," *Journal of the History of the Behavioral Sciences* 12 (1976), 208.

4. THE NETHERLANDS AS A COLONIAL MODEL

1. The Duke of Brabant to De Jonghe d'Ardoye, March 23, 1859, quoted in Jean Stengers, "Léopold II et le modèle colonial hollandais," in id., *Congo. Mythes et réalités. 100 ans d'histoire* (Paris, 1989), 20.

2. For all this, see Jean Stengers, "Léopold II," passim.

3. Spenser St. John to Brooke. Brooke, 7 September 1862, quoted in Jean Stengers, "Léopold II," 20.

4. For a more detailed study of Chailley-Bert, see my "The Dutch colonial model in French colonial theory, ± 1890–1914," in *Proceedings of the Second Meeting of the French Colonial Historical Society* (Athens, Ga., 1977), 107–180.

5. Challé-Bert [*sic!*], *Les Hollandais à Java* (Rouen, 1898), 4.

6. Ibid., 16.

7. See Paul Leroy-Beaulieu, *De la colonisation chez les peuples modernes* (Paris, 1886).

8. Challé-Bert, "Hollandais," 15.

9. J. Schumpeter, *Zur Soziologie der Imperialismen* (Berlin, 1919); E. de Seillière, *Philosophie de l'impérialisme* (Paris, 1903).

10. J. Seeley, *The Expansion of England* (Leipzig, 1884; Tauchnitz, ed.), 17.

11. Cf. E. Renan, *Oeuvres complètes*, 10 vols. (Paris, 1947–1961), I, 390; H. Taine, *Notes sur l'Angleterre* (Paris, 1871); P. de Coubertin, *L'Education en Angleterre* (Paris, 1888); for Germany: Ch.E. McClelland, *The German Historians and England. A Study in 19th Century Views* (Cambridge, England, 1971); A. Hillgruber, *Bismarcks Aussenpolitik* (Freiburg, 1972).

12. For German opinions on this, see below, notes 25–28; for French opinions, see my "The Dutch colonial model in French colonial theory, ± 1890–1914" (note 4); for English opinions, see the works of Money (note 13), Wallace (note 16), and H.S. Boys, *Some Notes on Java and Its Administration by the Dutch* (Allahahbad, 1892).

13. J.W.B. Money, *Java, or How to Manage a Colony*, 2 vols. (London, 1861), I, 3.

14. Ibid., I, 103.

15. Ibid., I, 157.

16. A.R. Wallace, *The Malay Archipelago*, 2 vols. (London, 1869), I, 148.

17. Ibid., I, 152.

18. Cf. K.L. Gillion, *Fiji's Indian Immigrants* (Oxford, 1962).

19. Cf. R. Reinsma, "De autobiografie van Jan Jacob Rochussen," *Bijdragen en Mededelingen van het Historisch Genootschap* 73 (1959), 55 and 134; J. Chailley-Bert, *Le Recrutement des fonctionnaires des colonies* (Paris, 1895), 10.

20. Cf. E.R. Scidmore, *Java. The Garden of the East* (New York, 1897), 112.

21. For this and the following, see especially Jean Stengers, "Léopold II," passim; and id., "King Leopold's Imperialism," in R. Owen and B. Sutcliffe, eds., *Studies in the Theory of Imperialism* (Harlow, 1972).

22. Léon Le Febve de Vivy, *Documents d'histoire précoloniale belge (1861–1865). Les idées coloniales de Léopold duc de Brabant* (Brussels, 1955), 20–21.

23. See, for example, the *Comptes rendus de l'Institut Colonial International* at Brussels, since 1895 (22 vols.), the *Bibliothèque Coloniale Internationale*, the *Bulletin de Colonisation Comparée* (Brussels, 1909–1914); J. Jooris, *Aperçu politique et économique sur les colonies néerlandaises aux Indes Orientales* (Liège, 1883); O. Collet, *L'Or aux Indes Néerlandaises* (Brussels, 1905); and many other studies by the same author (*Le Café, Le Tabac*, etc.).

24. H. Brunschwig, *L'Avènement de l'Afrique Noire* (Paris, 1863), 184.

25. F. Fabri, *Bedarf Deutschland der Colonien* (Gotha, 1879), 40.

26. Ibid., 96.

27. Wilhelm Hübbe-Schleiden, *Überseeische Politik* (Hamburg, 1881), 53.

28. Ibid., 96.

29. Quoted by Jean Stengers, "L'impérialisme colonial de la fin du XIXe siècle: mythe ou réalité?", *Journal of African History* 3 (1962), 487.

30. See, for example, H.-U. Wehler, *Bismarck und der Imperialismus* (Cologne, 1972); H.A. Turner, "Bismarck's imperialist venture," in P. Gifford and R. Louis, eds., *Britain and Germany in Africa* (New Haven and London, 1967).

31. Cf. R.F. Betts, "L'influence des méthodes hollandaises et anglaises sur la doctrine coloniale française à la fin du XIXe siècle," *Cahiers d'Histoire* 3 (1958), 35.

32. P. Dassier, "Java, sa population, son commerce," *Bulletin du Comité de l'Asie Française* III (1903), Nr. 29, 339; M. Dubois, *Systèmes coloniaux et peuples colonisa-*

teurs. Dogmes et faits (Paris, 1895), 84; P. Gonnaud, *La colonisation hollandaise à Java* (Paris, 1905), 569.

33. The most important are:

1891 V. de Ternant, "Les colonies néerlandaises," *Bulletin de la Société des Etudes Coloniales et Maritimes*, 209–237, 265–287, 330–348.

1892 M. d'Argout, *Java, Singapore et Manille.*

1893 J. Chailley-Bert, *La Hollande et les fonctionnaires des Indes Néerlandaises.*

1897 L. Lejeal, "L'Administration coloniale dans les Indes Néerlandaises," *Bulletin de la Société des Etudes Coloniales et Maritimes* (September 1897).

1898 J. Leclercq, *Un séjour dans l'île de Java. Le pays, les habitants, le système colonial.* This well-known Belgian traveller published many works in France.

1900 J. Chailley-Bert, *Java et ses habitants.*

1902 P. Dassier, "Aperçu politique et économique des Indes Néerlandaises," *Bulletin du Comité de l'Asie Française*, 17, II.

1904 F. Bernard, *A travers Sumatra (De Batavia à Atjeh).*

1905 P. Gonnaud, *La colonisation hollandaise à Java.*

1909 J. Joûbert, "Les Indes Néerlandaises à l'Exposition," *Revue Française de l'Etranger et des Colonies*, 25.

1910 A. Cabaton, *Les Indes Néerlandaises.*

34. Day, *Dutch*, 254, note 2. For the evolution of Dutch colonial policy, see "The giant that was a dwarf" (Chapter 6, this volume).

35. Dubouzet, "Etablissements hollandais en Asie." *Revue Coloniale* I (1843), 154.

36. E. Cardon, "La Hollande et ses colonies," *Revue du Monde Colonial* 9 (1843), 65.

37. A. de Jonquières, "Des possessions coloniales de la Hollande, en 1859," *Revue Algérienne et Coloniale* (1859,) 37.

38. J. Itier, "Notes pour servir à une déscription de Java," *Revue Coloniale* 9 (1946), 98.

39. Le Comte de Beauvoir, *Java, Siam, Canton. Voyage autour du monde* (Paris, 1869), VI, "Le système colonial," 165–197. For the critical remarks, see 186.

40. Beauvoir, "Java," 196.

41. Th. Duret, *Voyage en Asie. Le Japon, La Chine, La Mongolie, Java, Ceylan, l'Inde* (Paris, 1874), 199–202.

42. Leroy-Beaulieu, *Colonisation*, 292.

43. Ibid., 292.

44. Ibid., 293.

45. Ibid., 299.

46. V. de Ternant, "Les Colonies Néerlandaises," *Bulletin de la Société des Etudes Coloniales et Maritimes* (1891), 210.

47. Ibid., 223.

48. Ibid., 212.

49. P. Gonnaud, *La colonisation hollandaise à Java* (Paris, 1905), 504.

50. Ibid., 437.

51. Ibid., 471.

52. Cf. Leroy-Beaulieu, *Colonisation*, 286–287; Comte de Saint-Foix, *Rapport sur l'exposition internationale industrielle d'Amsterdam* (Paris, 1885), 426; Dassier, *Aperçu*, 361; Duret, *Voyage*, 199; A. de Pina, *Deux ans dans le pays des épices (Iles de la Sonde)* (Paris, 1880), 95; *Congrès Colonial International de Paris* (1889), 12–13.

53. Cf. Argout, *Java*, 31; and Leclercq, *Séjour*, 256.

54. Cf. Gonnaud, *Colonisation*, 517; Jonquières, *Possessions*, 311; Ternant, *Colonies*, 347.

55. Cf. P. Darby de Thiersant, "L'armée coloniale de l'Inde Néerlandaise," *Revue Maritime et Coloniale* 84 (1885), 5; Cabaton, *Indes*, 719.

56. Cf. Cabaton, *Indes*, 19; Leclercq, *Séjour*, 293.

57. Cf. Chailley-Bert in *La Quinzaine Coloniale* 3 (1898), 48; Dubouzet, *Etablissements*, 155; Duret, *Voyage*, 191; L. Lejeal, *Administration*, 288.

58. J. Challé-Bert [*sic!*], *Les Hollandais à Java* (Rouen, 1898), 15.

59. R.F. Betts, *Assimilation and Association in French Colonial Theory* (London, 1961).

60. Cf. Betts, *Assimilation*, passim; and *Congrès Colonial International de Paris*, 1889, 87 ff.

61. L. de Saussure, *Psychologie de la colonisation française dans ses rapports avec les sociétés indigènes* (Paris, 1899), 3.

62. J. Harmand, *Domination et colonisation* (Paris, 1910), 88.

63 *Congrès Colonial International de Paris* (1889), 93.

64. Harmand, *Domination*, 88.

65. Cf. Duret, "Voyage," 196; *Congrès International de Sociologie Coloniale, Rapports et procès-verbaux des séances* (Paris, 1901), 189.

66. Lamothe, "Le gouvernement de l'Insulinde: Java," *Bulletin du Comité de l'Asie Française* 5 (1905), 53, 316.

67. Lamothe, "Gouvernement," 318; Cabaton, *Indes*, 370.

68. P. Dassier, "Aperçu politique et économique des Indes Néerlandaises," *Bulletin du Comité de l'Asie Française* 2 (1902), Nr. 17, 362; cf. Gonnaud, *Colonisation*, 462.

69. Leclercq, *Séjour*, 262.

70. Beauvoir, *Java*, 168; Dassier, *Aperçu*, 359; Joûbert, "Indes Néerlandaises," 714; Lejeal, *Administration*, 285.

71. Girardet, *Idée Coloniale*, 76; cf. also Leroy-Beaulieu, *Colonisation*, 744.

72. Cf. Cohen, *Rulers*, 37–38 and 226, note 3.

73. E. Boutmy, *Le recrutement des administrateurs coloniaux* (Paris, 1895), 26–27, 91–98; cf. Girardet, *Idée coloniale*, 303–304, note 6.

74. Cf. Jean Jolly, *Dictionnaire parlementaire* III (Paris, 1960), 249. On the importance of Chailley-Bert, see also Chr. Andrew, *Theophile Delcassé and the Making of the Entente Cordiale* (London, 1968), 104–109; Betts, *Influence*, XIV; Betts, *Assimilation*, 85.

75. Persell, "Chailley-Bert," 276 ff.

76. J. Chailley-Bert, *Où en est la politique coloniale de la France. L'âge de l'agriculture* (Paris, 1896).

77. J. Chailley-Bert, *Java*, Frontispiece.

78. Cf. C. Fasseur, "Van suikercontractant tot kamerlid, bouwstenen voor een biografie van Fransen van de Putte (de jaren 1849–1864)," *Tijdschrift voor Geschiedenis* 88 (1975), 333–354.

79. Chailley-Bert, *Java*, 7.

80. Ibid., 177.

81. *Comptes rendus de la Société de Géographie* (1898), 2, 59.

82. Chailley-Bert, *Java*, 194.

83. Ibid., 151.

84. Challé-Bert [*sic!*], *Hollandais*, 4.
85. *Comptes rendus de la Société de Géographie* (1898), 2, 58.
86. Chailley-Bert, *Recrutement*, 86.
87. Chailley-Bert, *Java*, 151.
88. Ibid., 323.
89. Ibid., 326.
90. *La Quinzaine Coloniale* 3 (1898), 49.
91. Challé-Bert [*sic!*], *Hollandais*, 13.
92. Ibid., 15.
93. Ibid., 20.
94. *La Quinzaine Coloniale* 3 (1898), 49.
95. Cf. Challé-Bert [*sic!*], *Hollandais*, 4; Persell, *Chailley-Bert*, 178.
96. Challé-Bert [*sic!*], *Hollandais*, 18.
97. Comptes Rendus de la Société de Géographie (1898), 59.

5. THE DEBATE ON FRENCH IMPERIALISM, 1960–1975

1. H. Brunschwig, *Mythes et réalités de l'impérialisme colonial français, 1871–1914* (Paris, 1960).

2. D.K. Fieldhouse, ''Imperialism: A historiographical revision,'' *Economic History Review* 14 (1961), 187–209; R. Robinson and J. Gallagher with Alice Denny, *Africa and the Victorians. The Offical Mind of Imperialism* (London, 1967).

3. J. Marseille, *Empire colonial et capitalisme français; histoire d'un divorce* (Paris, 1984).

4. The most important are J. Meyer et al., *Histoire de la France coloniale I, Des origines à 1914* (Paris, 1991); J. Thobie, *Histoire de la France coloniale II, 1914–1990* (Paris, 1990); P. Pluchon, *Histoire de la colonisation française I* (Paris, 1991); and D. Bouche, *Histoire de la colonisation française II* (Paris, 1991).

5. J. Ferry, *Le Tonkin et la Mère-Patrie* (Paris, 1980), cited by Brunschwig, *Mythes*, 102.

6. G. Hanotaux, *Pour l'empire colonial français* (Paris, 1933), 41.

7. J.F. Cady, *The Roots of French Imperialism in Eastern Asia* (New York, 1954), 294: ''The taproot of French imperialism in the Far East from first to last was national pride—pride of culture, reputation, prestige and influence''; Th.F. Power, *Jules Ferry and the Renaissance of French Imperialism* (New York, 1944), 183–85, 194–99. But see also J. Laffey, ''Les racines de l'impérialisme français en Extrême-Orient,'' *Revue d'Histoire Moderne et Contemporaine* 16 (1969), 282–289.

8. Brunschwig, *Mythes*, 185.

9. Marcel Emerit in *Annales E.S.C.* 17 (1962), 1206–1209.

10. On the tariffs, see J. Chastenet, *Histoire de la Troisième République*, 7 vols. (Paris, 1952–1963), II, 250–254. On the crisis of 1873 with respect to the colonies, see G.W.F. Hallgarten, *Imperialismus vor 1914*, 2 vols. (Munich, 1964), II, 97; J. Valette, ''Note sur l'idée coloniale vers 1871,'' *Revue d'Histoire Moderne et Contemporaine* 14 (1967), 190. On the situation of French industry, see H. Körner, *Kolonialpolitik und Wirtschaftsentwicklung* (Stuttgart, 1965), 41; and A. Gerschenkron, ''Economic Backwardness in Historical Perspective,'' in D.F. Hoselitz, ed., *The Progress of Underdeveloped Areas* (Chicago, 1952), 22 ff.

11. See C.W. Newbury, ''The protectionist revival in French colonial trade: The case of Senegal,'' *Economic History Review* 21 (1968), 345; S.B. Clough, *France: A History of National Economics, 1789–1939* (New York, 1939), 214–240; D. Salem, ''Sur quelques conséquences du retour de la France au protectionnisme à la fin du XIXe siècle,'' *Revue d'Histoire Economique et Sociale* 45 (1967), 326–380.

12. See Power, *Ferry*, 195.

13. Salisbury, in an interview with the French ambassador in 1897, *Documents Diplomatiques Français*, 1st Series, XIII, 117, cited by J. Stengers, ''L'impérialisme colonial de la fin du XIXe siècle: mythe ou réalité,'' *Journal of African History* 3 (1962), 487. See also Newbury, *Revival*, 348. This need for protection was, naturally, mainly a consequence of the relative backwardness of French industry (on this, see the literature cited in note 10). In the first place, the colonies had to serve as controlled export markets (from which stemmed their generally negative trading balance). Although the significance of the colonial trade as a whole was small (see Brunschwig, *Mythes*, 91), exports to the colonies could be of great importance for certain industries, such as textiles.

14. See Betts, *False Dawn*, 81; Newbury, *Revival*, 348.

15. P. Leroy-Beaulieu, *De la colonisation chez les peuples modernes* (Paris, 1874).

16. On this, see above all H. Brunschwig, ''Politique et économie dans l'empire français d'Afrique noire, 1870–1914,'' *Journal of African History* 11 (1970), 401–417; and C. Coquery-Vidrovitch, *Le Congo français au temps des grandes compagnies concessionnaires 1898–1930* (Paris, 1972).

17. J.F. Laffey, ''Roots of French imperialism in the nineteenth century: The case of Lyon,'' *French Historical Studies* 6 (1969), 80. Lyon and municipal imperialism are also dealt with in the later studies by John Laffey, ''Municipal imperialism in nineteenth-century France,'' *Historical Reflections/Réflections Historiques* 1 (1974), 1, 81–114; ''Municipal imperialism: The Lyon Chamber of Commerce, 1914–1925,'' *The Journal of European Economic History* 4 (Spring 1975), 95–120; ''Municipal imperialism in decline: The Lyon Chamber of Commerce, 1925–1938,'' *French Historical Studies* 9 (1975), 329–353; ''Municipal imperialism in France: The Lyon Chamber of Commerce, 1900–1914,'' *Proceedings and Addresses of the American Philosophical Society* 119 (1975), 8–23.

18. Cited by Laffey, ''Racines,'' 299.

19. On this, see J. Ganiage, *Les origines du protectorat français en Tunisie, 1861–1881* (Paris, 1959), 145, 644 and 156, 655–656. A sequel to Ganiage's work is J. Rosenbaum, *Frankreich in Tunesien. Die Anfänge des Protektorates 1881–1886* (Zürich, 1971).

20. J. Bouvier, ''A propos des origines de l'impérialisme,'' *La Pensée* 100 (1961), 60. See Stengers, ''Impérialisme,'' 480.

21. P. Guillen, ''Les milieux d'affaires français et le Maroc à l'aube du XXe siècle,'' *Revue Historique* 239 (1963), 397–422. On the important role of the banks, see also P. Guillen, ''L'implantation de Schneider au Maroc,'' *Revue d'Histoire Diplomatique* 79 (1965), 165; and Gerschenkron, ''Backwardness,'' 12 ff.

22. Cited by Stengers, ''Impérialisme,'' 490. On the legendary riches of the Sudan, see H. Brunschwig, ''Politique,'' 403; J. Stengers, ''Une facette de la question du Haut-Nil: Le mirage soudanais,'' *Journal of African History* 10 (1969), 579–623; A.S. Kanya-Forstner, *The Conquest of the Western Sudan. A Study in French Military Imperialism* (Cambridge, England, 1969), 264 ff.; Ph. D. Curtin, ''The lure of Bambuk gold,'' *Journal of African History* 14 (1973), 623–631; H. Brunschwig, ''Le Dr Colin, l'or du Bambouk

et la 'Colonisation moderne,' " in id., *L'Afrique noire au temps de l'Empire français* (Paris, 1988), 65–94.

23. See Kanya-Forstner, *Conquest*, 264; and Stengers, "Facette," 585.

24. Hillaire Belloc, *The Modern Traveller* (1898), cited by G. Shepperson, "Africa, the Victorians and imperialism," *Revue Belge de Philologie et d'Histoire* 40 (1962), 1228.

25. C.M. Andrew and A.S. Kanya-Forstner, "The French Colonial Party: Its composition, aims and influence, 1889–1914," *Historical Journal* 14 (1971), 103. This excellent article was the first important supplement to Brunschwig's survey (*Mythes*, 111–139). On the origin of a colonial faction in the Chamber, see E. Schmieder, "La Chambre de 1885–1889 et les affaires du Tonkin," *Revue Française d'Histoire d'Outre-Mer* 53 (1966), 153–215. Andrew and Kanya-Forstner have continued their interesting research in: "The French Colonial Party and French colonial war aims, 1914–1918," *Historical Journal* 13 (1974), 79–106; "The Groupe Colonial in the French Chamber of Deputies, 1892–1932," *Historical Journal* 17 (1974), 837–866; "Hanotaux, the Colonial Party and the Fashoda strategy," *Journal of Imperial and Commonwealth History* 2 (1975), 55–104. About the "Union Coloniale Française," see also S. M. Persell, "Joseph Chailley-Bert and the importance of the *Union Coloniale Française*," *Historical Journal* 17 (1974), 176–184.

26. Andrew and Kanya-Forstner, "Party," 104.

27. Ibid., 27. An early example of similar Mediterranean-imperial dreams in 1868 is to be found with Prévost-Paradol. See J. Ganiage, *L'expansion coloniale de la France sous la Troisième République, 1871–1914* (Paris, 1968), 41. On this, see also Andrew and Kanya-Forstner, "Party," 120; J.P.T. Bury, "Gambetta and overseas problems," *The English Historical Review* 82 (1967), 277–295. About Etienne, see H. Sieberg, *Eugene Etienne und die französische Kolonialpolitik 1887–1904* (Cologne, 1968).

28. Andrew and Kanya-Forstner, "Party," 107.

29. R.G. Brown, *Fashoda Reconsidered. The Impact of Domestic Politics on French Policy in Africa, 1893–1898* (Baltimore, Md., 1970), 139. See also Andrew and Kanya-Forstner, "Party," 126 ff.

30. There often was opposition between Foreign Affairs and the Colonies. See for example, C. Coquery-Vidrovitch, "L'intervention d'une société privée à propos du contesté franco-espagnol dans le Rio Muni: la Société d'Explorations Coloniales, 1899–1924," *Cahiers d'Etudes Africaines* 13 (1969), 67; and Brown, *Fashoda*, 32; but also C.M. Andrew, *Theodore Delcassé and the Making of the Entente Cordiale* (London, 1968), 30.

31. J. Bouvier, "Les intérêts financiers et la question d'Egypte, 1875–1876," *Revue Historique* 224 (1960), 75–104; and Bouvier, "Origines," 127.

32. M. Bruguière, "Le Chemin de fer du Yunnan: Paul Doumer et la politique d'intervention française en Chine, 1889–1902," *Revue d'Histoire Diplomatique* 77 (1963), 278.

33. Guillen, "Implantation," 165–167.

34. See Bouvier, "Intérêts," 104; Bouvier, "Origines," 129; and Coquery-Vidrovitch "Intervention," 67.

35. Brunschwig, *Mythes*, 185.

36. Gambetta to Ferry, 13 May 1881, cited by Brunschwig, *Mythes*, 55. See also C.J. H. Hayes, *A Generation of Materialism 1871–1900* (New York, 1963; 1st ed., 1941), 220: "Basically the new imperialism was a nationalistic phenomenon." J. Stengers,

"Leopold II et la rivalité franco-anglaise en Afrique, 1883–1884," *Revue Belge de Philologie et d'Histoire* 47 (1969), 479: "Cette fièvre patriotique et chauvine qui, en fin de compte, a tout décidé (. . .)."

37. Clemenceau, *Débats parlementaires*, 31 July 1885, cited by R. Girardet, *Le Nationalisme français, 1871–1914* (Paris, 1966), 108.

38. Girardet, *Nationalisme*, 108.

39. On this exchange offer, see Hayes, *Generation*, 217. On Gambetta, see G. Wormser, *Gambetta dans les tempêtes, 1870–1877* (Paris, 1964), 229 ff. On Ferry, see F. Pisani-Ferry, *Jules Ferry et le partage du monde* (Paris, 1962), 76 ff.

40. See for example H. Brunschwig, "Note sur les technocrates de l'impérialisme français en Afrique noire," *Revue Française d'Histoire d'Outre-Mer* 54 (1967), 185.

41. Lyautey compared Africa and the Far West in a speech of 12 July 1907, cited by R.F. Betts, "The French colonial frontier," in C.K. Warner, ed., *From the Ancien Régime to the Popular Front* (New York, 1969), 136.

42. *Le Constitutionnel*, 7 October 1882, cited by Stengers, "Impérialisme," 475. See also H. Brunschwig, "La négociation du traité-Makoko," *Cahiers d'Etudes Africaines* 5 (1965), 5–57.

43. *Le Temps*, 23 November 1882, cited by Stengers, "Impérialisme," 475.

44. H. Brunschwig, "Les origines du partage de l'Afrique occidentale," *Journal of African History* 5 (1964), 121–125. This is a review article of J.D. Hargreaves, *Prelude to the Partition of West Africa* (London, 1963). Stengers attributes great importance not only to the Brazza-Makoko treaty, but also to the introduction by France of a policy of protectorates in West Africa, in January 1883. See Stengers, "Imperialisme," 477 ff.

45. C.W. Newbury and A.S. Kanya-Forstner, "French policy and the origins of the scramble for West Africa," *Journal of African History* 10 (1969), 253–276. See also Kanya-Forstner, *Conquest*, 265; H. Brunschwig, *Le partage de l'Afrique noire* (Paris, 1971), 153–156. A general discussion of this controversy can be found in W.R. Louis, *The Gallagher and Robinson Controversy* (London, 1976); and G.N. Sanderson, "The European partition of Africa: Coincidence or conjuncture?" *Journal of Imperial and Commonwealth History* 3 (1974), 54.

46. Brown, *Fashoda*, 31 ff. See also G.N. Sanderson, *England, Europe and the Upper Nile, 1882–1899* (Edinburgh, 1965), 361; Ganiage, *Expansion*, 43; M. Michel, *La Mission Marchand 1895–1899* (Paris, 1972). On Hanotaux, see Andrew and Kanya-Forstner, "Hanotaux" (cf. above, note 25); P. Grupp, *Theorie der Kolonialexpansion und Methoden der imperialistischen Aussenpolitik bei Gabriel Hanotaux* (Bern, 1972); A.A. Heggoy, *The African Policies of Gabriel Hanotaux 1894–1898* (Athens, Ga., 1972). Brunschwig does ascribe significance to public opinion, but considers that this was driven on by nationalism and not by interest in the colonies. On the contrary, in regard to that, there was only "ignorance et indifférence." Brunschwig, "Partage," 165. On the development of the colonial idea in France, see Raoul Girardet, *L'Idée coloniale en France de 1871 a 1962* (Paris, 1972); D.B. Marshall, *The French Colonial Myth and Constitution-Making in the Fourth Republic* (New Haven, Conn., 1973); and H. Brunschwig, "Vigné d'Octon et l'anticolonialisme sous la Troisième République (1871–1914)," *Cahiers d'Etudies Africaines* 54 (1974), 265–298.

47. Caprivi in the *Reichstag*, 12 May 1890; see before 74.

48. Stengers, "Imperialisme," 485. On this, see also Sieberg, Etienne, 149; and J.-B. Duroselle, *L'Europe de 1815 à nos jours* (Paris, 1967), 341.

49. On this, see especially H. Gollwitzer, *Europe in the Age of Imperialism, 1880–*

1914 (London, 1969). Cf. Newbury and Kanya-Forstner, ''Policy,'' 275: ''The age of imperialism was not an age of reason and French policies were nothing if not the product of their age''; and Sieberg, *Etienne*, 149.

50. Albert Duchêne, *La Politique coloniale de la France: Le ministère des Colonies depuis Richelieu* (Paris, 1928), 263, cited by C.W. Newbury, ''The formation of the Government General of French West Africa,'' *Journal of African History* 2 (1960), 112.

51. See R. Robinson and others in *Journal of African History* 2 (1961), 158–160.

52. Newbury, ''Formation,'' 111.

53. Sanderson, *England*, 390.

54. J.L. de Lanessan, *Principes de colonisation* (Paris, 1897), cited by Duroselle, *Europe*, 337.

55. With the exception of the Gambetta Cabinet (14 November 1881–26 January 1882) when a ministry united trade and colonies under Minister Maurice Rouvier. On nationalism in the navy, see H. Brunschwig, *L'Avènement de l'Afrique noire* (Paris, 1963), 172.

56. G. Taboulet, ''Le voyage d'exploration du Mekong (1866–1868): Doudart de Lagrée et Francis Garnier,'' *Revue Française d'Histoire d'Outre-Mer* 57 (1970), 10. In later expeditions, commercial considerations also played a role. See J. Valette, ''L'expédition de Francis Garnier au Tonkin,'' *Revue d'Histoire Moderne et Contemporaine* 16 (1969), 190; and Laffey, ''Racines,'' 283 ff. The most thorough and extensive treatment of French expansion in Vietnam is by D. Brötel, *Französischer Imperialismus in Vietnam. Die koloniale Expansion und die Errichtung des Protektorates Annam-Tongking 1880–1885* (Zurich, 1971). On similar expansion in Senegal, see B. Schnapper, *La politique et le commerce français dans le Golfe de Guinée de 1838 à 1871* (Paris, 1961), 203.

57. Kanya-Forstner, *Conquest*, 8. See also J.S. Ambler, *The French Army in Politics, 1945–1962* (Columbus, Ohio, 1966), 10.

58. Kanya-Forstner, *Conquest*, 270. On the great role of the soldiers, see also M. Crowder, *West Africa under Colonial Rule* (London, 1968), 70–77.

59. W.B. Cohen, ''The lure of Empire: Why Frenchmen entered the Colonial Service,'' *Journal of Contemporary History* 4 (1969), 107. This is a chapter from his more recent, larger study on the French colonial rulers: W.B. Cohen, *Rulers of Empire* (Stanford, Calif., 1971).

60. J. Gottmann, ''Bugeaud, Gallieni, Lyautey,'' in E.M. Earle, ed., *Makers of Modern Strategy* (Princeton, N.J., 1944), 234. See also the comment of John Stuart Mill on imperialism as ''a vast system of outdoor relief for the younger sons of the upper classes,'' cited in K. Zilliacus, *Mirror of the Past* (London, 1944), 32.

61. Sanderson, *England*, 390. On the colonial literature as a source of inspiration, see Cohen, ''Lure,'' 113–114.

62. On this, see K. Munholland, ''Rival approaches to Morocco; Delcassé, Lyautey and the Algerian-Moroccan border, 1903–1905,'' *French Historical Studies* 5 (1968), 328–343.

63. See Brunschwig, ''Partage,'' 166.

6. THE GIANT THAT WAS A DWARF OR: THE STRANGE CASE OF DUTCH IMPERIALISM

1. K. Hancock, *Survey of British Commonwealth Affairs, Vol. 2. Problems of Economic Policy, Part 1* (London, 1940), 1–2.

2. J.A. Hobson, *Imperialism: A Study* (London, 1902), 25.

3. Ibid., 15.

4. Ibid., 65.

5. J. Gallagher and R. Robinson, ''The imperialism of free trade,'' *Economic History Review*, Second Series 6 (1953) 1–15.

6. Cf. J. Gallagher and R. Robinson, ''The partition of Africa,'' in *New Cambridge, Modern History* 10 (Cambridge, 1962); R. Robinson, ''Non-European foundations of European imperialism: Sketch for a theory of collaboration,'' in R. Owen and B. Sutcliffe, eds., *Studies in the Theory of Imperialism* (London, 1972), 118–140.

7. H. Brunschwig, *Mythes et réalités de l'impérialisme colonial français, 1871–1914* (Paris, 1960). For a fuller discussion of this, see ''The debate on French imperialism, 1960–1975'' (Chapter 5, this volume).

8. J. Marseilles' *Empire colonial et capitalisme français. Histoire d'un divorce* (Paris, 1984) throws a new light on the economic aspects of French imperialism.

9. H.-U. Wehler, *Bismarck und der Imperialismus* (Cologne, 1969).

10. J.-L. Miège, *L'Impérialisme colonial italien de 1870 à nos jours* (Paris, 1968).

11. R.J. Hammond, *Portugal and Africa, 1815–1910. A Study in Uneconomic Imperialism* (Stanford, Calif., 1966).

12. G. Clarence-Smith, *The Third Portuguese Empire, 1825–1975. A Study in Economic Imperialism* (Manchester, 1985).

13. J. Stengers, ''King Leopold's Imperialism,'' in R. Owen and B. Sutcliffe, eds., *Studies in the Theory of Imperialism* (London, 1972), 248–275.

14. As quoted in M. Kuitenbrouwer, *Nederland en de opkomst van het moderne imperialisme. Koloniën en buitenlandse politiek, 1870–1902* (Amsterdam, 1985), 195.

15. Cf. H. Roland Holst, *Kapitaal en arbeid in Nederland*, 2 vols. (Amsterdam, 1902).

16. C. Fasseur, *Kultuurstelsel en koloniale baten* (Leiden, 1975), passim.

17. Quoted in H.W. van den Doel, *Het Rijk van Insulinde* (Amsterdam, 1996), 244.

18. Cf. I. Schöffer, ''Dutch expansion and Indonesian reactions: Some dilemmas of modern colonial rule (1900–1942),'' in H.L. Wesseling, ed., *Expansion and Reaction* (Leiden, 1978), 78–100; C. Fasseur, ''Een koloniale paradox. De Nederlandse expansie in de Indonesische Archipel in het midden van de negentiende eeuw (1830–1870),'' *Tijdschrift voor Geschiedenis* 92 (1979), 162–187; H.L. Wesseling, ''Myths and realities of Dutch imperialism,'' in *Proceedings of the Second Indonesian-Dutch Historical Conference Leiden 1978* (Jakarta, 1979).

19. Kuitenbrouwer, *Nederland en de opkomst van het moderne imperialisme* (see note 14).

20. Ibid., 8–9.

21. R. Betts, *The False Dawn. European Imperialism in the Nineteenth Century* (Oxford, 1976), 81.

22. Cf. Fasseur, ''Koloniale paradox'' (see note 18).

23. R. Robinson, ''The excentric idea of imperialism, with or without empire,'' in W.J. Mommsen and J. Osterhammel, eds., *Imperialism and After. Continuities and Discontinuities* (London, 1986), 286.

24. T. August, ''Locating the Age of Imperialism,'' *Itinerario* 10 (1986), 2, 85–97.

25. Cf. Gallagher and Robinson, ''Imperialism of free trade,'' 1–15.

26. Cf. P.M. Kennedy, ''Why did the British Empire last so long?'', in id., *Strategy and Diplomacy, 1870–1945. Eight Studies* (London, 1983), 197–218.

7. THE BERLIN CONFERENCE OF 1884–1885: MYTHS AND REALITIES

1. Kwame Nkrumah, *Challenge of the Congo* (New York, 1967), X.

2. Quoted in H.L. Wesseling, *Divide and Rule. The Partition of Africa, 1880–1914* (Westport, Conn., 1996), 29.

3. Ibid., 98.

4. Cf. G. de Gourcel, "The Berlin Act of 26 February 1885," in S. Förster, W.J. Mommsen, and R. Robinson, eds., *Bismarck, Europe and Africa. The Berlin Africa Conference 1884–1885 and the Onset of Partition* (Oxford, 1988), 247–262.

5. Quoted in W. Langer, *European Alliances and Alignments, 1871–1890* (New York, 1950), 298.

6. Quoted in ibid., 313.

7. See my "The Netherlands and the partition of Africa" (Chapter 8, this volume).

8. Quoted in R. Girardet, *L'Idée coloniale en France, 1871–1962* (Paris, 1972), 63.

9. O. von Bismarck, *Die gesammelten Werke*, 15 vols. (Berlin, 1924–32) VIII, 646.

10. Ibid., XIII, 386.

11. R. Robinson and J. Gallagher with A. Denny, *Africa and the Victorians: The Official Mind of Imperialism*, 2nd ed. (London, 1981).

12. Quoted in Langer, *European Alliances*, 308.

13. Quoted in R.R. James, *Rosebery* (New York, 1963), 249.

14. For the 1898 agreement, see C. Hirschfield, *The Diplomacy of Partition: Britain, France and the Creation of Nigeria, 1890–1898* (The Hague, 1979).

15. Quoted in J. Stengers, "L'Impérialisme colonial de la fin du XIXe siècle: mythe ou realité?," *Journal of African History* 3 (1962), 469–491.

16. Cf. J. Stengers, "A propos de l'Acte de Berlin, ou comment naît une légende," *Zaïre* (1953), 839–844.

17. R.R. Palmer, *A History of the Modern World*, 4th ed. (New York, 1971), 690.

18. Cf. Stengers, "Acte de Berlin," 841.

19. D. Schäfer, *Weltgeschichte der Neuzeit*, 2 vols., 3rd ed. (Berlin, 1908), II, 340.

20. See W.J. Mommsen, "Bismarck, the concert of Europe and the future of West Africa," in Förster, Mommsen, and Robinson, *Bismarck*, 151–170.

21. *Algemeen Handelsblad*, 21 November 1884.

22. Cf. G.N. Sanderson, "The European partition of Africa: Coincidence or conjuncture?," *Journal of Imperial and Commonwealth History* 3 (1974), 1–54.

23. Cf. R. Anstey, *Britain and the Congo in the Nineteenth Century* (Oxford, 1961), 54 ff.

24. Quoted in Langer, *European Alliances*, 295.

25. See J.D. Hargreaves, "The Berlin Conference, West African boundaries, and the eventual partition," in Förster, Mommsen, and Robinson, *Bismarck*, 313–320.

26. J.S. Keltie, *The Partition of Africa* (London, 1903).

27. Cf. J.D. Singer and M. Small, *The Wages of War, 1816–1965: A Statistical Handbook* (New York, 1972).

28. Quoted in Robinson and Gallagher, *Africa and the Victorians*, 303.

8. THE NETHERLANDS AND THE PARTITION OF AFRICA

1. The name of Banana was given by the Dutch "who first christened it." See H.H. Johnston, *The River Congo* (London, 1884), 22.

2. See especially, for this early history of the Dutch trade in the Congo area, A.F. Schepel, ed., *West-Afrika 1857/1858, Reisjournaal van Lodewijk Kerdijk* (Schiedam, 1978); K. Franssens, "De vestiging van 'Kerdijk en Pincoffs' te Banana, 1857–1859," *Mededelingen der zittingen van de Koninklijke Akademie voor Overzeese Wetenschappen* 22 (1976), 683–697; W. Holman Bentley, *Pioneering on the Congo* (London, 1900); R.T. Anstey, *Britain and the Congo in the Nineteenth Century* (Oxford, 1962); Chr. Jeannest, *Quatre années au Congo* (Paris, 1883); Robidé van der Aa, *Afrikaansche Studien. Koloniaal bezit en particuliere handel op Afrika's Westkust* (The Hague, 1871). According to Franssens ("Vestiging," 692), the Dutch trader Albert Schut had been active in Loanda long before 1850. He later became the head of the Kerdijk and Pincoffs' factory at Ambriz. See also B. Oosterwijk, *Vlucht na Victorie. Lodewijk Pincoffs, 1827–1911* (Rotterdam, 1979), 41, who states that Schut had taken the Portuguese nationality and operated as "Oliveira and Schut."

3. H.M. Stanley, *The Congo and the Founding of Its Free State*, 2 vols. (London, 1885), I, 76, and 83.

4. See Schepel, *West-Afrika*, 8 ff.

5. Sj. Hofstra, "Eenige gegevens over het schip 'Lodewijk' en over den handel van Rotterdam op West-Afrika in de negentiende eeuw," *Rotterdams Jaarboekje* (Rotterdam, 1938).

6. The first factory in Ambriz was probably bought from Samsom in late 1857. The second was founded at Quisembo, the third at Ponte da Lenha (Autumn 1858) the fourth at Banana (1858–1859): see Oosterwijk, *Vlucht*, 46–47. There is much difference of opinion about the exact number of factories Kerdijk and Pincoffs had altogether. Stanley counted almost 80 (Stanley, *Congo*, 73); Hofstra (*Gegevens*, 194) estimated 35 to 40; H. Blink, *Het Kongoland en zijne bewoners* (Haarlem, 1891), 159, mentions 75. J. Chavanne, *Reisen und Forschungen im alten und neuen Kongostaate in den Jahren 1884 und 1885* (Jena, 1887), 83, reported a total of 158 factories in the Congo at 83 locations, of which 55 were Dutch, 33 English or American, 20 French, 41 Portuguese, 6 German, 2 Spanish, and one Brazilian. Onno Zwier van Sandick, who worked some time for the (N.) A.H.V. in the Congo, mentioned 41 factories (of which 13 were closed) as well as some branches. See O.Z. van Sandick, *Herinneringen van de Zuid-Westkust van Afrika* (Deventer, 1881), 117–118. According to Blink, *Kongoland*, 166, the Dutch firm in 1890 employed 103 Dutchmen, 64 Portuguese, and about 2,000 blacks. In 1878–1880 there were 50 or 60 employees in Banana, usually half Dutch, half Portuguese (Bentley, *Pioneering*, 70).

7. Almost all observers considered the Dutch firm as the most important. See, for instance, Blink, *Kongoland*, 156; Chavanne, *Reisen*, 83; P. J. Veth, *Daniël Veth's Reizen in Angola* (Haarlem, 1887), 132; E. Peschuël-Loesche, *Kongo-Land* (Jena, 1887), 225; F. Latour da Veiga Pinto, *Le Portugal et le Congo au XIXe siècle* (Bordeaux, 1972), 79; Bentley, *Pioneering*, 70. According to Van Sandick (*Herinneringen*, 43), the English firm Hatton and Cookson, from Liverpool, outdid the Dutch around the year 1880. The data are clearly referring to different periods. I return below to the subject of priority in the Congo trade.

8. Robidé van der Aa, *Afrikaansche Studiën*, 129–130.

9. Blink, *Kongoland*, 171.

10. Van Sandick, *Herinneringen*, 46.

11. Ibid., 40. According to Bentley (*Pioneering*, 72) gin was "the sole currency of the place."

12. See Oosterwijk, *Vlucht na victorie.*

13. J. Hudig, "In memoriam L. Pincoffs," *Rotterdams Jaarboekje* (1912), 178 ff. On the other hand, he could not, as a Jew, become a member of the club "Amicitia," and the ladies of Rotterdam begged the forgiveness of other ladies whenever the Pincoffs were included in the guest list: ibid., 182; H. Muller, *Muller. Een Rotterdams Zeehandelaar. Hendrik Muller Szn, 1819–1898* (Schiedam, 1977), 307; W. C. Mees, *Man van de daad. Mr Marten Mees en de opkomst van Rotterdam* (Rotterdam, 1946), 404.

14. Muller, *Muller*, 308.

15. Ibid., 308.

16. After the death of Prince Henry, Prince Alexander became chairman. There were 10 provincial and 18 municipal committees as well as 2 subcommittees in the East and West Indies. See Blink, *Kongoland*, 30 ff; and K. Franssens, "Nederland na de Aardrijkskundige Conferentie van Brussel (1877–1879)," *Bijdragen over de Aardrijkskundige Conferentie van 1876* (Brussels, 1976), 501–516.

17. There is a complete list in C.M. Kan, *Het internationaal onderzoek der Afrikaansche binnenlanden* (Utrecht, 1877), 86.

18. Blink, *Kongoland*, 32 ff.

19. P.J. Veth, *Daniël Veth's reizen in Angola* (Haarlem, 1887); J. Feith, *Het Verhaal van den Afrika Reiziger* (Amsterdam, 1910).

20. Franssens, "Nederland," 505; Kan, *Onderzoek*, 16–17.

21. F. Bontinck, *Aux Origines de l'Etat indépendant du Congo* (Louvain, 1966), 40. Pincoffs called Stanley's plans in a meeting of the committee "irréalisables" (Franssens, "Nederland," 310); A. Roeykens, *Les Débuts de l'oeuvre africaine de Léopold II, 1876–1879* (Brussels, 1955), 373. Cf. also F. Bontinck, "Les Archives de la *Nieuwe Afrikaansche Handelsvennootschap* conservées à Schaarsbergen (Pays-Bas)," *Bulletin des Séances de l'Académie Royale des Sciences d-Outre-Mer* (Brussels, 1970), 179.

22. Franssens, "Nederland," 510.

23. See, for the Stanley-Pincoffs controversy, also Franssens, "Nederland," 310 ff.

24. Roeykens (*Débuts*, 379): "La Providence lui avait singulièrement facilité la chose (. . .)."

25. This characterization is found in an article of the journalist Oldenkott in 1868, cited in Mees, *Man van de daad*, 405.

26. Oosterwijk, *Vlucht*, 161.

27. Mees, *Man van de daad*, 466.

28. Muller, *Muller*, 318.

29. H. Blink, "De Nederlanders aan Afrika's Zuid-Westkust," *Eigen Haard* 46 (1890), 732; Muller, *Muller*, 303 ff; Oosterwijk, *Vlucht*, 141–142, 208, 228, 234.

30. Muller, *Muller*, 310.

31. The history of the activities of Hendrik Muller in this respect is described in detail in his biography (see note 13).

32. J. Woltring, ed. *Bescheiden betreffende de buitenlandse politiek van Nederland, 1848–1919. Tweede Periode, 1871–1898*, III (1881–1885) (The Hague, 1967), 329.

33. Ibid., 335.

34. Ibid., 336.

35. Ibid., 345. According to Latour da Veiga Pinto (*Portugal*, 79), it had the disposal of "une véritable petite armée." On fights with the Portuguese, see Oosterwijk, *Vlucht*, 261–262, and 139–140. Marc Michel (*La Mission Marchand, 1895–1899* (Paris, 1972),

100, note 6) says that Greshoff, the agent of the N.A.H.V., was a "véritable puissance" whom the Bakongo nicknamed *Fouman Tangon*, or "The Sungod."

36. For this, see R. Robinson and J. Gallagher with Alice Denny, *Africa and the Victorians* (London, 1961), 33, 168; and the review by Jean Stengers, "L'Impérialisme colonial de la fin du XlXe siècle: mythe ou réalité," *Journal of African History* 3 (1962), 469.

37. Anstey, *Britain and the Congo*, 31. Oosterwijk (*Vlucht*, 89) gives a higher estimate for the Dutch share, but his figures are rather obscure. See also Latour da Veiga Pinto, Portugal, 80. Robidé van der Aa (*Afrikaansche Studiën*, 129) mentions some export of textiles from Twente. See, for this, also R.A. Burgers, *100 jaar G. en H. Salomonson* (Leiden, 1954), 213.

38. J. Woltring, ed., *Bescheiden betreffende de buitenlandse politiek van Nederland, 1848–1919. Tweede Periode, 1871–1898, II (1874–1880)* (The Hague, 1965), XII.

39. Van Bylandt to Rochussen, 12 December 1882, in Wolting, *Bescheiden*, II, 345; Latour da Veiga Pinto, Portugal, 237 ff.

40. *Archief Kamer van Koophandel Rotterdam*, 1882, 54 and 54a. According to Latour da Veiga Pinto (*Portugal*, 239), the Anglo-Portuguese Treaty did not get a bad reception in The Hague and the attitude of the Dutch government was "extrêmement mesurée" (*Portugal*, 240), despite the vehement press campaign. Asser, however, refers to a vigorous Dutch protest and gives Van der Does credit for contributing much to the rejection of the treaty: T.M. Asser, "De Congo-Akte," *De Gids* 49 (1885), 324. According to S.E. Crowe, *The Berlin West-African Conference, 1884–1885* (London, 1942), 23, the Netherlands was second only to France in its resistance to the treaty.

41. On 3 April 1884.

42. *Verslag der Handelingen der Staten-Generaal, 1883–1884*, I, 326–327 (hereafter *Handelingen*).

43. Gericke van Herwijnen to Van der Does de Willebois, 4 July 1884, in Wolting, *Bescheiden*, III, 677.

44. Van der Does de Willebois to Van der Hoeven, 31 October 1884, in ibid., 722.

45. Ibid., 709.

46. Ibid., 710–711.

47. Ibid., 713–714.

48. Ibid., 727.

49. Muller, *Muller*, 372.

50. Wolting, *Bescheiden*, III, 710.

51. Ibid., 713.

52. For the diplomatic complications of the *Nisero* incident, see ibid., passim.

53. Ibid., 713.

54. Ibid., 714.

55. *Affaires du Congo et de l'Afrique occidentale, Documents Diplomatiques* (Paris, 1885), 60 ff. See also G. de Courcel, *L'Influence de la Conférence de Berlin de 1885 sur le droit international* (Paris, 1935), 92 ff.

56. Muller, *Muller*, 376.

57. See Brunschwig (*Partage*, 64), who wrongly dates the "gin-debate" to 22 instead of 13 December 1884. Every month steamers from Hamburg delivered thousands of bottles of rum and gin "made in Germany" (Holman Bentley, *Pioneering*, 72).

58. Wolting, *Bescheiden*, III, 738–739.

59. See, for the literal text, *Affaires du Congo*, 181.

60. Texts in ibid., 82 ff.

61. Wolting, *Bescheiden*, III, 752–753.

62. Ibid., 784–785, 804; *Affaires du Congo*, 148–152, 170–174, 189–195, 228–233, 265–266, 274–276.

63. Wolting, *Bescheiden*, III, 784–785, 806.

64. Muller to Van der Does de Willebois, 30 November 1884, in ibid., 759–761.

65. After the United States, Germany, England, Italy, and Austria-Hungary, but before Spain, France, Russia, Sweden-Norway, Portugal, Denmark, and the last one, Belgium. Text of the Convention in *Affaires du Congo*, 248–250.

66. Van der Does de Willebois to the king, 27 February 1885, in Wolting, *Bescheiden*, III, 806.

67. *Handelingen*, 1884–1885, II, 342.

68. *Jaarverslag van de N.A.H.V.*, Archives of the N.A.H.V., Box 72, Nr. 167. Algemeen Rijksarchief.

69. *Jaarverslag over 1884 van de Kamer van Koophandel te Rotterdam.*

70. *Tijdschrift van het Koninklijk Nederlands Aardrijkskundig Genootschap*, 2nd Series, Part 3 (1886), 206–207.

71. *Algemeen Handelsblad*, 4 March 1885. About Asser's role in Berlin, see also Asser, "De Congo-Akte" (cited in 40).

72. See for this, for example, S.J.S. Cookey, *Britain and the Congo Question, 1885–1913* (London, 1968), 12 ff.; and S. Miers, "The Brussels Conference of 1889–1890," in P. Gifford and W.R. Louis, eds., *Britain and Germany in Africa* (New Haven, 1967), 83–118.

73. Namely, on 3 April 1884 in the Lower Chamber, on 24 April 1884 in the Upper Chamber, on 30 December 1884 again in the Upper Chamber and, finally, on 25 February 1885 in the Lower Chamber.

74. Asser, "Congo-Akte," 330.

75. See C. Smit, *De buitenlandse politiek van Nederland*, 2 vols. (The Hague, 1945), II, 142.

76. *De Maasbode*, 15 January 1885.

77. P. Leroy-Beaulieu, *De la colonisation chez les peuples modernes* (Paris, 1874).

78. Cf. H.L. Wesseling, "Myths and realities of Dutch imperialism," in *Proceedings of the Second Indonesian-Dutch Historical Conference Held at Ujung Pandang, 1978* (Jakarta, 1979).

9. TOWARD A HISTORY OF DECOLONIZATION

1. The word "decolonization" seems to have been coined in 1932 by a German scholar, Moritz Julius Bonn. See M.E. Chamberlain, *Decolonization. The Fall of the European Empires* (Oxford, 1985), 1. About the word, see also M. Michel, "Y a-t-il eu impréparation de la France à la décolonisation?", in *Enjeux et puissances. Mélanges en l'honneur de J.-B. Duroselle* (Paris, 1986), 184.

2. Cf. D.A. Low, *Lion Rampant. Essays in the Study of British Imperialism*, 2nd ed. (London, 1974), 149; P. Kennedy, *Strategy and Diplomacy, 1870–1945* (London, 1983), 202.

3. W.H. Morris-Jones and G. Fischer, eds., *Decolonization and After. The British and French Experience* (London, 1980); P. Gifford and Wm. R. Louis, eds., *The Transfer of Power in Africa. Decolonization, 1940–1960* (New Haven, Conn., 1982); *Les Chemins de la décolonisation de l'empire colonial français* (Paris, 1986); L. Blussé et al., *India and Indonesia from the 1920s to the 1950s. The Origins of Planning* (Leiden, 1986). Of course, the pioneer studies by R. von Albertini, *Dekolonisation* (Cologne, 1986; English translation, New York, 1971), and H. Grimal, *La Décolonisation* (Paris, 1965; new ed., 1985; English translation, London, 1978) should also be mentioned.

4. J. Gallagher, *The Decline, Revival and Fall of the British Empire* (Cambridge, England, 1982); D.A. Low, *The Contraction of England* (Inaugural lecture, Cambridge, England, 1984); R.F. Holland, *European Decolonization, 1918–1981. An Introductory Survey* (London, 1985); T. Smith, *The Pattern of Imperialism. The United States, Great Britain and the Late Industrializing World since 1815* (Cambridge, Mass., 1981); J.A.A. van Doorn and W.J. Hendrix, *The Process of Decolonization, 1945–1975. The Military Experience in Comparative Perspective*. (Comparative Asian Studies Programme 17, Rotterdam, 1987); J. Bank, "Exercities in vergelijkende dekolonisatie; Indonesië in Zuid-Oost Azië, Nederland in West-Europa," *Bijdragen tot de Taal-, Land- en Volkenkunde* 141 (1985), 19–35; P.C. Emmer, "De contractie van het Westen; de dekolonisatie na 1945," in J.L. Heldring, H. Renner, and R.B. Soetendorp, eds., *Geschiedenis na 1945* (Utrecht, 1985); M. Kuitenbrouwer, "Dekolonisatie en revolutie in vergelijkend perspectief: Indonesië, India en Indochina," in J. van Goor, ed., *The Indonesian Revolution* (Utrecht, 1981).

5. See, for example, N. Mansergh, ed., *The Transfer of Power in India*, 12 vols. (London, 1970–1983); S.L. van der Wal, ed., continued by P.J. Drooglever, *Officiële bescheiden betreffende de Nederlands-Indonesische betrekkingen, 1945–1950*, 13 vols. (The Hague, 1971–1986).

6. See H. Brunschwig, "The decolonization of French black Africa," in Gifford and Louis, *Transfer of Power*, 211–224.

7. The impact or lack of impact of the events in Asia on the decolonization of Africa is now a matter of discussion, particularly among British historians; see, for example, D.A. Low, "The Asian mirror to tropical Africa's independence," and Wm. R. Louis and R. Robinson, "The United States and the liquidation of the British Empire in tropical Africa, 1941–1951," both in Gifford and Louis, *Transfer of Power*, 1–30, and 31–56, resp.; also Gallagher, *Decline*, and Holland, *European Decolonization*, passim.

8. Cf. R. Girardet, *L'Idée coloniale en France, 1871–1962* (Paris, 1972); D.B. Marshall, *The French Colonial Myth and Constitution-Making in the Fourth Republic* (New Haven, Conn., 1973); H.L. Wesseling, "Post-imperial Holland," *Journal of Contemporary History* 15 (1980), 125–142.

9. F. Brockway, *The Colonial Revolution* (New York, 1973), 75. See also J. Darwin, "British decolonization since 1945: A pattern or a puzzle," *Journal of Imperial and Commonwealth History* 12 (1984), 187–209.

10. Cf. R. Robinson, "Non-European foundations of European imperialism: Sketch for a theory of collaboration," in R. Owen and B. Sutcliffe, eds., *Studies in the Theory of Imperialism* (London, 1972), 117–140; R. Robinson, "The excentric idea of imperialism, with or without Empire," in W.J. Mommsen and J. Osterhammel, eds., *Imperialism and After. Continuities and Discontinuities* (London, 1986), 267–289.

11. Cf. Low, *Contraction*, 12; and, for the opposite view, Holland, *European Decolonization*, 191.

12. In Indonesia the Republic was able to quickly put down the 1948 communist uprising, the so-called "Madiun Affair." On the importance of this, See, for example, Van Doorn, *Process*, 10; and Kuitenbrouwer, "Dekolonisatie," 101.

13. A.G. Hopkins, "European expansion into West Africa: A historiographical survey of English-language publications since 1945," in P.C. Emmer and H.L. Wesseling, eds., *Reappraisals in Overseas History* (Leiden, 1979), 54–68. Cf. also D.K. Fieldhouse, "Decolonization, development, and dependence: A survey of changing attitudes," in Gifford and Louis, *Transfer of Power*, 483–512.

14. See on this subject, for example, L. Blussé, H.L. Wesseling, and G.D. Winius, eds., *History and Underdevelopment* (Leiden, 1980).

15. J. Gallagher and R. Robinson, "The imperialism of free trade," *Economic History Review*, 2nd Series, 6 (1953), 1–15. According to Winks the term "informal empire" was used already in 1934 by Charles R. Fay; see R.W. Winks, "On decolonization and informal Empire," *American Historical Review* 81 (1976), 544.

16. Cf. Wesseling, "Post-imperial Holland" (Chapter 10, this volume). On the impact of the Dutch example ("le complexe hollandais") on French decolonization, see J. Marseille, *Empire colonial et capitalisme français. Histoire d'un divorce* (Paris, 1984), 359 ff.

17. Cf. B.R. Tomlinson, "Continuities and discontinuities in Indo-British economic relations: British multinational corporations in India, 1920–1970," in Mommsen and Osterhammel, *Imperialism and After*, 154–166.

10. POST-IMPERIAL HOLLAND

1. See J.C.H. Blom, "The Second World War and Dutch society: Continuity and change," in A.C. Duke and C.A. Tamse, eds., *Britain and the Netherlands, VI. War and Society* (The Hague, 1977), 234.

2. See J.A.A. van Doorn and W.J. Hendrix, *Ontsporing van geweld* (Rotterdam, 1970), 151.

3. C.G.S. Sandberg, *Indië verloren, rampspoed geboren* (The Hague, 1914).

4. See H. Baudet, "The economic interest of the Netherlands in the Netherlands East Indies," in *Papers of the Dutch-Indonesian Historical Conference Held at Noordwijkerhout, The Netherlands 19–22 May 1976* (Leiden, 1978), 234–249.

5. See H.L. Wesseling, "Le modèle colonial néerlandais dans la théorie coloniale française, 1880–1914," *Revue Française d'Histoire d'Outre-Mer* 63 (1976), 241.

6. Baudet, "Economic interest," 436.

7. H. Colijn, *Koloniale vraagstukken van heden en morgen* (Amsterdam, 1928).

8. Quoted in H.W. van den Doel, *Het Rijk van Insulinde* (Amsterdam, 1996), 244.

9. See R. von Albertini, *Dekolonisation* (Zurich, 1966), 563.

10. See, on this, Henri Baudet, "The Netherlands after the loss of empire," *Journal of Contemporary History* 4 (1969), 127–141.

11. See A. Lijphart, *The Trauma of Decolonization* (London, 1966).

12. S.L. van der Wal, ed., *Besturen overzee* (Franeker, 1977).

13. J.B.D. Derksen and J. Tinbergen, "Berekeningen over de economische betekenis van Nederlandsch-Indië voor Nederland," *Maandschrift van het Centraal Bureau voor de Statistiek* (1945).

14. J.B.D. Derksen, *Nederlandsch-Indië als afzetgebied van Nederlandse arbeidskrachten en de werkverruiming in Nederland door Nederlandsch-Indië* (Wageningen, 1938), 39 and 42.

15. See W. Brand, ''Heroriëntatie van vroeger in Indonesië werkende bedrijven,'' in H. Baudet, ed., *Handelswereld en wereldhandel* (Rotterdam, 1969), 143–173.

16. See *Zeventig jaren statistiek in tijdreeksen, 1899–1969* (The Hague, 1970), 14–15.

17. See Brand, ''Heroriëntatie,'' 143–173.

18. *Zeventig jaren statistiek*, 92–95.

19. See, on this, H. Verwey-Jonker, ed., *Allochtonen in Nederland* (The Hague, 1973), 47–110.

20. See, on all this, the official government paper *De problematiek van de Molukse minderheid in Nederland* (1978).

21. Baudet, ''The Netherlands,'' 127.

22. See H.L. Wesseling, ''Dutch historiography on European expansion since 1945,'' in P.C. Emmer and H.L. Wesseling, eds., *Reappraisals in Overseas History* (Leiden, 1979).

23. F. Weinreb, *Collaboratie en Verzet*, 3 vols. (Amsterdam, 1969).

11. OVERSEAS HISTORY, 1945–1995

1. See, for example, M. Mörner and T. Svensson, eds., *The History of the Third World in Nordic Research* (Göteborg, 1986).

2. See C. Fasseur, ''Leiden and Empire: University and Colonial Office, 1825–1925,'' in W. Otterspeer, ed., *Leiden Oriental Connections, 1850–1940* (Leiden, 1989), 187–203.

3. J. Romein, *Aera van Europa* (Leiden, 1954), and *De eeuw van Azië* (Leiden, 1956).

4. L. Blussé, ''Japanese historiography and European sources,'' in P.C. Emmer and H.L. Wesseling, eds., *Reappraisals in Overseas History* (Leiden, 1979), 193–222.

5. Zie T.O. Ranger, ''Towards a usable African past,'' in C. Fyfe, ed., *African Studies Since 1945: a Tribute to Basil Davidson* (London, 1976), 17–29.

6. See A.G. Hopkins, ''European expansion into West Africa: A historiographical survey of English-language publications since 1945,'' in Emmer and Wesseling, *Reappraisals*, 56.

7. F. Braudel, *La Méditerranée et le monde méditerranéen à l'époque de Philippe II*, 3rd ed., 2 vols. (Paris, 1976), I, 17.

8. For practical as well as for theoretical reasons we will not discuss here the history of the Americas and the Caribbean. As far as Asia is concerned we will limit ourselves to the two big ex-colonies, India and Indonesia, where the rise of a national historiography has been the most impressive.

9. J. Nehru, *The Discovery of India* (London, 1956), 28.

10. See S. Ray, ''India: After independence,'' *Journal of Contemporary History* 2 (1967), 125–142.

11. H.A.J. Klooster, *Indonesiërs schrijven hun geschiedenis. De ontwikkeling van de Indonesische geschiedbeoefening in theorie en praktijk, 1900–1980* (Leiden, 1985).

12. J. Bastin, *The Study of Modern Southeast Asian History* (Kuala Lumpur, 1959).

See also his *The Western Element in Modern Southeast Asian History* (Kuala Lumpur, 1963).

13. J.C. van Leur, *Eenige beschouwingen betreffende den ouden Aziatischen handel* (Middelburg, 1934); and J.C. van Leur, *Indonesian Trade and Society: Essays in Asian Social and Economic History* (The Hague, 1955).

14. Van Leur, *Trade and Society*, 162. For a more detailed discussion of Van Leur's work, see "Overseas history in the Netherlands after the Second World War" (Chapter 12, this volume).

15. Ibid., 268–289.

16. K.M. Panikkar, *A Survey of Indian History* (London, 1947); W.F. Wertheim, "Asian history and the western historian. Rejoinder to Professor Bastin," *Bijdragen tot de Taal-, Land- en Volkenkunde* 119 (1963), 149–160.

17. G.W.F. Hegel, *The Philosophy of History* (New York, 1944), 99.

18. E. Sik, *The History of Black Africa*, 2 vols. (Budapest, 1966), I, 17.

19. H. Trevor-Roper, *The Rise of Christian Europe* (London, 1965), 9.

20. H. Brunschwig, "Un faux problème: l'ethnohistoire," *Annales E.S.C.* 20 (1965), 291–300.

21. J. Vansina, *De la tradition orale. Essai de méthode historique* (Tervueren, 1961).

22. In some of his later works Vansina was somewhat more skeptical. See P. Salmon, *Introduction à l'histoire de l'Afrique* (Brussels, 1986), 126 ff.

23. See Brunschwig, "Une histoire de l'Afrique noire est-elle possible?", in *Mélanges en l'honneur de Fernand Braudel*, 2 vols. (Toulouse, 1973), I, 75–87.

24. See T. Ranger, "Usable Past," 17.

25. *The Blackwell Dictionary of Historians* (Oxford, 1988), 308, s.v. Oliver, R.

26. C. Coquery-Vidrovitch, *Le Congo au temps des grandes compagnies concessionnaires* (Paris, 1972); Y. Person, *Samori: une Révolution dyula*, 3 vols. (Dakar, 1968–1976). See also H. Brunschwig, "French historiography since 1945 concerning black Africa," in Emmer and Wesseling, *Reappraisals*, 84–97.

27. See T. Lindblad, "Computer applications in expansion history: A survey," *Second Bulletin of the ESF-Network on the History of European Expansion. Supplement to Itinerario* 12 (1988), 2–61.

28. C.R. Boxer, *The Portuguese Seaborne Empire, 1418–1825* (New York, 1969); C.R. Boxer, *The Dutch Seaborne Empire, 1600–1800* (London, 1965); J.H. Parry, *The Spanish Seaborne Empire* (New York, 1966).

29. K. Glamann, *Dutch-Asiatic Trade 1620–1740*, 2nd ed. (The Hague, 1980); N. Steensgaard, *The Asian Trade Revolution of the 17th Century. The East India Companies and the Decline of the Caravan Trade* (Chicago, 1974); K.N. Chaudhuri, *The Trading World of Asia and the English East India Company, 1660–1760* (Cambridge, England, 1978); P. Curtin, *The Atlantic Slave Trade: A Census* (Madison, Wis., 1969); P. Chaunu and H. Chaunu, *Séville et l'Atlantique, 1504–1650*, 12 vols. (Paris, 1956–1960); B. Bailyn, *Voyagers to the West; Emigration from Britain to America on the Eve of the Revolution* (London, 1987). A recent synthesis in G.V. Scammell, *The First Imperial Age: European Overseas Expansion, c. 1400–1715* (London, 1989).

30. F. Braudel, *Civilisation matérielle, économie et capitalisme, XVe–XVIIIe siècle*, 3 vols. (Paris, 1979).

31. I. Wallerstein, *The Modern World System: Capitalist Agriculture and the Origins of the European World-Economy in the Sixteenth Century* (New York, 1974).

32. See J. de Vries, *The Economy of Europe in an Age of Crisis, 1600–1750* (Cambridge, England, 1976), 192–193.

33. See R. Floud and D. McCloskey, eds., *The Economic History of Britain since 1700*, 2 vols. (Cambridge, 1981), I, 87–92.

34. See P. O'Brien, ''European economic development: The contribution of the periphery,'' *Economic History Review* 35 (1982), 9.

35. J.A. Hobson, *Imperialism: A Study* (London, 1902).

36. Ibid., 85.

37. R. Robinson and J. Gallagher with A. Denny, *Africa and the Victorians. The Official Mind of Imperialism* (London, 1961).

38 H. Brunschwig, *Mythes et réalités de l'impérialisme colonial français*, 1871–1914 (Paris, 1960).

39. For this, see ''The debate on French imperialism, 1960–1975,'' and ''The giant that was a dwarf'' (Chapters 5 and 6, this volume).

40. L.A. Davis and R.A. Huttenback, *Mammon and the Pursuit of Empire. The Political Economy of British Imperialism, 1860–1912* (Cambridge, England, 1986).

41. For a more recent interpretation, see P.J. Cain and A.G. Hopkins, *British Imperialism. Innovation and Expansion 1688–1914* (London, 1993); and id., *British Imperialism. Crisis and Reconstruction, 1914–1990* (London, 1993).

42. See J. Bouvier and R. Girault, eds., *L'Impérialisme français d'avant 1914* (Paris, 1976).

43. J. Marseille, *Empire colonial et capitalisme français: histoire d'un divorce* (Paris, 1984).

44. Gallagher and Robinson, ''Imperialism of free trade'' (see note 5 of Chapter 6 of this volume).

45. R. Robinson, ''Non-European foundations of European imperialism. Sketch for a theory of collaboration,'' in R. Owen and B. Sutcliffe, eds., *Studies in the Theory of Imperialism* (London, 1972), 117–140.

46. See W.J. Mommsen and J. Osterhammel, eds., *Imperialism and After: Continuities and Discontinuities* (London, 1986).

47. For this, see ''Toward a history of decolonization'' (Chapter 9, this volume).

48. A.G. Frank, ''The development of underdevelopment,'' in R.I. Rhodes, ed., *Imperialism and Underdevelopment: A Reader* (New York, 1960), 5–16. See also L. Blussé, H.L. Wesseling, and G.D. Winius, eds., *History and Underdevelopment* (Leiden, 1980).

49. W. Rodney, *How Europe Underdeveloped Africa* (London, 1972).

50. See A.G. Hopkins, ''Clio-Antics: A horoscope for African economic history,'' in Fyfe, *African Studies*, 31–48.

51. P.M. Kennedy, ''Why did the British Empire last so long?'', in id., *Strategy and Diplomacy, 1870–1945: Eight Studies* (London, 1983), 197–218.

52. See also R. Robinson, ''The excentric idea of imperialism, with or without Empire,'' in Mommsen and Osterhammel, *Imperialism and After*, 267–289.

53. P.C. Emmer and H.L. Wesseling, ''What is overseas history?'', in Emmer and Wesseling, *Reappraisals*, 3.

54. See T. Skocpol and M. Somer, ''The uses of comparative history in macrosocial inquiry,'' *Comparative Studies in Society and History* 22 (1980), 174–197.

55. Cf. also Eric R. Wolf's *Europe and the People Without History* (Berkeley, Calif., 1982); P. Curtin, *Cross Cultural Trade in World History* (Cambridge, Mass., 1985); and W. McNeill's *The Rise of the West: a History of the Human Community* (Chicago, Ill., 1963), III.

56. J. Huizinga, ''A definition of the concept of history,'' in R. Klibansky and H.J. Paton, eds., *Philosophy and History* (Oxford, 1936), 8.

12. OVERSEAS HISTORY IN THE NETHERLANDS AFTER THE SECOND WORLD WAR

1. See, for example, Charles-Olivier Carbonell, *Histoire et historiens. Une mutation idéologique des historiens français, 1865–1885* (Toulouse, 1976); and Pim den Boer, *Geschiedenis als beroep. De professionalisering van de geschiedbeoefening in Frankrijk, 1880–1914* (Nijmegen, 1987).

2. Cf. J. Romein, *In opdracht van de tijd. Tien voordrachten over historische thema's* (Amsterdam, 1946).

3. *Sources inédites de l'histoire du Maroc*, edited by the Duc de Castries, 6 vols. (Paris, 1906–1923).

4. See C. Fasseur, *De indologen. Ambtenaren voor de Oost* (Amsterdam, 1993); and W. Otterspeer, ed., *Leiden Oriental Connections, 1850–1940* (Leiden, 1989).

5. Cf. J.C. Heesterman, ''The precarious rise and survival of Sanskrit and Indian studies,'' and H. 't Hart, ''Imagine Leiden without Kern,'' both in Otterspeer, *Oriental Connections*, 115–125, and 126–140.

6. One could think of the well-known studies of Immanuel Wallerstein on this subject.

7. For the development of Indonesian historiography, see H.A.J. Klooster, *Indonesiërs schrijven hun geschiedenis. De ontwikkeling van de Indonesische geschiedbeoefening in theorie en praktijk, 1900–1980* (Dordrecht, 1985).

8. J.W. Berkelbach van der Sprankel and C.D.J. Brandt, eds., *De pelgrimstocht der mensheid*, 4th ed. (Utrecht, 1952).

9. Cf. J. Romein, *De eeuw van Azië. Opkomst, ontwikkeling en overwinning van het modern-aziatische nationalisme* (Leiden, 1956); and W.F. Wertheim, *Indonesian Society in Transition: A Study of Social Change* (The Hague, 1956); id., *East-West Parallels. Sociological Approaches to Modern Asia* (The Hague, 1964); id., *Evolutie en revolutie: de golfslag der emancipatie* (Amsterdam, 1971).

10. G.J. Resink, *Indonesia's History Between the Myths. Essays in Legal History and Historical Theory* (The Hague, 1968).

11. Cf., for example, J. Bastin, *The Study of Modern Southeast-Asian History* (Kuala Lumpur, 1959).

12. M.A.P. Meilink-Roelofsz, *Asian Trade and European Influence in the Indonesian Archipelago between 1500 and about 1630* (The Hague, 1962).

13 See J.C. van Leur, *Indonesian Trade and Society. Essays in Asian Social and Economic History* (The Hague, 1955).

14. For Van Leur and his work, see J. Vogel, *De opkomst van het indocentrische geschiedbeeld. Leven en werken van B.J.O. Schrieke en J.C. van Leur* (Hilversum, 1992).

15. Van Leur, *Trade and Society*, 261.

16. Ibid., 157–245.

17. Ibid., 268–290.

18. Ch. van der Woude and E. Rademakers-Wolf, ''Verslag van een onderzoek naar dissertaties met een historisch wetenschappelijke inslag,'' *Aanzet* (Mei 1986), 35–52.

19. Van der Woude and Rademakers-Wolf, ''Verslag,'' 43–46.

20. P. Blaas, "Nederlandse geschiedschrijving na 1945," in W.W. Mijnhardt, ed., *Kantelend geschiedbeeld. Nederlandse historiografie sinds 1945* (Utrecht, 1983), 37.

21. See the list in the leaflet *The Institute for the History of European Expansion* (Leiden, 1994).

22. See for the following also: G.J. Schutte, "De koloniale geschiedschrijving," in Mijnhardt, *Kantelend geschiedbeeld*, 289–310; N.A. Bootsma, "Indonesië, Suriname en de Antillen," in P. Luykx and N. Bootsma, eds., *De laatste tijd* (Utrecht, 1987), 299–345. Indispensable is W.Ph. Coolhaas, *A Critical Survey of Studies on Dutch Colonial History* (second edition revised by G.J. Schutte; The Hague, 1980). For the current bibliography, cf. the *Current Annotated Bibliography of Dutch Expansion Studies* (CABDES), published annually as number 3/4 of *Itinerario. European Journal of Overseas History*.

23. W.Ph. Coolhaas, *Generale missiven van Gouverneurs-Generaal en Raden aan Heren XVII der Verenigde Oostindische Compagnie* (The Hague, 1960–), continued by J. van Goor.

24. J.R. Bruijn, F.S. Gaastra, and I. Schöffer, *Dutch-Asiatic Shipping in the 17th and 18th Centuries*, 3 vols. (The Hague, 1979–1987).

25. J.L. Blussé, M.E. van Opstall, and Ts'ao Yungo-ho, eds., *De dagregisters van het Kasteel Zeelandia, Taiwan 1629–1662. Deel 1: 1629–1641* (The Hague, 1986).

26. A.C.J. Vermeulen, *The Deshima Dagregisters; Their Original Tables of Contents* (Leiden, 1986–), continued by P.G.E.I.J. van der Velde.

27. R.C. Kwantes, *De ontwikkeling van de nationalistische beweging in Nederlandsch-Indië. Bronnenpublicatie*, 4 vols. (Groningen, 1975–1982); S.L. van der Wal, *Het onderwijsbeleid in Nederlandsch-Indië, 1900–1940; een bronnenpublikatie* (Groningen, 1963); S.L. van der Wal, *De opkomst van de nationalistische beweging in Nederlands-Indië; een bronnenpublikatie* (Groningen, 1967); P. Creutzberg, *Het ekonomisch beleid in Nederlandsch-Indië. Capita Selecta. Een bronnenpublikatie*, 2 vols. (Groningen, 1972–1974).

28. S.L. van der Wal, *Officiële bescheiden betreffende de Nederlands-Indonesische betrekkingen, 1945–1950* (The Hague, 1971–), continued by P.J. Drooglever and M.J.B. Schouten.

29. P. Creutzberg, *Changing Economy in Indonesia: A Selection of Statistical Source Material from the Early 19th Century up to 1940* (The Hague, 1975–), continued by P. Boomgaard.

30. E. Gobée and C. Adriaanse, *Ambtelijke adviezen van C. Snouck Hurgronje, 1889–1936*, 3 vols. (The Hague, 1957–1965); W.A. Baud, *De semi-officiële en particuliere briefwisseling tussen J.C. Baud en J.J. Rochussen, 1845–1851*, 3 vols. (Leiden, 1983); F. Lequin, *The Private Correspondence of Isaac Titsingh*, 2 vols. (Amsterdam, 1990–1993); G.J. Knaap, *In deze halve gevangenis. Dagboek van Mr. Dr. L.F. Jansen, Batavia/Djakarta 1942–1945* (Franeker, 1988).

31. Cf. *Nieuwe Algemene Geschiedenis der Nederlanden*, 15 vols. (Haarlem, 1978–1983). A recent work of synthesis is J. van Goor, *De Nederlandse koloniën. Geschiedenis van de Nederlandse expansie, 1600–1975* (The Hague, 1993).

32. For example, L.Y. Andaya, *The Kingdom of Johor, 1641–1728* (Kuala Lumpur, 1975); A. Das Gupta, *Malabar in Asian Trade, 1740–1800* (Cambridge, England, 1967); O. Prakash, *The Dutch East-India Company and the Economy of Bengal, 1630–1720* (Princeton, N.J., 1985); S. Arasaratnam, *Merchants, Companies and Commerce on the*

Coromandel Coast, 1650–1740 (Delhi, 1986); A. Das Gupta, *Indian Merchants and the Decline of Surat, c. 1700–1750* (Wiesbaden, 1979).

33. See for example, C.R. Boxer, *The Dutch Sea-Borne Empire, 1600–1800* (London, 1965); K. Glamann, *Dutch-Asiatic Trade, 1620–1740* (The Hague, 1958); N. Steensgaard, *Carracks, Caravans and Companies. The Structural Crisis in the European-Asian Trade in the Early 17th Century* (Copenhagen, 1973).

34. Cf. R.A.J. van Lier, *Samenleving in een grensgebied, een sociaal historische studie over de maatschappij in Suriname* (The Hague, 1949); H. Hoetink, *Het patroon van de oude Curaçaose samenleving* (Assen, 1958).

35. Cf. F.W. Stapel, ed., *Geschiedenis van Nederlandsch-Indië*, 5 vols. (Amsterdam, 1938–1940).

36. H. Baudet and M. Fennema, eds., *Het Nederlands belang bij Indië* (Utrecht, 1983); J.Th. Lindblad, *Between Dayak and Dutch. The Economic History of Southeast Kalimantan, 1880–1942* (Dordrecht, 1988).

37. L.A. Davis and R.A. Huttenback, *Mammon and the Pursuit of Empire. The Political Economy of British Imperialism, 1860–1912* (Cambridge, England, 1986); J. Marseille, *Empire colonial et capitalisme français. Histoire d'un divorce* (Paris, 1984). There are two important works on Dutch colonial politics in the nineteenth century: C. Fasseur, *The Politics of Colonial Exploitation. Java, the Dutch, and the Cultivation System* (Ithaca, N.Y., 1992); and J. de Jong, *Van batig slot naar ereschuld. De discussie over de financiële verhouding tussen Nederland en Indië en de hervorming van de Nederlandse koloniale politiek, 1860–1900* (The Hague, 1989).

38. Taufik Abdullah, "The making of a schakel-society. The Minangkabau region in the late 19th century," in *Papers of the Dutch-Indonesian Historical Conference Held at Noordwijkerhout, The Netherlands 1976* (Leiden, 1978), 143–153.

39. See "The giant that was a dwarf" (Chapter 6, this volume).

40. M. Kuitenbrouwer, *The Netherlands and the Rise of Modern Imperialism. Colonies and Foreign Policy* (Oxford, 1991). For a discussion of the reactions to this book, see E. Locher-Scholten, "Dutch expansion in the Indonesian Archipelago around 1900 and the imperialism debate," *Journal of Southeast Asian Studies* 25 (1994), 91–111.

41. J. Breman, *Taming the Coolie Beast. Plantation Society and the Colonial Order in Southeast Asia* (Delhi, 1989).

42. J.A.A. van Doorn and W.J. Hendrix, *Het Nederlands-Indonesische conflict. Ontsporing van geweld*, 2nd ed. (Amsterdam, 1983).

43. L. de Jong, *Het Koninkrijk der Nederlanden in de Tweede Wereldoorlog*, 11 (The Hague, 1984–1986), and 12 (The Hague, 1988).

44. Cf. especially J.Th.M. Bank, *Katholieken en de Indonesische revolutie* (Baarn, 1983); J.J.P. de Jong, *Diplomatie of strijd. Het Nederlands beleid tegenover de Indonesische revolutie, 1945–1947* (Meppel, 1988); P.M.H. Groen, *Marsroutes en dwaalsporen. Het Nederlands militair strategisch beleid in Indonesië, 1945–1950* (The Hague, 1991).

45. See, for this, Bootsma, "Indonesië," 316–317.

Index

About the Author

H. L. WESSELING is Professor of General History at the University of Leiden and Rector of the Netherlands Institute for Advanced Study at Wassenaar. Previously he was the Director of the Centre for the History of European Expansion at Leiden (1975–1995). Dr. Wesseling is the author of *Divide and Rule: The Partition of Africa, 1880–1914* (Praeger, 1996), which has been translated into three languages.

ISBN 0-313-30431-9

90000>

EAN

9 780313 304316

HARDCOVER BAR CODE

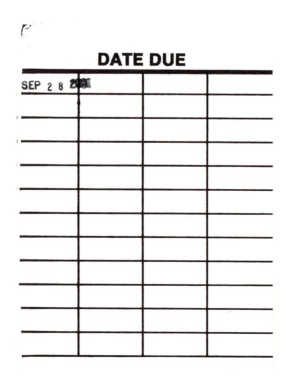